Citizenship and Migration

Citizenship and Migration

Globalization and the Politics of Belonging

Stephen Castles
Alastair Davidson

Routledge, New York

Published 2000 by
ROUTLEDGE
29 West 35th Street
New York, NY 10001

0–415–92713–7 (hardback)
0–415–92714–5 (paperback)

CIP information is available from the Library of Congress.

This book is printed on paper suitable for recycling and
made from fully managed and sustained forest sources.

Printed in Malaysia

Contents

Preface

The membership of individuals in modern democratic societies is marked by the status of citizenship. Those who belong in a given nation-state have documents certifying their membership (generally a certificate of birth or naturalization, and an identity card or passport). More importantly, citizens possess a wide range of civil, political and social rights. The pivotal right is that of participation in law-making and government, for it is this which makes the active citizen, who is supposed to be the basis of popular sovereignty. Such rights are balanced by a series of obligations to the community and state. Ideally, citizens are meant to belong to one nation-state only. In turn, the nation-state is meant to be inclusive of all the people living on its territory. The underlying assumption is that there is sufficient cultural homogeneity to allow agreement on the basic rules of conviviality, despite differing individual and group values. The democratic state needs the participation of all its members: everybody is meant to belong.

The reality has always been somewhat different. Most nation-states have had groups on their territory not considered capable of belonging, and therefore either denied citizenship or alternatively forced to go through a process of cultural assimilation in order to belong. Moreover, even those with formal membership have often been denied some of the rights vital to citizenship, so that they have not fully belonged. Discrimination based on class, gender, ethnicity, race, religion and other criteria has always meant that some people could not be full citizens. Securing the participation of previously excluded groups has been seen as the key to democratization.

But globalization creates new challenges for citizenship, both in established western democracies and in the emerging nation-states of Eastern Europe, Asia, Latin America and Africa. The growing international mobility of people questions the basis for belonging to the nation-state. The heterogeneity of cultural values and practices grows exponentially, so there is no time for processes of acculturation and assimilation. The boundaries of the nation-state are being eroded: millions of people have multiple citizenships and live in more than one country. Millions more do not live in their country of citizenship. Governments find that their power to control the economy, the welfare

system and national culture is being eroded. Global markets, transnational corporations, regional and supra-national bodies, and a new
pervasive international culture are all gaining in influence. The idea of
the citizen who spent most of his or her life in one country and shared
a common national identity is losing ground.

Millions of people are disenfranchised because they cannot become
citizens in their country of residence. Even more people, however,
have formal membership of the nation-state yet lack many of the rights
that are meant to go with this. Porous boundaries and multiple identities undermine ideas of cultural belonging as a necessary accompani-
ment to political membership. There are increasing numbers of *citizens
who do not belong*. This in turn undermines the basis of the nation-state
as the central site of democracy.

These are the central themes of this book. We will argue that basing
citizenship on singular and individual membership in a nation-state is
no longer adequate, since the nation-state model itself is being severely
eroded. Instead, new approaches to citizenship are needed, which take
account of collective identities and the fact that many people now
belong at various levels to more than one society. If democracy is to be
maintained and enhanced, all members of society must have a political
voice as a citizen. But belonging can no longer mean being part of a
national community, based on common history and culture. Much of
our discussion focuses on western nations, but we will also examine
issues of citizenship and difference in the Asia-Pacific region as an
example of the new issues arising in non-western countries.

The fundamental problem is to work out new rules for conviviality,
which provide not only the basis for equality, but also the conditions
for cross-cultural communication and the development of a new sense
of community. The solution must lie in a mode of citizenship that
reconciles the pressures of globalization with the reality that states will
continue, for the foreseeable future, to exist as the most important political unit. One aim must be to dissolve the nation part of the nation-state
and to replace it with a democratic state based on open and flexible
belonging. Citizenship should not be derived from the membership of
one or more cultural groups, but from residence on a state's territory.
Other significant links – such as origin in the territory, family bonds,
economic involvement or cultural participation – should also confer
citizenship rights, which may need to be differentiated according to the
type of linkage. A second aim is to devise forms of democratic political
participation that transcend state boundaries, for many vital decisions
are now made in regional, supra-national and transnational contexts.

New forms of belonging should not be based on culture, but neither can they ignore it. Citizenship rules must be based on the recognition that individuality is always formed in social and cultural contexts, and that individuals are always also members of social and cultural groups, with particular needs, interests and values. The liberal principle of abstracting from these contexts leads to a fiction of equality as citizens, which is belied by real differences in political and economic power. Democratic societies have addressed this by developing welfare states, but globalization makes it necessary to go a step further and to develop approaches to citizenship designed to achieve both individual equality and the recognition of collective difference. This requires a radical rethinking of citizenship rights. Our discussion in this book will concentrate on the issue of democratic belonging for ethnic minorities (both immigrants and indigenous peoples in former settler colonies), but reshaping citizenship for minorities inevitably affects the nature of citizenship as a whole.

This book is the result of several years of debate and cooperation between its two authors. The method has been for one of us to write a first draft for each chapter, which has been followed by intensive discussion and revision. Thus, each chapter contains ideas and analysis from both of us. In the end, however, we cannot claim full agreement on all the views expressed here. The main responsibility for Chapters 1, 3, 4, 5 and 6 lies with Stephen Castles, and for Chapters 2, 7, 8, 9 and 10 with Alastair Davidson.

Chapter 1 examines globalization and the dilemmas it creates for the nation-state and citizenship. Globalization erodes the autonomy of the nation-state, undermines the ideology of distinct and relatively autonomous cultures, and causes the increasing mobility of people across borders. This leads to crucial new questions on modes of polit- -ical and cultural belonging. These new factors destabilize traditional ways of balancing the contradictions that always beset the nation-state model: the contradictions between the inclusion and exclusion of various groups, between the rights and obligations of citizenship, and – most important – between political belonging as a citizen and cultural belonging as a national. Finally, we look at four recent theoretical responses to the challenges presented for citizenship by globalization.

Chapter 2 focuses on theories of citizenship and their adequacy in a situation of global change. The essential concern of citizenship has always been the empowerment of people over the natural and social environment, but the form and content of that empowerment changes according to the historical and societal context. Since the democratic revolutions of the eighteenth and nineteenth centuries, citizenship has meant first and foremost the assertion of popular will, and then a list of the rights inherent in all people as equals. Democracy implies the *active citizen*, able to participate in the exercise of political power, rather than just the *passive citizen* as a bearer of rights. The problem, however, has always been to stipulate who belongs to the people and is therefore entitled to be a citizen. The historical conflation of the citizen and the national involved a process of homogenization of minorities. The population mobility and cultural interchange inherent in globalization leads to an irreducibility of multicultural difference, which makes the linking of nationality and citizenship anachronistic. The challenge is to integrate the global, regional and local dimensions of belonging into a new political model.

Chapter 3 sets the scene for understanding the links between immigration, minority formation and citizenship. In it, we examine the immigration experience of a range of countries, including permanent settlement countries like the USA and Australia; former guestworker importers such as Germany; former colonial powers like France and Britain; and new immigration countries both in Southern Europe and Asia. We discuss the significance of 'ethnic minority' status and look at statistical indicators of the size of minorities. We argue that nation-states have an intrinsic drive towards the creation of cultural difference and the radicalization of minorities. This arises from the dualism between the nation as a cultural community and the state as a political community. We go on to look more specifically at the legal, economic, social, spatial and cultural factors that underpin minority formation.

In Chapter 4, we consider how immigrants can become citizens in various countries, that is, the rules for naturalization and for access to citizenship through birth or residence. In many cases, these rules are changing rapidly in response to the problems thrown up by mass immigration. One new aspect is the emergence of forms of 'quasi-citizenship' or 'denizenship' through which immigrants gain many of the rights of citizenship without formal membership. Another important factor is the rights created through international agreements and supranational bodies. Overall, there are signs of convergence of rules for access to citizenship in western countries, yet actual practices still differ considerably.

Chapter 5 goes on to look at what it actually means to be a citizen, using Marshall's triad of civil, political and social rights. We show that the situation of various groups varies considerably and is strongly linked to processes of racialization. Social citizenship is particularly significant, since it is a precondition for real chances of political participation. Globalization leads to increasing inequality and to new forms of social exclusion that affect minorities most severely. We argue that it is necessary to add two additional categories of rights – gender and cultural rights – in order to achieve full citizenship for members of minorities.

In Chapter 6, we discuss ethnic mobilization and the emergence of new political subjects. Community formation is often the result of experiences of exclusion from mainstream society. It consists of processes of home-building and place making, the development of ethnic economies, the building of religious institutions and the assertion of national identities. Different types of ethnic consciousness emerge, including assimilation, separatism, diasporic identities and transnational consciousness. Minority communities and consciousness are the breeding ground for political associations and movements, which affect political institutions and political culture in many different ways.

Chapter 7 argues that new forms of citizenship are beginning to develop in response to the problems posed by globalization and population mobility. These new forms are contested and incomplete, but they show the possibility of post-national belonging. We examine two of the most important approaches. The first is multiculturalism. Our discussion focuses on the USA and Australia, which have very different understandings of the concept. Yet, in both cases, multiculturalism has changed the ideological and legal basis for citizenship, although it has fallen short of bringing about the fundamental changes needed to empower citizens in a globalizing world. The second example is the role of regional economies – especially the European Union – in changing citizenship. The creation of supra-national laws and powerful legal institutions shifts power away from the national level. This makes it necessary to seek ways of achieving active citizenship through democratic supra-national political institutions and practices.

Chapter 8 extends the analysis to emerging nation-states outside the traditional western sphere through a discussion of citizenship in the Asia-Pacific region. Most of the world's nations aspire to democracy and citizenship, yet historical conditions for the development of democratic ideas and practices vary widely. We look at the extent to which new immigrants can become citizens, and find that the emphasis on ethnic homogeneity is often far stronger than in western countries. As for the quality of being a citizen, the rights of citizenship are extremely restricted in most non-western countries. A long struggle lies ahead not only for the rights of minorities, but also to create genuine citizenship for everybody.

Chapter 9 presents some ideas for new forms of citizenship, which go beyond current models – even the multicultural and regional ones. A post-national state must be able to accommodate a multiplicity of notions of the good. This requires a continuing debate between individuals and communities on an agreed set of democratic procedures and goals. A basic requirement for success is a shared civic culture of tolerance and trust, based on a differential set of human rights that could protect what is most sacred for each group from the potential tyranny of the majority. Group representation would be needed in order to allow minority voices to be heard. At the same time, the state would have to guarantee social, economic and educational standards adequate to ensure genuine participation for all. This model would require not only institutional structures acceptable to all, but also mechanisms to facilitate communication across cultural difference. Such a model would put a premium on political mobilization and active citizenship.

Finally, Chapter 10 points out that conditions in large areas of the world – most of Africa, Central and South Asia and parts of Latin America – are such that active citizenship and transnational democracy seem almost out of reach. Citizenship presupposes a functioning state, the rule of law and basic human rights guarantees. All these are absent in countries that are home to the majority of the world's population. Indeed, globalization has in many places led to a dramatic decline in economic, social and political standards. The result is often a situation of chaos, in which weak and oppressive states compete for influence with fundamentalist movements and criminal organizations. However, globalization also means that such conditions in the poorer parts of the world inevitably spill over into the rich countries, undermining social and political achievements. The struggle for democratic citizenship must therefore have a global perspective, with the aim of creating the conditions for full participation everywhere. Citizenship or chaos are the stark alternatives at the beginning of the new millennium.

The authors wish to acknowledge the help received from many colleagues. In particular, Stephen Castles thanks Ellie Vasta for her comments and support, and Rainer Bauböck for the insights he has provided over many years and for getting him involved in citizenship studies. Some of the research for this book took place in the context of the project *Intercultural Relations, Identity and Citizenship*, funded by the Volkswagen Foundation and the Australian Research Council. Stephen Castles also thanks his colleagues on this project: Gianni Zappalà and Colleen Mitchell at the University of Wollongong; Catherine Wihtol de Wenden, Vasoo Vuddamalay and Sabrina Guérard at CERI in Paris; and Michael Bommes, Matthias Liedtke and Ingrid Schumacher at IMIS, University of Osnabrück.

Alastair Davidson wishes to thank Maryellen Davidson, head of the Civics Education Program at the Board of Studies of Victoria; Professors Bryan Turner (Deakin), Dominique Schnapper (EHESS, Paris) and Said Bouamama (IFAR, Lille); Professor Renate Holub and her colleagues of the Western European Studies Program at UCLA Berkeley; and his colleagues on the Globalization, Identity and Citizenship Program at the Institute for Social Research at Swinburne University of Technology – in particular Professor Ken Young and Dr Kathleen Weekley for their careful comments on Chapter 8 and Dvora Liberman and David Hudson for their skilful help with wordprocessing and editing.

Colleen Mitchell of the Centre for Asia Pacific Social Transformation Studies, University of Wollongong, checked and edited the manuscript. Finally, the authors thank the publisher, Catherine Gray of Macmillan for her support, patience and helpful comments. We also thank an anonymous reviewer for many helpful suggestions.

1

The Crisis of Citizenship

In that summer of 1914, when the rulers of human destinies drew European humanity from the playing fields of universal suffrage to the already prepared arena of universal military service, the town of Visegrad provided a small but eloquent example of the first symptoms of a contagion which would in time become European and then spread to the entire world. (Andric, 1994 [1945], p. 265)

Today we are experiencing the weakening of civic feeling and of political bonds. There is nothing to guarantee that the modern democratic nation will in future have the capability of maintaining the social bond, as it has done in the past.... It seems impossible for democracies to demand of their citizens to defend them with their lives. In democracy there is no longer any supreme sacrifice: the individuals and their interests have taken the place of the citizens and their ideals. (Schnapper, 1994, p. 11, translation by Castles)

Until a few years ago, the notion of citizenship was little discussed outside university political science courses. Being a citizen was just a matter of common sense in the fortunate minority of the world's countries that might be considered to be democracies. It was 'normal' to be a citizen, which meant having the rights to vote and to stand for political office, enjoying equality before the law and being entitled to various government services and benefits. Being a citizen also meant having the obligations to obey the laws, to pay taxes and – in extreme situations – to defend one's country. As for the rest of the world, it was a widespread aspiration to move towards the western model of citizenship. As the President of Mongolia, Punsalmaaggiyu Orchirbat, said when he visited Paris, the symbolic birthplace of the modern nation, 'In 1990 we embarked on a great journey to join the common course of mankind – democracy and human rights, the market economy and economic development' (*Le Monde/Guardian Weekly*, 5 May, 1996). Those were the icons of progress. The nation-state had become the global norm for political advancement, and citizenship was seen as an integral aspect of prosperity and modernization.

There are, however, signs that citizenship has in recent years become problematic. Several countries have revised their laws and practices concerning the rights and obligations of citizens. Others have changed their rules for access to citizenship for immigrants, children of immigrants and other minorities. New countries emerging from the dissolving multiethnic states of real socialism have sought to define and establish appropriate rules of citizenship. Other new countries forged out of former colonies have dissolved into anarchy because of a failure to build an inclusive national identity and a stable state. The notion of citizenship has become the focus of political and academic discourse, with a spate of books, debates and conferences. Citizenship campaigns have sprung up, which claim that extending citizenship to certain groups, or changing the substance of certain aspects of citizenship, could help to solve major social problems. Why this sudden interest in something that seemed so obvious? Is it the result of major changes in the political and social context? Or is it that we have become sensitive to possible omissions and problems implicit in the common-sense notion of citizenship?

The answer is both. The global context of citizenship is changing dramatically, but so is the way in which we perceive it. These two trends are linked: there have always been some fundamental ambiguities in the notion of citizenship, but these did not seem to matter much as long as the political context appeared fairly coherent and stable. That context was, of course, the nation-state: the development of modern citizenship was inextricably linked with the emergence of the nation-state in Western Europe and North America from the seventeenth century onwards. The current crisis of citizenship is thus closely linked with the challenges facing the nation-state model at the end of the twentieth century. These affect – in specific ways – not only the classical nation-states of Western Europe, but also the nation-building societies of North America and Oceania, and the new industrial countries of Asia and Latin America.[1]

Globalization and the nation-state

The essence of the nation-state is the institution of citizenship: the integration of all the inhabitants of a territory into the political community, and their political equality as citizens. Of course, relatively few nations match this democratic ideal. How many countries have not had a violent change in government during the twentieth century? It is hard to think of more than seven! In how many states do the people really have a choice about who forms the government and what it does? Yet most heads of state claim that their country is democratic, and most politically aware people aspire to this.

The European and North American nation-states that emerged from the seventeenth to the nineteenth centuries were astonishingly effective, in both internal and external terms. Their political systems facilitated the integration of diverse groups into cohesive populations and provided the conditions for capitalist industrialization. They were able to dominate and colonize the rest of the world, and to impose economic relations and cultural values that were to transform all the disparate societies and bring them into a global system. These nation-states continued the work of the great centralizing monarchies: Spain, Portugal, France and England. However, they quickly transcended the absolutist model, marginalizing those countries that did not make the transition to the modern nation-state on time. Colonialism was crucial to the emerging nation-states: exploiting the natural resources and the labour power of dominated peoples made industrialization possible. When the 'late nations' such as Germany and Italy began to seek 'their place in the sun', and the colonized peoples demanded freedom, the result was the conflicts that were to lead to the most violent century in history.

This dialectic of progress and violence indicates some of the ambivalences inherent in the nation-state model. Can it work if all the societies of the world constitute themselves as nation-states and seek equality in a global system? Or is it premised on the domination of weaker countries, and the stigmatization and exclusion of the Other? It is vital to deconstruct the contradictions of the nation-state model if we are to find ways of achieving more democratic types of citizenship and more equitable and peaceful international relations. However, the project of this book is more modest: we aim to analyse just one – albeit the most important – aspect of the nation-state in the light of some of the challenges it faces in the current epoch. Our theme is citizenship and the ways in which it is being questioned and reshaped by current global transformations.

Globalization is widely seen as one of the most important determinants of the human condition in the contemporary world, so we need to characterize it here, as the context for debates on citizenship. Globalization is a term used to summarize the following trends:

- The emergence of a global economy based on the activities of transnational corporations and on international markets for capital, commodities, services and futures.
- The very rapid introduction of new information technologies that are revolutionizing communication, production and trade, and facilitating the international dissemination of cultural values.
- The formation of regional economies and markets characterized by the free movement of capital, goods and labour across nation-states' borders. The European Union (EU) is the most developed example, while the North American Free Trade Area and the Asia-Pacific Economic Cooperation Forum permit free movement in some respects but not others.
- The development of supra-national institutions and legal norms to regulate economic and political relations (the EU, the World Court, the European Court of Justice, the World Trade Organization and so on).
- The growing significance of democracy and human rights as near-universal norms of governance in the international community.
- The emergence of a global commitment to a common set of values and standards of the Good as a result of global information transfer and cross-cultural awareness.

The development of global systems of production and trade is not in itself new – it is a central aspect of modernity as embodied in the world-wide empires of the great European powers that reached their zenith in the pre-1914 era of imperialism. What is new today is the all-embracing character of global relationships, the speed of reaction through electronically networked markets and media, and the decline of central control as the role of national governments diminishes. Globalization is characterized by a lightning-quick transmission of information through new media. Television images of human disasters in Central Africa bring that world into the living-rooms of rich countries. However, the converse is also true: the idealized lifestyles of Beverly Hills are flaunted before the world's poor.

It is doubtful, however, whether the global media explosion is really breeding a global consciousness. Most of its images exist only in a fantasy realm completely divorced from the lives of 80 per cent of the globe who view them. This rupture between mental or cultural life and lived life is marked by the fact that, of some billion international trips per year, most are made by a relatively small group of privileged people from rich countries. The bulk of the world's population either stay where they were born, or move to adjoining countries much like their own. It is important to avoid an over-facile definition of globalization based on the experience of privileged minorities, as found for example in the work of Ohmae (1995). Most people still do not have a wide experience of different cultures of that direct sort that allows them to make sense of media grabs.

Even more significant is the fact that economic, social, educational and health conditions still vary immensely. Even in the USA, income inequality grew sharply in the 1980s: the rich got richer, there were more poor people, and the middle classes were eroded (Reich, 1991, pp. 196–207). This trend applies in virtually all the older industrial countries, where the decline of welfare states has exacerbated the social polarization. Growing inequalities in wealth can also be found in newly industrializing countries. Economic development under conditions of free markets and non-interventionist states seems inevitably to lead to greater inequality. Modernization theories claim that higher living standards will 'trickle down' to disadvantaged groups, yet it is far from clear that this is happening. The most glaring inequality, however, is still that between the industrial countries (both old and new) and those areas which have not been able to achieve sustained economic development. In many areas of Africa and Asia, real income is falling. This means declines in educational opportunities, health standards and even life expectancy. Whole nations are being excluded from the new global order.

A recent text on global inequalities makes this devastatingly clear, mortality tables showing an 18:1 greater chance of dying before the age of 5 years in poor against rich countries, and a life expectancy of 54.5 years compared with 80 years. More than 90 per cent of children attend secondary school in rich countries, against fewer than 20 per cent in poor countries (Bradshaw and Wallace, 1996, Chapter 2; Streeten, 1996). Another study points out that in the 1980s, real minimum wages fell by up to 50 per cent in Africa and Latin America. In the 42 poorest countries, the expenditure on health fell over 50 per cent and that on education over 25 per cent. Resource transfer to poor countries went from a positive 43 billion dollars in 1981 to a negative 33 billion dollars in 1988. Comparative income gaps have widened, the average per capita income in an advanced country being 58 times that in the least developed countries, where over half the world's population live on 5.6 per cent of world income (Turk, 1993, pp. 17–18; Khor, 1996). Like many other texts, these sources suggest that globalization is making the discrepancy worse. There is a 'relentless growth' in the number of the 'absolute poor' reaching 1.3 billion in 1993 (Global Commission, 1995, pp. 21–3).

Globalization is characterized by new forms of inclusion in and exclusion from societal relationships. Castells (1996, p. 3) argues that 'our societies are increasingly structured around a bipolar opposition between the Net and the Self'. He emphasizes the role of new information technologies in creating global networks of wealth, power and images. These networks can 'selectively switch on and off individuals, groups, regions and even countries' according to their relevance in fulfilling instrumental goals. This system is economically efficient but incapable of giving meaning to people's lives. To escape such abstract universalism, people increasingly seek meaning through particularistic identities based on ethnicity, religion, regionalism or nationalism.

This explains why many contemporary conflicts are not concerned primarily with 'rational' economic and social interests. The defence of local or sectional interests against globalizing forces may be based on cultural symbols connected with dignity and identity. Resistance movements may appear particularistic and even backward-looking because discourses of universalism appear to have been monopolized by globalizing forces. At worst, the result is a new 'tribalism' in which populations retreat from universal to exclusive localist outlooks and a new anarchy or chaos dominates outside rich countries (Global Commission, 1995, pp. 16–17). There is a massive increase in violence, crime, war and drug addiction (UNRISD, 1995). In some places, barbarism rules: torture, rape, cannibalism and other bizarre expressions of violence become commonplace (Kaplan, 1996b; Touati, 1996; Zheng, 1996). We can thus discount any notion that globalization spells the homogenization of experience throughout the globe on the lines of that in advanced countries.

Globalization affects citizenship in many ways. This can be summarized by pointing to three main aspects, of which two are contextual and the third more direct. First, globalization questions the notion of the relative autonomy of the nation-state, upon which each separate national citizenship is based. Globalization breaks the territorial principle, the nexus between power and place. Wieviorka (1994, p. 25) has drawn attention to the 'decomposition of national industrial societies'. The 'national industrial society', as it evolved in the nineteenth and twentieth centuries, articulated three elements – society, state and nation – in a particular form. 'Society' referred to an economic and social system based on rational (as opposed to traditional or religious) principles, within a bounded national territory. 'State' referred to a political system based on secular (and usually democratic) principles, capable of regulating economic and political relations and change. 'Nation' referred to a 'people' defined on the basis both of belonging to the territory of the state and having a common cultural and ethnic background (Lapeyronnie *et al.*, 1990, pp. 258–62). Politics, the economy, social relations and culture were congruent in that they all took the nation-state as their main point of reference. The nation-state was seen as a discrete unit within a world of nation-states. The whole of classical sociology takes this 'national society' for granted (Lapeyronnie *et al.*, 1990, p. 259). Even the critics of capitalism based their politics on national units: social-democratic demands for economic reform and welfare policies addressed the state; communists called for world revolution but were organized nationally.

Globalization has destabilized the 'national industrial society'. The central dynamics of economic life now transcend national borders and have become uncontrollable for national governments. Deindustrialization of the older industrial nations has led to profound social changes and has eroded the membership basis of the labour movement. The nation-state is still the basic unit for welfare systems, but no government can pursue welfare policies that ignore the pressures of global markets. This alters the terms for socialist parties: even if they can get elected to power, they may have to abandon their traditional objectives and adopt economic rationalism. Capital may appear to have won the class struggle, but this leads not to Fukuyama's (1992) 'end of history' but instead to forms of social and political disorganization that threaten the security of the well-off and the stability of democratic states. What, then, does it mean to be a citizen if the autonomy of the nation-state is being eroded, and the vote that one wields cannot influence key political decisions because they are no longer made by national parliaments?

The second aspect of globalization is that it has undermined the ideology of distinct and relatively autonomous national cultures. These were always a myth because virtually every nation-state has been made up of a number of ethnic groups, with distinct languages, traditions and histories. Homogenization is at the core of the nationalist project. The internal Other has to be made into a national before he or she can become a citizen. As Renan pointed out in 1882 in his famous discourse 'What is a nation?' (Renan, 1992), forgetting the history of ethnic distinctiveness and the (often repressive) process of overcoming it is vital to national identity. Moreover, no frontier has ever been completely impervious to cultural influences: even Enver Hodja's Albania could not completely encapsulate itself against the influences of western culture, as the rush to migrate to Italy after 1989 showed. All cultures are hybrids. Nonetheless, ideas of national cultural distinctiveness have underpinned nation-building and patriotism.

Globalization has changed all this: rapid improvements in transport and communications have led to an unprecedented degree of cultural interchange. The industrialization of media production puts enormous pressure on national and local cultures. Dominance by global cultural factories, for example Hollywood, means the diffusion of specific value systems connected with consumerism, individualism and US lifestyles. At the same time, however, we witness a re-ethnicization of culture at a subnational level. This trend appears as a form of resistance to both the nationalization and the globalization of culture. Collectivities that constitute themselves around cultural claims may be based not only on ethnicity, but also on regional location, gender, sexual preferences and lifestyles. National culture is being squeezed between the global and the local.

The third aspect is the central theme of this book: globalization means the rapidly increasing mobility of people across national borders. The period since 1945 and especially since 1980 has been marked by large-scale migrations of all kinds: temporary and permanent movements; labour migrations and refugee exoduses; individual and family flows; highly skilled specialists and manual workers (Castles and Miller, 1998). Such migrations have led to settlement in nearly all highly developed countries and in many parts of the less-developed regions. Populations have become more heterogeneous and culturally diverse. Cultural difference and social marginalization are often closely linked, creating ethnic minorities with disadvantaged and relatively isolated positions in society. In addition to long-term migration, mobility takes on other forms that may have a considerable impact on local cultures and economies: tourism, the short-term movement of business executives and experts, and the mobility of young people in search of education and training.

The mobility of people has always been an inherent part of colonialism and industrialization. Sailors, soldiers, traders, administrators and settlers were sent out to manage and exploit the colonized Others, who were constructed through racist ideologies as being inferior and threatening. As the flow of colonial profits back to the metropoles helped to provide the capital for industrialization, new mass migrations started. At first, these were movements of impoverished rural workers into the new industrial towns. As these reserves dried up, however, workers were pulled in across national borders: Irish to Britain; Poles and Italians to Germany, France and Switzerland; and Eastern and Southern Europeans to fuel the industrial take-off of the USA. These migrants were eventually, to a large extent, absorbed into the national populations, and their children became citizens.

Two things are new about current migrations. The first is their sheer scale: they affect all regions and most countries of the world simultaneously. The speed at which new ethnic minorities have emerged has confounded policy makers and undermined laws and practices concerned with integration and citizenship. The second is the ethnocultural characteristics of many of the immigrants: they come from areas that are increasingly distant – not only in kilometres, but also in cultural terms. They often originate in former colonies or areas of military presence of the receiving countries: North and West Africans in France; Caribbeans, Indians, Pakistanis and Bangladeshis in Britain; Mexicans, Filipinos, Koreans and Vietnamese in the USA; and so on. Many recent migrants, however, come from areas where the linkages are based on more tenuous experiences of economic and cultural penetration: Arabs to the USA; South East and South Asians to Japan; Chinese to virtually all developed countries. The highly historical success of the western nation-states in establishing the domination of the Third World has created mechanisms that now question the nation-state; this domination has led to linkages that facilitate the movement of not only capital and commodities, but also people and ideas – in both directions.

Key questions

The colonized Other is returning to the metropoles and becoming part of their populations and societies. In every city of Western Europe and North America, ethnic heterogeneity has become an inescapable reality. This Other has no shared past with the people of the receiving society. The cultural background, as seen in the contrast between Christian and Islamic traditions, may be very different. In the case of migrants from former colonies, the culture of the Other may partially mirror that of the receiving society, yet the dialectical unity of exploiter and exploited may contain a fundamental difference in experience. This situation raises crucial questions:

● Can these Others be submitted to a process of acculturation (as were previous internal minorities), which will reduce them to nationals and thus qualify them for membership in the nation-state?

- Or is such a process unthinkable in the era of globalization, with its multiple identities and diasporic communities?
- Has the pace of intermingling of ethnic groups become so rapid that there is no time for the process of forgetting different histories, which Renan saw as being crucial to national identity?
- Does this mean that the nation-state and citizenship will have to be modified to fit the new reality of the collective presence of the irreducible Other in multiethnic societies?
- If so, what can be the characteristics of possible new forms of political belonging?
- What political action is needed to develop these new forms?

These are the central questions of this book. Before discussing them further, it is necessary to return briefly to the problems that have always been implicit in the notions of the nation-state and citizenship.

Ambiguities of citizenship

Citizenship is one of the key institutions of contemporary societies, at the very core of both democracy and national identity, yet it has always been ambiguous in various ways. First, it implies not only inclusion, but also exclusion: the citizenship of certain types of person implies the non-citizenship of others. In the Greek *polis*, slaves, foreigners and, above all, women were excluded. In the modern states that emerged in the nineteenth century, the very size of the society precluded direct democracy. Suffrage was linked to the assumption of the capability of a man to participate rationally in the public sphere and to represent the people dependent upon him (women, children, servants and employees). In a wider sense, those elected to office had to be capable of representing the social category or interest group from which they derived. Citizenship was restricted to male householders belonging to the dominant religion and ethnic group. The political movements of excluded groups (women, workers, religious minorities and indigenous peoples) have seen access to the franchise as the main instrument of their emancipation.

Today, the problem of *formal exclusion* from citizenship applies above all to immigrants. By 1995, the total foreign population of European Organization for Economic Co-operation and Development countries was 19.4 million, of whom only 6.7 million were EU citizens. There were 2 million North Africans, 2.6 million Turks and 1.4 million people from former Yugoslavia (OECD, 1997, p. 30). A large number of these were actually born in their country of residence yet had not become citizens, due to the principle of *ius sanguinis* (nationality by descent). Even in North America and Australia, where naturalization is easier to obtain, there is a relatively large number of resident non-citizens. These are people who belong to society as workers, tax-payers and parents, yet are denied full political participation. Even illegal immigrants may be long-term residents but do not enjoy many basic rights. This negates the basic principle of liberal democracy that all members of society should be included as citizens.

There is, however, another dimension, that of *de facto* exclusion: in most countries, there are significant groups, usually marked by race, by ethnicity or by being indigenous peoples, who are denied full participation as citizens. They may have the right to vote, but social, economic and cultural exclusion denies them the chance of gaining political representation or of having any real say in the decisions that affect their lives. This situation is in part a reflection of the fact that the substantial meaning of citizenship itself has become extended in recent times as civil and political rights have been joined by social rights (Marshall, 1964). Put differently, a certain level of social and economic welfare is needed before people can take advantage of formal political rights. Today, it may be argued that collective cultural rights needed to be added to Marshall's triad. *De facto* exclusion presents new challenges for the politics of inclusion, leading to calls for 'differential citizenship' (Young, 1989, 1990) and 'multicultural citizenship' (Kymlicka, 1995).

A second ambiguity of citizenship concerns the relationship between *rights* and *obligations*. This is most evident in the close link between universal suffrage and universal military service (referred to in the quotation from Ivo Andric's epic novel on Bosnia at the beginning of this chapter). Dominique Schnapper's important work on citizenship constantly emphasizes the notion of the 'warrior-citizen' (Schnapper, 1994, p. 49). This link is problematic: it excludes women, who, with a few exceptions (such as in Israel), have not been seen as being capable of defending their nation by violent means. It also implies that democratic nations can only be consolidated internally by hostility towards external groups, that is, by constructing a *Feindbild*, or by the concept of an enemy (see Hoffmann, 1994). Moreover, linking suffrage with conscription can be a means of excluding internal minorities, who may be accused of 'unclear loyalties' in the event of a conflict. A model of citizenship for a global society can hardly be based on the willingness to indulge in inter-state warfare, although it might require willingness to support the use of force to prevent conflict or human rights abuses.

Both of the above ambiguities are the expression of a more fundamental contradiction: that between *citizenship* and *nationality*, or between the notion of the *citizen* as an individual abstracted from cultural characteristics, and that of the *national* as a member of a community with common cultural values. In liberal theory, all citizens are meant to be free and equal persons, who as citizens are homogeneous individuals (Rawls, 1985, pp. 232–4). This requires a separation between a person's political rights and obligations, and their membership of specific groups, based on ethnicity, religion, social class or regional location. The political sphere is one of universalism, which means equality and abstraction from cultural particularity and difference. Difference is to be restricted to the 'non-public identity' (Rawls, 1985, p. 241).

This, however, conflicts with the reality of nation-state formation, in which becoming a citizen has depended on membership in a community. The nation-state is the combination of a political unit that controls a bounded territory (the state) with a national community (the nation or people) that has the power to impose its political will within those boundaries. A citizen is always also a member of a nation, a *national*. Thus, citizenship is meant to be universalistic and above cultural difference, yet it exists only in the context of a nation-state, which is based on cultural specificity – on the belief in being different from other nations. Historically, this tension has been expressed in measures to incorporate minority groups into the 'national culture'. Today, it is a major issue for indigenous peoples as well as for immigrants: can they only belong to the nation if they reject their own language and traditions and conform to the dominant ones?

It is clearly vital to distinguish between the nation and the ethnic group. There are currently some 200 nation-states in the world, yet over 6000 languages (Moynihan, 1993, p. 72). Language is in most cases an indicator of a cultural community and thus frequently of an ethnic group; if even a fraction of these groups were to seek to become nations, the potential for conflict would be enormous. As Moynihan (1993, pp. 63–106) shows, there is an inherent contradiction between two basic principles of the United Nations (UN): the principle of national sovereignty and that of the self-determinationof peoples.

But the difference between the nation and the ethnic group is not always obvious, especially in the Anglo-American literature. For example, Seton-Watson describes a nation as 'a community of people, whose members are bound together by a sense of solidarity, a common culture, a national consciousness' (Seton-Watson, 1977, p. 1). Connor defines a nation as 'a group of people who *believe* they are ancestrally related. It is the largest grouping that shares that belief' (Connor, 1991, p. 6, emphasis in original, quoted here from Moynihan, 1993, p. 1). Ethnicity is usually defined as a sense of group belonging based on ideas of common origins, history, culture, experience and values. Ethnicity is seen as 'cultural', in contradistinction to 'biological' notions of race (see Castles and Miller, 1998, pp. 30–2).

The distinction between ethnic group and nation in Anglo-American interpretations is usually a practical one based on sovereignty: an ethnic group that controls a bounded territory becomes a nation and establishes a nation-state. Factors of shared history and culture are then complemented by a common economy and legal system. Anthony Smith sums this up as follows:

> A nation can therefore be defined as a named human population sharing an historic territory, common myths and historical memories, a mass, public culture, a common economy and common legal rights and duties for all members. (Smith, 1991, p. 14)

Since, however, there are few homogeneous nation-states, the question is how the varying ethnic groups in a territory are to be moulded into one nation. This may take place through the forcible imposition of the culture of the dominant group on the others, for example through the prohibition of minority languages, schools and festivals, as in the case of present-day Kurds in Turkey. The process may be a more gradual and consensual one, in which groups grow together through economic and social interaction, and the development of a common language and shared institutions, such as schools, church and military service. There is a fine line between the nation based on repression and that based on historical consensus. Most have elements of both and are open to subsequent challenge by movements of territorial minorities, as recent European history has shown.

Continental European views on the difference between nation and ethnic group have followed a rather different line, based on the famous distinction between the *Kulturnation* (cultural nation, also known as the ethnic nation) and the *Staatsnation* (state nation, also known as the civic nation). These notions developed as ideological expressions of the struggle for dominance between Germany and France in the nineteenth century.

Germany was a backward patchwork of principalities and mini-states with absolutist rulers until the end of eighteenth century. Nation-state formation did not come through internal impulses, but as a reaction to conquest by the Napoleonic armies. As Habermas points out, national consciousness was based not on democratic civil liberties and popular sovereignty, but on 'the romantically inspired middle-class notion of a *Kulturnation*, a nation defined by its culture' (Habermas, 1994a, p. 146). Romanticism portrayed individuals as part of an organic whole; freedom meant not individual rights but the acceptance of one's role in the greater organism. The state was the embodiment of this superior meaning, which could only be interpreted by great leaders. Democracy had no place in the model (Hoffmann, 1994, pp. 108–30).

The French *Staatsnation*, on the other hand, developed through the democratic revolution of 1789. It was seen as being based not on common culture but on a common will, as expressed both in Rousseau's idea of the 'general will' and in Renan's famous expression of the nation as '*le plébiscite de tous les jours*' (the daily plebiscite). The implication is that citizens of a nation form a community because they constantly express the will to do so. The nation should therefore be understood as a political project capable of transcending the tension between universalism and particularism (Schnapper, 1994, pp. 83–114). The common will creates and maintains the political unit, whatever conflicts there are within it. This idea provides the basis for a republican form of government, which should be capable of assimilating ethnic or religious minorities.

Yet the claim of transcending culture is dubious, for the French experience was actually based on linguistic homogenization, political centralization and compulsory assimilation. Shared endeavour and suffering in war were seen as the nation-building experiences *par excellence*. 'Political nation-units are generally born in the fracas of war' (Schnapper, 1994, p. 45). Even Renan emphasizes alongside the principle of consent that of common history and culture (see Schnapper, 1994, p. 168). The republican model worked well as long as the dominant group was willing to assimilate others, and the economy was able to provide a reasonable level of social integration to all. But how well has the republican model coped with globalization and the immigration of the Other? We will return to this in later chapters.

A final ambiguity to be noted is contained in the concept of 'naturalization', used in English, French and certain other European languages to refer to the administrative act whereby a foreigner is accepted as a citizen. Naturalization implies that being a member of a certain nation-state is laid down by 'natural laws', perhaps linked to natural environment or racial descent. Foreigners can only 'become natural' to the new host country through a long process (taking between 5 and 12 years in most countries), which may be seen as an exception to the normal rule of lifelong membership.

Fehér and Heller (1994) have pointed out that becoming acceptable as a citizen has nothing to do with nature but is instead based on a process of cultural adaptation; 'culturalization' would therefore be a more appropriate term. However, naturalization can be taken to mean being assimilated into an order that is 'the only natural one' for the place concerned. Failure to assimilate would then label the immigrant as a deviant or an enemy. The confusion between nature and culture is endemic in discourses on citizenship and the nation-state. The concept of naturalization is in blatant contradiction to the idea of citizenship as culturally neutral and open to all members of a society. Curiously, the German-speaking countries, which are highly restrictive in their policies of access to citizenship, use the more neutral term of '*Einbürgerung*', which literally means 'making into a citizen'.

Dealing with globalization: some approaches

Throughout this book, we will be looking at ideas on how citizenship should be reshaped in response to globalization and cultural diversity. Here we will mention just two positions, which can perhaps be seen as the opposing poles in the debate. Between them lies a wide range of interpretations and suggestions, to be found in a growing body of literature. These two positions are:

- The idea that the substance of citizenship and the nation-state are changing anyway through the inexorable forces of globalization, so that little further action is needed.
- The belief that the nation-state, although weakened by internal and external contradictions, is still the only political unit capable of maintaining democratic citizenship.

There is also, of course, the position that nothing fundamental has changed, and that national politics can go on as before. This view is widely held by conservative commentators and politicians. It leads to isolationism and to policies that are dangerously out of touch with both global markets and global cultural transformations. We have already advanced reasons for rejecting this position and will not discuss it further here.

The first position – that global forces of themselves bring about reforms in citizenship patterns – can be associated both with the technocratic ideas of global managerialism and with political theories that focus on the growing role of supra-national human rights norms. We will discuss the former using the work of the Japanese management expert Kenichi Ohmae, and the latter with reference to a study by Harvard sociologist Yasemin Soysal.

In his book, *The Borderless World*, Ohmae argues that a supra-national power has already emerged; he calls it the Interlinked Economy (ILE), which consists of the 'Triad' (the USA, Europe and Japan), joined by new industrial economies such as Taiwan, Hong Kong and Singapore.

> It has become so powerful that it has swallowed most consumers and corporations, made traditional national borders almost disappear, and pushed bureaucrats, politicians and the military towards the status of declining industries. (Ohmae, 1991, p. xi)

This may come as something of a surprise to the officials of the EU or the generals of the Pentagon, and indeed – even more so – to asylum-seekers trying to cross the borders of Fortress Europe, but this is not what Ohmae is concerned with: his borderless world applies to the transnational corporations and their executives and specialists. He is talking about what he sees as an inevitable trend:

> The policy objective for the ILE will be ensuring the free flow of information, money, goods and services as well as the free migration of people and corporations. Traditional governments will have to establish a new single framework of global governance. (Ohmae, 1991, p. xii–xiii)

For Ohmae, the global economy is driven by the free choices of customers, which dictate a radical opening of economies. The task of government is to end protectionism and to 'ensure that its people have a good life by ensuring stable access to the best and the cheapest goods and services from anywhere in the world' (Ohmae, 1991, p. 12). The burgeoning flow of information is turning people into 'global citizens', who are aware of all that is happening around the world – with regard to tastes and preferences, styles of clothing, sports and lifestyles (Ohmae, 1991, pp. 18–22). Thus, Ohmae reduces the philosophical notion of the 'good life' to the right to buy the most stylish and best-quality consumer goods. Global citizenship is about reducing the role of government in order to permit untrammelled play to the transnational corporations.

Yet it is not so easy to dismiss this vision. Ohmae is right to claim that much economic power has passed from states to corporations and to markets. His argument is a post-nationalist one, when he claims that power in the great companies can no longer effectively be based in one country or on one national culture. He shows that successful management requires the abandonment of 'the headquarters mentality', and a real decentralization of decision making to global networks. This is in turn only possible if corporations can free themselves of the national culture of their founders and develop their own transnational culture, that is, 'a system of values that all employees in all countries and regions unquestionably accept' (Ohmae, 1991, p. 89).

Ohmae's 'borderless world' is a comfortless place for those who believe in national autonomy. Developing countries that seek to build up their economies through protectionism are doomed to failure; in Ohmae's view, they should throw open their borders to a free transfer of commodities and capital, whatever the social costs (which he never mentions). The 'borderless world' is also bad news for anyone who believes in democracy. Governments are increasingly powerless, so the right to elect them has little meaning. There are no democratic mechanisms in the global marketplaces and transnational corporations. The theme is not even discussed in Ohmae's book – he clearly sees it as irrelevant. Ohmae's global citizen is imbued with consumerism, not democratic values.

Ohmae is an adviser to some of the world's most powerful corporations, so his views may be seen as a significant expression of the technocratic logic of advanced sectors of capital. He is pointing to real trends that contain serious threats to any notion of democratic citizenship. The analysis shows the difficulties faced by democratically elected authorities constituted at the nation-state level when they seek to influence the global economy. The answer can only lie in the development of democratically elected supra-national bodies capable of developing countervailing power to control economic interests at the global level.

A very different notion of 'post-national membership' is put forward in the book *Limits of Citizenship* by Yasemin Soysal. She argues that:

> A new and more universal concept of citizenship has unfolded in the post-war era, one whose organising and legitimating principles are based on universal personhood rather than national belonging. (Soysal, 1994, p. 1)

Soysal criticizes political sociologists for remaining fixated on the
bounded nation-state as the locus for rights. Her study finds that:

> the classical formal order of the of the nation-state and its membership is not in
> place. The state is no longer an autonomous and independent organisation closed
> over a nationally defined population. Instead, we have a system of constitution-
> ally interconnected states with a multiplicity of membership. (Soysal, 1994,
> pp. 163–4)

The main focus of Soysal's book is a comparative study of incorporation patterns and changes in the societal membership of immigrants
in Western European countries. Soysal (1994, p. 29) argues that 'world-
level pressures towards more expanded individual rights have lead to
the increasing incorporation of foreigners into existing membership
schemes'. At the same time, the extension of membership beyond
national citizens transforms the existing models, 'making national citizenship less important'. A number of questions may be raised with
regard to Soysal's analysis. Does it overstate the extent to which immigrants in Western European countries such as Germany have in fact
gained most of the rights of citizenship without actual formal access to
citizenship? In fact, immigrants are in many places still denied significant social and political rights, being open to deportation for a range of
reasons. Does Soysal overemphasize the importance of 'world-level
pressures' in securing rights for immigrants, while paying little attention to the role of political mobilization by immigrant groups themselves in gaining greater equality?

The main issue that concerns us here, however, is Soysal's conclusion that the emergence of universal personhood is rapidly eroding the
territorially bounded nation-state. In her view, this type of nation-state
was the dominant form for only a fairly short time: from about the mid-
nineteenth century to the mid-twentieth century. Soysal's model of
'post-national belonging' is based on universal human rights, as laid
down in conventions and declarations of supra-national bodies like the
UN, which are gradually incorporated into the constitutions and laws of
nation-states. Thus, universal entitlements are still basically delivered
by the nation-state but are no longer limited by formal citizenship. The
furthest-going expression of the trend is the transnational citizenship
laid down within the EU.

This perspective does correspond with current trends and may have
important consequences for citizenship in future, but Soysal seems to
overstate the extent to which it has been already achieved, and may be
overly optimistic about the strength of the tendency. International

human rights conventions are often not ratified: for example, the 1990 UN Convention on the Rights of Migrant Workers and Members of their Families has only been signed by a handful of emigration countries. Moreover, they may not be implemented where they are ratified, and above all are ignored by the countries where abuses are worst. The number of countries where democracy and human rights prevail is fairly small, and there are strong trends towards exclusionary nationalism and racism in many places. The EU is an important development, but little progress has been made on extending European citizenship rights to the large minorities from outside the EU. The trend in Europe is towards the exclusion of non-EU citizens. In principle, as Soysal points out, that could be consistent with improving the rights of those who have been admitted, but it is far from clear that this is the main tendency at present (see Chapters 4 and 7 for more discussion of EU citizenship).

It thus seems misplaced to argue that 'post-national citizenship' has been or is about to be achieved. The nation-state is still the key reference point for citizenship, and is likely to remain so. Global citizenship has to be built around the reality of a world of nation-states, despite the globalization of economy and culture. Let us therefore turn now to the position that the nation-state is still the only conceivable unit for democratic citizenship, even though it is under pressure through global change. We will again contrast a mainly economic perspective – that of Robert B. Reich – with a political sociology approach – that of Dominique Schnapper.

In his book, *The Work of Nations*, Reich (who was the US Secretary for Labour in the First Clinton Administration) presents a compelling analysis of the effects of globalization:

> As almost every factor of production – money, technology, factories, and equipment – moves effortlessly across border, the very idea of a national economy is becoming meaningless. (Reich, 1991, p. 8)

The question that Reich raises is whether there can be a national society in the absence of a national economy. Citing Adam Smith's *Wealth of Nations*, Reich states, 'the idea that the citizens of a nation shared responsibility for their economic wellbeing' was closely linked to the rise of the democratic nation-state (Reich, 1991, p. 18). As long as economic affairs were organized on national lines, there was a certain degree of common interest that transcended class divisions: successful industrial economies could pass on some of their wealth to workers through higher wages, access to consumer goods and improved welfare systems. This in turn strengthened feelings of national solidarity.

Globalization and technological change shatter the basis of national solidarity. Reich argues that class structure has been transformed through the decline of manufacturing industries in countries such as the USA. Three categories of workers are emerging (Reich, 1991, pp. 171–84):

● routine production workers, the declining group of employees in manufacturing enterprises;
● in-person servers, people performing simple and repetitive tasks, such as retail sales workers, waiters and waitresses, health-care personnel and the growing army of security guards;
● 'symbolic analysts', all the problem-solving, problem-identifying and strategic-brokering activities, which require high-level skills and training.

The first two categories are oriented towards local or national labour markets, while the symbolic analysts function increasingly in global labour markets. It is irrelevant for them whether they work for a US, a Japanese or a transnational company. Moreover, the symbolic analysts have a strong grip on economic power. They can ensure that their earnings grow while the wages of the production workers and in-person servers are strictly limited. This explains the enormous growth of income inequality in the USA over the past 20 years. As real wages and working conditions worsen for most of the population, symbolic analysts have been able to reduce their own personal taxation. This explains the fiscal crisis of the welfare state. The wealthy one-fifth of the population have, according to Reich, effectively seceded from the rest (Reich, 1991, pp. 282–300). They have moved into separate towns and suburbs, protected by private police. They have ceased to contribute to public expenditure, instead financing their own privatized schools, health-care systems and leisure facilities. Above all, they dominate political power and see no reason to share it with the rest of the nation. Politics thus oscillates between the 'zero-sum nationalism' of those who want to turn the clock back, and the 'impassive cosmopolitanism' of people who, as citizens of the world, may feel no particular bond with any society (Reich, 1991, pp. 301–15).

For Reich, the only answer lies in a reassertion of national solidarity. This may be stimulated by 'the inability of symbolic analysts to protect themselves, their families and their property from the depredations of a larger and ever more desperate population outside' (Reich, 1991, p. 303). The main factor, however, must be 'a new patriotism', founded less upon economic self-interest than upon 'loyalty to place'. This could be the starting point for 'a positive economic nationalism', in which each nation's citizens would take responsibility for ensuring that their compatriots had full and productive lives, while also cooperating with other countries for mutual advantage. This would require a sense of national purpose, based on historical and cultural connections to a common political endeavour (Reich, 1991, pp. 311–12). The problem with this conclusion is that it is completely voluntaristic: having demonstrated the powerful forces that are undermining the national bond, Reich postulates that these can be countered by an act of a collective will that, according to his own analysis, no longer exists.

Dominique Schnapper's book, *La Communauté des Citoyens*, was awarded the Prize of the French National Assembly in 1994 for its passionate defence of republican values. Schnapper's analysis combines a reassertion of Rousseau's principle of the common will as the basis of the social bond, with a critique of the contradictions of increasing rationalization of societal relationships that leans heavily on Weber. Schnapper laments the decline of the nation as a political form in the various areas where it originated: Western Europe and North America. She also mentions the 'dysfunctions' connected with the imposition of the nation-state form elsewhere in the world, but this is not her main theme. As the quotation at the beginning of this chapter indicates, Schnapper asserts that the nation-state is being seriously weakened by both external and internal factors (Schnapper, 1994, pp. 11, 185).

The external stresses are connected with globalization and the development of supra- and infra-national units. A global political order, as represented by the UN, limits national independence and sovereignty. The need for common action to achieve collective security, to combat terrorism and to stop drug smuggling also makes inter-state cooperation essential. At the economic level, international markets and the increasing importance of global regulatory bodies such as the International Monetary Fund and the General Agreement on Tariffs and Trade render autonomous national economic policies impossible. Administrative and legal decisions by European bodies restrict the power of national parliaments and governments. At the same time, the emphasis on local interests and cultures creates demands for regional autonomy or representation (Schnapper, 1994, pp. 186–8).

Internally, Schnapper argues, the nation is weakened by an inherent contradiction. Democracy is based on the principle that citizens should be genuinely capable of exercising their rights of participation. This requires not just formal equality, but also a degree of real equality of socioeconomic conditions. Thus, the logic of democratic participation leads inevitably to a welfare state. This in turn engenders a new 'productivist–hedonist logic', which, by emphasizing the interests of the individual, undermines the basic political project of the nation. People come to see the state simply as an instrument that manages the economy and distributes social benefits. *Civisme* (civic or public feeling) gets lost. There is a trend towards depoliticization, which constitutes a constant menace for democratic nations (Schnapper, 1994, pp. 190–1).

These external and internal changes lead to a contradiction:

> between the objective integration of people in a virtually global space and their social habitus, that is their feeling of collective identity, as well as their political participation, which continue to be mainly expressed at the level of the nation. (Schnapper, 1994, p. 189)

The nation becomes degraded to an emotional bond, which can give a subjective meaning to people's existence. This opens the ways for a 're-ethnicization', in which people perceive themselves to be members of an emotional community based on shared history and culture, rather than political citizens who participate in a democracy. Schnapper argues this with reference to Germany's shift from *Verfassungspatriotismus* (Habermas' term for loyalty to a constitutional political community) to a more nationalistic model after the demise of the German Democratic Republic in 1989. She implies, however, that the same trend applies in France, Britain and elsewhere (Schnapper, 1994, pp. 194–6).

Peace and international cooperation appear as problems for the nation-state. 'Every war or threat of war is a factor of integration' (Schnapper, 1994, p. 197). Now that the Soviet threat has gone, Schnapper complains of trends towards pacifism and a lack of *civisme*. She observes a trend towards a decline of the great public institutions – school, army, judiciary, public services – which were intended to teach the values of the nation and democracy. The depoliticization and re-ethnicization of the nation-state undermine the republican project of the individual integration of immigrants and other minorities by means of common political values. This is replaced by separatist consciousness: national identity (for the majority), ethnic identities (for the minorities) and new forms of religious identity (sects and so on) help people to cope with feelings of

powerlessness and disenchantment caused by the increasing rationalization, anonymity and bureaucratization of large-scale societies.

Schnapper presents a powerful analysis of the crisis of democratic
citizenship, yet her critique remains problematic. Although she claims
to be presenting a general argument for a political concept of the
nation, her picture is clearly that of the French republican model. She
is one-sided in her portrayal of the nation, emphasizing its rationality
and its capacity for creating a social bond between people of differing
origins. She neglects past repressions needed to homogenize ethnically
diverse populations, and current racism towards immigrants and
minorities. She idealizes conscription and war as means of national
integration, but ignores the suffering that flowed from this notion of the
warrior-citizen. (In this context, the French government's decision to
abolish conscription in 1996 must have appeared as a threat to civic
values.) Schnapper seems oblivious to the dialectic of rationality and
barbarism that bedevils the history of European nations. The development of communities of warrior-soldiers armed to the teeth against
(real or imagined) external enemies led inexorably to ever-more
horrific wars.

The main problem is that Schnapper suggests no way of
resolving the crisis of the nation-state. She explicitly rejects the notion
of a multicultural society, arguing (without giving any reasons) that
multiculturalism offers merely a 'magical' or apparent solution to the
contradiction between the two great values of modernity: individual
equality inscribed in the principle of citizenship, and *authenticity* tied
to a specific culture. In the same way, Schnapper argues that decentralization and local democracy are insufficient to unite citizens around
a project that creates a common will (Schnapper, 1994, p. 201). In the
end, she states that it seems possible that the project of the democratic
nation has become exhausted, but she offers not even a glimpse of a
way forwards.

From differing perspectives, all four authors discussed here provide
convincing evidence that the nation-state is in serious difficulties.
Ohmae argues from a rather crude economic determinism that nation-
states should not control the workings of global markets. The democratic citizen does not appear in his world-view, while his notion of the
'global citizen' refers to the mobile corporate executive. Soysal's
notion of 'post-national belonging' and her assertion that universal
personhood is rapidly replacing citizenship in the nation-state seem
optimistic in view of the continuing limitation on the rights of migrants
and minorities. Reich gives an incisive critique of the polarization of

US society, but fails to provide a convincing strategy for recreating national solidarity. Schnapper presents a thorough analysis of the stresses faced by nation-states, but is unable to suggest any political solution. In the end, all four analyses lead to inaction, Ohmae and Soysal because they indicate that new modes of political integration are appearing by themselves, Reich and Schnapper because they see no option to the nation-state, even though they show that it is no longer viable in its existing form.

Conclusion

Clearly, globalization and the increasing mobility of people raise new issues for the nation-state and citizenship, and existing models no longer provide the answers. The main thesis of this book is that a theory of citizenship for a global society must be based on the separation between nation and state. Such a theory must, in other words, evacuate the nation part of the concept of the nation-state. This means a new type of state that is not constituted exclusively or mainly around the nexus of territoriality and belonging. Citizenship should therefore not be connected to nationality (that is, to the idea of being one people with common cultural characteristics); citizenship should be a political community without any claim to common cultural identity.

Yet in a world of migrants and ethnic groups, citizenship cannot be blind to cultural belonging. The political mechanisms that make people into citizens must take account both of their equal rights as individuals and their needs, interests and values as members of social and cultural collectivities. Reconciling the individual and the collective is the key problem of citizenship for a globalized society and will be discussed extensively in this volume. The traditional answer of liberal theory – that citizenship refers only to the individual abstracted from his or her sociocultural specificity – is no longer adequate.

Citizenship for a global society also requires a new notion of state borders. These cannot be abolished, as distinct states will remain the rule for the foreseeable future, but borders cannot be rigid, in view of the mobility intrinsic in modernity and globalism. A notion of *porous borders* is required, with admission rules and rights based on people's real societal membership (compare Bauböck, 1994). Such a system would break with the outmoded norm of singular membership in a nation-state and recognize the growing prevalence of dual or multiple membership. There must be a link between admission procedures (to the state territory and to citizenship) and the contents of citizenship. This may require differentiated forms of rights, which take account of people's differing needs and values, as well as new forms of representation and participation.

It is now time to turn to a more fundamental discussion of theories of citizenship, before looking in more detail at the issues raised by the new cultural diversity.

Note

1. An earlier version of some parts of this chapter has been published in Bauböck, R. and Rundell, J. (eds) 'Globalisation and the ambiguities of national citizenship', *Blurred Boundaries* (Aldershot: Ashgate, 1998).

2

Theories of Citizenship

The new global context discussed in Chapter 1 gives rise to new challenges for human beings: they need to cope with and control the new context, and impose a rule of law upon it. They require a new form of citizenship to do this. What then do we need for citizenship in a global world?

Answers to the question of what it means to be a citizen are as old as political theory itself. Yet despite many changes in detail, we can identify only three major reformulations, behind which lies something even more constant. It is only through understanding what citizenship has always concerned that we can grasp why the major reformulations have been made. Even more importantly, it is only through grasping what has been constant in citizenship theory that we can understand the need for a contemporary reformulation that marks a rupture with all the ways in which we have previously considered citizenship.

To be a citizen is first to act to empower oneself against the environment into which one is born (Bobbio, 1990a, pp. 52–3). The nature of that context decides what is needed to empower oneself against it rather than to be a victim or to be subject to its forces. The existential refusal of subjection means that a citizen seeks mastery over whatever pushes him or her back into subjection. The logic is always to expand the number of acts asserted as rights to act the more the context becomes complex (Bobbio, 1990a, pp. 68–9). Citizenship thus tends to an imperious assertion of the mastery of humankind over all environments. Ultimately, it is a calculation about the context that decides what combination of acts is necessary to empower individuals against or over that context. What they will do depends on what they think the world is. It is clear that, over history, that understanding has changed, as has our understanding of what it is to be a citizen.

Yet a constant factor has always been that the way to be empowered is to subject the chaotic, arbitrary and irrational to rules that individuals and collectivities make. Freedom consists in making laws for ourselves (Rousseau, 1971, p. 524). Thus, citizenship means acts that establish a rule of law and not of men. However, the management of the context through the establishment of law – which thus tends to end all tyranny – has always implied a belief in the capacity of reason to arrive at an understanding of what is to be done to master the natural or uncontrollable world. Citizenship as empowerment and dominance over a threatening context rests on a primacy accorded to human reasoning capacity.

Who can speak and who has the capacity to reason has itself rested on the context, and as that context has changed so has the attribution of the right to reason and to establish the laws of conviviality. Broadly speaking, we can detect two main traditions concerning reason. The first is élitist and hostile to popular wisdom, the second democratic and based on popular wisdom. This latter is the only position easily reconciled with the desire to be empowered, since only that position is consistent with power from below. Where the last word rests with experts, there is only power from above, and that must disempower those below. Logically, citizenship as empowerment must tend to be expansive and inclusive as it seeks to solve ever-widening and complex problems involving an ever-greater number of people. A world of change can only be a world where the concept of reason itself grows and adapts.

This very expansion renders reason fragile and uncertain. It thus itself becomes ever more open to renegotiation with regard to its terms. It is notable that in history, as the world became more complex, it was less and less assumed that, as a totality, it could ever be truly described. On the other hand, it was essential to pretend that the total story was true, rather than a myth, to make sense of it and to take the actions that provided empowerment and made life liveable. Thus, when the notion of a citizen first emerged, it did so among people who believed that what we call myths were true statements about the world. Gradually, those 'religious' beliefs where all was explained in, for example, a Creation myth revealed themselves to be inadequate to explain the world. Nevertheless, an agreed story or 'myth' about how the world worked as a whole (a hypothesis) was still necessary in order to decide how to master it. 'Science' merely demystified or deconstructed the parts. It could show what was wrong about parts of the master myth of the context, but never what was right about it.

Summed up, citizenship has always been about empowerment in and over a baffling and changing world context. It has involved more and more acts, rights and obligations as people have increasingly seen what was necessary in order to be empowered. That process will not stop since its object is security and contentment (Montesquieu, 1964, p. 598) in a world of change. Its own refusal of reason as science in favour of reason as negotiated consensus, infinitely renewable, tempers its consequent militant assertion of the will of those who 'dare to think'. The latter is certainly an imperial quality in which the refusal of subjection in favour of freedom can quickly slide into a warrior ethic, but it also means a mild and weak approach to knowledge, and a refusal of totalitarian sureties.

We will illustrate these generalizations by a brief examination of the oldest theories of citizenship, those which were developed in ancient Greece and Rome. Most of the structure of those theories is still relevant to any discussion of citizenship today, but the content is no longer of relevance because the context has completely changed.

The Athenian model

First, there was the theme of bringing peace and order out of chaos. Plato pointed to Zeus' deep concern with peace within communities faced with chaos when he instructed Hermes, his winged messenger, to impart to 'men the qualities of respect for others and a sense of justice, so as to bring order into our cities and create a bond of friendship and union' (Plato, 1987, p. 54). Then there was the theme of men uniting together to establish their rule of law as equals. According to Aristotle, citizens established a state to ensure their survival as a self-sufficient community in a process of negotiation involving all participants (see, for example, Aristotle, 1986, pp. 60–1, 169–71, 456–7), whose collective life depended on defending that conviviality against threats. Finally, there was the theme of militant propagation and defence of the rule of law.

These qualities of citizenship were already present in the famous funeral oration given by Pericles in Athens in 429 BC for soldiers who had fallen in the defence of democracy against the Spartans. He started by praising first the ancestors who had handed on a 'free country', and then the fathers and men who had constructed a state organized in such a way that it was perfectly able to defend itself in peace and war. Pericles proceeded to explain to the 'assembly of citizens and foreigners'

why they had died by their desire to protect a political order that made
them what they were:

> Let me say that our system of government does not copy the institutions of our
> neighbours... Our constitution is called a democracy because power is in the
> hands not of a minority but of the whole people. When it is a question of settling
> private disputes, everyone is equal before the law, when it is a question of putting
> one person before another in positions of public responsibility what counts is not
> membership of a particular class, but the actual ability which a man possesses.
> No-one, so long as he has it to be of service to the state, is kept in political obscu-
> rity because of poverty. And, just as we do not get into a state with our next-door
> neighbour if he enjoys himself in his own way, nor do we give him the kind of
> black looks which, although they do no real harm, still do hurt people's feelings.
> We are free and tolerant in our private lives; but in public affairs we keep to the
> law. This is because it commands our deep respect. We give our obedience to
> those who we put in positions of authority, and we obey the laws themselves,
> especially those which are for the protection of the oppressed, and those
> unwritten laws which it is an acknowledged shame to break. (Thucydides, 1964,
> pp. 116–17)

In this is encapsulated the essence of being a citizen, when first the
term was used. The people made themselves into a citizenry by establishing a rule of law to defend themselves within and without. They
believed that their system of government or state, which issued those
laws, was something that others should imitate, and that their own
laws, written and unwritten, should be obeyed. The citizen was a
warrior on both accounts. Citizenship as a creation of community is
always created against the representation of disorder, but where can the
threat come from once the rule of law to which all are obedient has
been established under their control? It can only come from those who
are outside the citizenry. In principle, the militant warrior-citizen thus
faced those without with as much fierceness as he was full of 'friendship' for those within.

Of course, not all those called 'foreigners' by Pericles were in practice enemies. Indeed, there were clearly always friendly outsiders, or
non-citizens, within the state; the Athenians were explicitly aware of
that. Thus, lines had to be drawn between those ready to accept a city's
written and unwritten laws and those not. Those outsiders who
accepted such public values and their underlying rationality were therefore sharply distinguished from those who could not or did not do so.
Indeed, at the limit there existed those who could not communicate at
all with the citizens. They were the barbarians, who could only
stammer 'bababa'. In the Athenian notion of a citizen we can already
see the primacy given to reason understood as 'our discourse', or the

story a citizenry tells about itself. We can also clearly see the confusion in such a 'collective memory' of myth and history. The democratic practice of Athenians was traced back to Zeus giving instructions to a winged messenger called Hermes; men were the heirs to the Gods.

What was notable in the Greek battle against chaos of a human sort through uniting politically to establish its contrary, a rule of law, was its recognition of the practical limits to citizenship. The writ of a rule of law might begin in a community where it could be enforced over practically all aspects of social life – despite Pericles' tolerance of the private – but it was difficult to enforce where there was no community of shared experience. In the mythical discourse of the Greeks, most of those ancient communities were small city-states, with tiny populations, who could come together even physically in a square to make collective decisions and vote on them (Ehrenberg, 1950, p. 515; Larsen, 1954, p. 1). This has become known as direct democratic procedure, even if state functions were vested in a limited number of people. According to such a theory, the private space where particular rules were needed was small. Technically, even the affairs of the bedroom could be discussed and legislated on by the whole people. The issue was, who were the 'whole people'?

In practice, even before such cities established empires and started to disintegrate, there were always too many people for the myth that all could be involved in deciding matters of state to hold. Apart from foreigners who came to trade, there were those taken as slaves, and also women and children. Most were regarded as existing in a strictly private realm, and were excluded from the making of the laws under which they could live. Two favoured arguments to justify their exclusion were that they were unable to fight to defend the state, or could not be trusted to do so, and that they did not have the reason to adhere to its values and thus represented chaos within (see Hartsock, 1984, pp. 123–50; Irigaray, 1984, pp. 27–50). This illustrates how close any rationalization for exclusion is to the logic that requires citizen law to control chaos. The fierce war against the external enemy who threatens chaos is accompanied by a battle against other chaotic value systems within: those of foreigners, women and children, who are regarded as slaves of their own unreason.

It is important to insist on this logic of citizenship even in the Athenian political project, because Athens is often extolled as the model of democratic citizenship. Instead, it illustrates the contradiction and Achilles heel of citizenship. The latter starts with a laudable desire for conviviality established by a consensus among equals. This is considered so desirable that the ultimate virtue is to defend it against any threat from attack. While its logical goal is universal and perpetual peace, until all humans accept the procedures it involves, they may represent the Other as chaos, or the negation of order and the rule of law. Even an 'open republic' that any outsider can join presumes rules for those who already belong to it; a rule for admission to belonging and thus rules of exclusion, and finally rules for those who do not and will not belong.

While citizenship is clearly tendentially democratic and inclusive, the speed of its progress towards such inclusion will depend on the openness of its rules of admission. Yet at the same time, it tends to a militant defence of what it has achieved and will do so until its values are generally accepted. Citizenship's limits can too easily be seen in the Aristotelian endorsement of a particular myth that is not limited to Athens but is implicit in citizenship more generally.

Although Aristotle, the foremost theoretician of citizenship in Athens, expressly stated that citizens were a group who, to bring order from chaos, united to make laws for a common good, and that politics thus preceded community, he described that process mythico-historically as the politics of familial groups united through blood into clans, who needed to establish a commonweal. He wisely recognized that that story could not be squared with reality (who knew where one's forefathers came from?). To establish who had, and did not have, the right to make laws in a constituted state that already existed, however, Aristotle insisted that only those who could establish kinship (blood) ties with someone else already entitled to those rights could be a citizen. This, of course, kept all foreigners as non-citizens *ad infinitum*. They did not and could not belong. The absurdity of such a view was clear to Aristotle, who knew that practical realities – the context – demanded that there be other ways to obtain citizenship, by grant for example.

This was the significant first formulation of the legal rights of citizenship known as the *ius sanguinis*. What is notable is that, even then, it was seen as impracticable.

Multiethnic citizenship in Ancient Rome

Citizenship takes on a completely new meaning in ancient Rome: it is no longer bound to membership of a specific *polis*, and even less so to belonging to a community based on kinship. As Rome expanded from a city-state to a vast empire, it developed a form of citizenship capable of incorporating people of quite diverse cultural origins. Under the Republic, Etruscans and various other peoples of the Italian peninsula were incorporated as citizens, followed by Greeks and Gauls. Citizenship was also broadened in social terms: liberated slaves were granted citizenship, often remaining in the household of their former masters. In some cases, thousands of enslaved prisoners of war were freed and made into citizens. Such slaves came from Greece, Syria, Gaul and the Danube region – their ethnic origin was irrelevant. Under the Empire, Roman citizenship was conferred on individuals and groups who had served Rome, such as auxiliary troops or tribes seen as useful in defending the Imperial frontiers. Caracalla's Edict of 212 AD granted citizenship to nearly all free people living in the Empire (Schnapper, 1994, pp. 86–7; Demandt, 1995, pp. 24–6).

If citizenship in Greece meant belonging to a city, Rome extended the meaning of both notions. Roman citizenship meant membership in a political community, based on legally defined rights and duties. According to Demandt (1995, p. 23), citizenship was not defined in terms of common history or culture, and could be conferred on anyone, whatever his origin. In contrast, Balibar (1993, p. 197, following Nicolet, 1976) argues that Rome included all who shared a common culture, but that this culture could be extended to embrace anyone who was granted citizenship, which was hereditary and marked belonging to the 'ruling class of the universe'. In any case, the crucial point in terms of the history of citizenship is that Rome marked the first appearance of the citizen as a legal subject with civil and personal rights. This opened the way to the inclusion of foreigners and laid the basis for the principle of universalism in citizenship rights (Schnapper, 1994, pp. 87–8).

Conquered peoples were treated with mildness and not forced to give up their local customs and languages, yet Rome appears to have had no notion of cultural pluralism. Common law, languages, technology and cultural practices were powerful instruments of integration. Plinius estimated that 53 peoples that had once lived in Latinium had disappeared completely. Adopting Roman ways of doing things was closely linked to integration into the legal community. Latin was generally used in the western part of the Empire, while Greek and Aramaic were used in the east. Latin had a powerful influence in eroding older languages, and the languages of many modern Western European countries derive from it. Religious openness facilitated the integration of conquered people: polytheism made it possible to add Greek, Syrian or Germanic gods to the panoply of Roman deities. However, conflict arose when monotheistic peoples were added to the Empire. The Jews repeatedly rebelled against polytheism and were forcibly repressed. The Christianization of Rome – especially the conversion of Emperor Constantine in 312 AD – undermined the principle of tolerance that had been so important to the success of Roman civilization, paving the way for the dissolution of the Empire (Demandt, 1995, pp. 26–37).

Rome was able to create a legal and political community that had no need for myths of common origins. However, Roman citizenship implied neither equality nor participation in public life. An inclusive form of membership was possible just because citizenship no longer required a face-to-face community, as in the Greek *polis*. The modern principle of democratic representation through elections was, however, yet to emerge. Rome was ruled by an oligarchy based on economic and military power. Only the wealthy could become magistrates or senators. Roman citizenship did not imply active citizens who exercised political power, but passive citizens with rights and duties within a *Rechtsstaat*. It may thus be seen as a step forward compared with the Greek *polis* in terms of inclusiveness, but a step backward in terms of democracy.

Nation-state citizenship: the social contract

Whatever the merits of the Athenian system, its impracticability in a changed context meant a reformulation of the notion after the fall of the Roman Empire. The world in which the Athenians sought to impose their rules extended only to tiny city-states, smaller than even the smallest nation-state that had emerged by the seventeenth century. Fortunately, that changed context is much easier for us to understand, since it is the context in which we still live. This is the context of a world of nation-states that has emerged to become universal over four centuries, with some 200 states. In a sense, the great seventeenth-century political philosophers Hobbes, Locke, Rousseau and Kant wrote, in terms that are familiar, about what concerns us today.

The shared reality is that of large modern states covering huge territories. Even in the seventeenth century, people were born into such systems of power, whose links were lost in a labyrinthine web leading back to people they might never see. It was the incomprehensible nature of those power systems that individuals and groups sought to control, thus constituting themselves as citizens. It was because they experienced a real 'war of all against all', as Hobbes (1968) put it, that they wished to create an orderly lawful world, and challenged the rules and values of the existing systems.

While there were clearly variations in the modern states that made up the world of the seventeenth century, their basic characteristic was that they were ruled by absolute monarchs, who regarded all in their state as their possessions. These monarchs had started as the strongest feudal warlords in a world of near anarchy between regions. They had imposed themselves over the others in a more extended area, which was labelled France or Great Britain; done deals over the division of the spoils in a Mafia-like fashion; and held on to their pre-eminence by brutal power that was challenged again and again. They had systematized that world through dynastic marriages, alliances maintaining a balance of power, rudimentary systems of centralized armed force, taxation and, in some cases by the seventeenth century, centralized legal systems.

Their subjects had no control over the ensuing arbitrariness and violence that marked their lives. Vast bands of vagabonds infested the forests and occasionally descended on the towns to wreak mayhem. For most people, life was nasty, brutish and short. Their sovereign monarchs claimed the right to their relatively untrammelled power on the ground that it was given by God, that they were like patriarchs and that their subjects were like their children. A familial model of society and the state held sway. It was legitimated by reference to the neo-Aristotelian theory that described an organic growth of larger societies from clan and tribal origins, linked by kinship. There could be some support for that view in the emergence of the early modern state from the local power systems of the middle ages, but it was nonetheless a fratricidal family.

Citizenship theory of the new sort thus arose against a background of existing state power. Unlike the Greek theory that portrayed citizenship as an organic growth out of a community, and in which the enemy of the citizen was the amorphous Other beyond the walls, modern theory saw citizenship as the assertion of individuals against a tyrannical state power. It was simultaneously a rejection of the notion that everyone was part of a family in which the sovereign power was the father (Bobbio, 1989, pp. 3ff). Thus, against naturally given hierarchies of authority and reason, it asserted only socially accorded hierarchies of authority and reason. This ultimately ended in the assertion of the common sense of the people against all expertise (Locke, 1959).

The existing state fought all these pretensions until forced either to concede to them or to compromise with them. The most successful example of the state being forced to compromise was in the Glorious

English Revolution of 1688, which brought William of Orange to power as a constitutional monarch. This was the culmination of an almost century-long popular struggle to establish a rule of law that embodied some accountability of the law-making sovereign to those over whom he ruled. All the basic ingredients were there: a tyrannous state; revolutionary people who overthrew the monarch by force and imposed their views in a Bill of Rights and an Act of Settlement; a clever state machine; and above all a judiciary that was appointed, so to speak, as the guardian of the law (those rights in the documents above). It took another tyrant and another revolution, that of America in 1776, as well as another assertion of the right of popular wisdom or common sense to rule, before that judicial supremacy was superseded by a claim to political supremacy of the citizens (Paine, 1987, p. 65).

What this illustrated was an enduring theme in modern citizenship theory. Democracy is always a battle against the state to control it, not simply the once and for all establishment of a good constitution, but that lesson had still to be learnt concretely, as it would be in the French Revolution. The more sophisticated lesson, that the edge was gained by never transferring the citizens' right to establish the rules of reason to other groups and institutions, was only learnt in the twentieth century. Where Hobbes had warned against succumbing to the pretensions of the common law to embody social wisdom and have the last say, the revolutionaries of 1688 began the sell-out to that notion which has put the English-speaking world behind other models ever since.

This is why what is known as social contract theory, mainly British and elaborated in the seventeenth century, is much less important than it was. The basic thrust of such theory was to insist that sovereign or state only ruled with the consensus of its subjects. However, it focused more on the moment of the constitution of a polity that put power in popular hands, than on the regular accountability of the sovereign to those who were ruled. It was thus possible to argue that a people might by agreement place all power in the hands of an absolute monarch because the latter could guarantee peace, without there being any notion that the people still decided what rights they had, beyond that of not having their lives taken away.

The French Revolution

The real turning point to a modern theory of citizenship – where the citizens make all the laws under which they live rather than just the basic law or constitution – came with the French Revolution of 1789. In contrast, the American Revolution of 13 years earlier was the last of the great social contractarian revolutions, inspired by Locke and Rousseau. Like the earlier English revolution, it was considered enough to establish a rule of law understood as the right to fair trial (equality before the law) for everyone rather than the right to equal treatment and equal conditions (equality in the law). To declare a right to pursue happiness was even more vague than declaring a right to equal opportunity and light years from any list of concrete rights to ensure those opportunities. The Americans assumed private property without adequately examining the implications of such doctrines. The kindest gloss we can put on this is that people only gradually discover their own hypocrisy and that it was not as obvious to their founding fathers (note the metaphor) as it was a century later to novelist Anatole France that there is something strange about a formal equality in which some live under bridges and others in palaces: 'The law in its majestic equality, forbids all men to sleep under bridges, to beg in the street, and to steal bread – the rich as well as the poor.'

It is in the debate on the rights of man and the citizen at the time of the French Revolution that we see with absolute clarity that the modern theory of the citizen in a nation-state insists on the citizens' rights against the state, and that this view is imposed by political force on those who give primacy to the law or duties and obligations towards the state. The experience of the common people, or the third estate as they were known, was that they were nothing, and they demanded that they be everything. For them, the extension of the modern state had meant tyranny. Indeed, their demands were built on the 'recent memory of despotism' (Stewart, 1963, p. 456), and as they felt this to be an encroachment on and denial of whatever freedoms they had had, they were determined that the system they set up would be subordinate to a recognition of their rights and dignity.

That is why the conservatives of 1789 argued bitterly against a Bill of Rights and for a Bill of Duties. They failed. Citizenship is thus first an assertion of popular will, and then a list of legal rights that are regarded as inherent in all people as equals. Only afterwards does it involve particular political arrangements and duties to the state. We see this in the Declaration of the Rights of Man and the Citizen, which states (Art. 1) that all men are equal in their rights, and (Art. 3) that sovereignty lies in the nation, whose general will is expressed in the laws. This is achieved through the participation of all equally directly or through representatives in making those laws (Art. 6).

In practically all of these early modern formulations, the words 'citizens', 'people' and 'nation' are used interchangeably. What must be noticed is that the regime of equality in rights that is imposed by a revolutionary people comprises above all those rights which guarantee 'human dignity' no matter what the objective difference of an individual. Thus, again and again in different versions of such declarations, we meet the assertion that, after life and liberty, each individual possesses himself and his property, and has a right to freedom of conscience, expression and organization so that he can participate in the debate leading to the making of the laws. The implicit democracy is a set of procedures designed to protect rights in a private realm, which are precisely rights of and to difference (Rials, 1988, pp. 475–751).

The modern citizen who emerges from the French Revolution – unlike his Greek forebear – divides his life into a public and private realm, the second being more important (Constant, 1990, p. 309). 'Freedom from' exists in the private realm. The public is a collective space where he unites with others as a people in designing laws for the common good. Unity is only expected in that public space of the republic. Here, we note another difference from the Greek model. The French people who overthrew the Bourbon tyranny and declared themselves citizens defined their own limits by reference to the modern state against which they stood. Its political/jurisdictional borders in 1789 decided who was united against it; it was thus the modern state that created the limits to a 'people'. The latter were in fact a host of cultures, often not even sharing a common language, who were united only by what they stood against, and by an agreement that certain mechanisms had to be established to control the arbitrariness of despotism. There was no social or familial common origin to the modern citizen. Instead, the nation that was so often referred to can be reduced ideologically to a claim to ancient politico-legal rights (which had usually never existed) and to a unity forged in defence of the 'open republic' that they had established as their defence against the chaos of tyranny.

We pause here to emphasize that any unity greater than that of a shared defence of civil and political rights and of democracy – even that of a shared language – was only developed from the battle of Valmy (1790) onwards, when a French citizen army defeated the powerful Prussian military. The refrain of the Marseillaise, '*Aux armes citoyens*', highlights the importance of the warrior aspect of citizenship against the outside threat. From a defence of their political arrangements against those dedicated to destroy them, including other states such as Britain, and a readiness to strike alliances with anyone who supported them, notably the USA, grew a sense of nationality – and not vice versa. As the 1793 French constitution made clear, anyone who agreed with the political arrangements in France could become a French citizen almost at will.

Most of those procedures existed more in theory than in practice, but even their declaration hinted at their claims to be ever more inclusive. Thus, the assertion of equality as a principle never to be vitiated by objective differences in status or wealth, while at first in fact excluding women, provided a basis for the latter's claim to admission to the polity. Again, while the procedures of representative democracy had to be fought for, and took a century to become really established, they were logically implicit in the claim to equality. Certainly, they were claimed as the rights of *man* and as *individuals* rather than groups, but the heterogeneous regions of France that clamoured for them saw them as a defence of local communities. The only national community was that of the 'open republic' (Delbruck, 1994, pp. 45–56).

The identification of citizenship with the creation and defence of a particular political order, basically that of representative responsible democracy under a rule of law, created a significant blind spot that took over 150 years to cure. As the creation of reasoning equals who agreed on procedures, the modern citizenry tended to ignore the origin of each individual member. Indeed, it started from the rejection of history in the myth of natural rights of man (Bobbio, 1990a, Ch. 1). The conditioning of past and culture were downplayed in an emphasis on the capacity of mind and will to free men from that past, which was usually seen as bad. Typically, Immanuel Kant, an admirer of Rousseau, who was most influential in the ideas of the promoters of the rights of man, saw this liberation from 'self-imposed tutelage' as coming through the act of 'daring to think' (for oneself). Thus, the past passed into thought as all men, as potentially reasoning beings, refused it and decided for themselves as autonomous reasoning beings what was best to do (Kant, 1784). Kant ascribed the refusal to do so as laziness resulting from too long obeying natural guardians – for Kant, like all good modern theorists of citizenship, was firmly against the familial model of society:

> A government based on the principle of benevolence towards the people, like the government of a *father* towards his sons, that is a *paternalistic government* (*imperium paternale*) in which the subjects, like children in their minority who cannot distinguish what is useful from what is harmful to themselves, are obliged to act only passively, to await the judgement of the head of state about the way in

which they must be happy, and expect only his bounty when he wants, is the worst *despotism imaginable* (a regime which denies all freedom to the subjects, who thus have no rights whatsoever). (Kant, 1985, p. 72, original emphasis)

The socialist critique and the rise of the welfare state

This reduction of human beings to will and mind worked passingly well for those classes who led the French and American Revolutions, but it was difficult for others less privileged to remain in control of the state on such terms. Objective discrepancies in wealth, status and education prevented their having any empowering say in making the laws. The nineteenth century thus became a battle between the liberal individualistic interpretation of citizenship epitomized in Kant and extolled by the middle classes, and a liberal socialist interpretation increasingly adhered to by an organized working class. In some thinkers, for example John Stuart Mill in England and Francesco de Sanctis in Italy, we can actually see the shift take place within their thought.

What rapidly became clear in the first half of the nineteenth century was that certain economic, social and educational conditions had to be met if the citizens were to participate in the debate and choose the representatives through whom they made the laws. Citizens came from different worlds, with different pasts, even once it was admitted that they should be equal at the voting booth. Where they came from socially and what histories they had could not be ignored.

The work of Georg Wilhelm Hegel, Ludwig Feuerbach and a young Karl Marx thus laid the ground for a reassessment of the nature of citizenship. The essential thrust of their work is, for our purposes, embodied in Feuerbach's claim that 'Suffering precedes thought', which broke radically from Kant's views. Metaphorically speaking, the stomach ruled the heart and mind, and if it were the central preoccupation, it would not be possible for citizens to participate as reasoning activists. Marx elaborated at length on this in *On the Jewish Question* (Marx, 1975, Part III, pp. 146ff). To the political state of the citizen could be opposed the reality of a bourgeois society, with all its inequalities in wealth and education (Bovero and Bobbio, 1979, Part II). To make the civil and political rights work to empower men, they would have to be underpinned by certain levels of economic wellbeing and education. The Marxist solution was another revolution to eliminate inequality from the realms hitherto regarded as private, especially those of work and property.

Independently, similar but less radical views were expressed by Mill in his chapters on socialism. We may typify these as being those of an honest bourgeois forced to face the facts by the working-class movements that had arisen to challenge the gross discrepancies in conditions in the industrial society emerging since the French Revolution (Mill, 1991). Thereafter, thinkers like Bosanquet and Hobhouse started to insist that, to make the active political citizen possible, economic, social and educational rights would have to be added to the civil and political rights found at that time only in the French and American constitutions. Hobhouse wrote with regard to his views:

> This, it will be said, is not Liberalism but Socialism. Pursuing the economic rights of the individual we have been led to contemplate a Socialistic organisation of industry. But a word like Socialism has many meanings, and it is possible that there should be liberal socialism, as well as a socialism that is illiberal. (Hobhouse, 1964, pp. 77, 87)

Indeed, it had become so clear by the 1920s that a citizen who controlled the state under which he or she was subject was impossible without such an extension of rights, that even in states where this was a distant pipe dream, theorists of citizenship tended to be liberal socialists. In Italy, the liberal-socialist movement that emerged in 1925 started to challenge the followers of Marx as opponents of the Fascist total state. Early liberalism in countries of new settlement such as Australia adopted similar ideas in the early years of this century.

Again, the motive power for these additions to the theory of the citizen was those who still felt disempowered by state and society, usually the organized working class. The ruling state machine was pressured into making such concessions both directly and indirectly as it sought to incorporate the working classes into the polity through extensions of the franchise. These were consequent on the principles of equality and consensus that had marked the modern notion of citizenship. They had been difficult to gainsay, but a successful resistance to the voice of the people becoming dominant had been fought for 50 years after the French Revolution. The argument had often been that to dare to think required an education, and that once that had been given, a person would be admitted to the franchise or active citizenship. Until then, he or she would enjoy only the rights of passive citizenship. Mill argued strongly for this view.

In fact, the nineteenth century forever discredited the idea that people can easily be schooled into right ideas. Instead, once educated they carried their threat of another revolution into the debate on the good and to the voting booths. Thus, it became imperative to buy them off with national educational, then welfare and finally health systems. This took place unevenly in the period 1880–1945. It was a tacit admission of the Marxist critique of the Enlightenment.

Today, it seems obvious that the core notion of the active neo-Kantian citizen is impracticable if that person is unable for economic, social or educational reasons to fulfil that role. However, it took over a hundred years before it was accepted in the first welfare states established after 1945. There were multiple reasons for this. One was the successful resistance of the privileged against the ill-organized poor, the 'masses'. The former were able to characterize such liberal-socialist views as standing against freedom in three ways. First, there was the argument that started in Mill's work: that unbridled democracy threatened individual liberties, so the 'roar of the people' was to be avoided or controlled. Second, such 'socialism' threatened the obliteration of rights to person and property. It was totalitarian even if it had majority support. Third, and this is more telling, it required the state regulation of society when citizenship rights had been established against the state; active citizens did not want a maximalist state, they wanted a minimalist one that guaranteed the pre-existing private realm.

The refutation of such views in practice and in theory took place mainly when Fascism dominated Europe in 1922–45. During that experience, it became clear that democracy and common sense if really expressed – and not controlled by state education – were opposed to totalitarianism. This argument could be and was extended to Stalinist Communism in 1945–55. The tendency of the modern total state to obliterate difference and the rights that protected it, made so obvious by Nazism, also made clear the distinction between a state socialism of a totally levelling sort and a demand for a threshold of welfare rights that would enable a person to be a thinking, acting citizen. Finally, it was increasingly recognized that a citizen might start by being vigilant against the state but that this was coupled with obligations to his or her fellows and the state itself once social welfare was regarded as a citizen right.

When Mill made his defence of liberty against Rousseauian democracy, he emphasized the role of representation in a large state as a mediating and moderating function rather than an expression of the will of the people. He thus made clear that certain levels of education would be required both for the franchise and for being a representative. He was decidedly hostile to popular wisdom (Mill, 1991, p. 19). This was in fact an élitist belief that some men (and women?) could see or understand more than others. This view was common in the nineteenth century, reaching its epitome in the Hegelian theory that history had been a succession of ever more wise civilizations, culminating in Hegel's great mind. The common position of liberalism and the fore-runners of extreme nationalism and Fascism was clear. Ultimately, the denial of the voice of the people in favour of expert leadership could and did lead to its converse, the *Führerprinzip*. Marcuse's devastating words are that 'we can say it is liberalism that "produces" the total-authoritarian state out of itself, as its own consummation at a more advanced stage of development' (Marcuse, 1969, p. 19). Such associations were frequently made in the 1930s, when it became more and more clear that limited liberalism, that is, liberalism without democracy, led to its converse.

If it remained obvious only to a few that representative democracy was the only sort possible in large modern states, and direct democracy had dangerous Napoleonic overtones, it was increasingly refor-mulated away from the managerial model of the nineteenth century. The basic procedures were still the same. Indeed, the 'state of the art' formulation of a leading liberal socialist remained in the 1980s (Bobbio, 1984, pp. 4–5):

1. Power is exercised by a very high number of people affected by it.
2. Decisions are made by the majority of that number.
3. Decisions are made between real alternatives by people able to make real choices.
4. That this means they have freedom of conscience, speech, organization and whatever else is necessary to the other procedures.
5. There are therefore rights guaranteed by a rule of law.

Such a definition would probably have been shared by Mill a hundred years earlier, but not by the majority of liberal theorists. What was new followed from the desire to make the people's voice heard and dominant rather than muted through expert representatives. What was demanded was democracy in more places, that is, a shift away from the central 'national' house of parliament to a semi-federal structure with many levels of regional and municipal government. Only a tiny minority of thinkers had shared such decentralizing local representative democracy notions in the nineteenth century. This demand for more democracy in more places, increasingly heard in the movements of resistance to Fascism, and later Communism, should not be confused with a demand for a return to direct democracy. This was regarded both as impracticable even in a self-managed large factory, and as allowing easy manipulation by totalitarianism.

Since the object was the empowering of popular reason against that of experts who knew how the world worked, these demands – which became a clamour in the early 1940s in Europe – highlighted the importance of minimal economic and social standards even in a free market economy. Indeed, it is worthwhile noting that the clamour was led by neo-Kantians, who knew full well Kant's commitment to the notion that the free market would spell peace through the moderation of commercial exchange. It was pointed out not only that it was impossible to have a real democratic debate and vote without the fundamental civil and political liberties and thus the rigid opposition of democracy and liberalism favoured by Anglo-Saxon commentators, but also that at least those economic, social and educational standards necessary to the active citizen had to be guaranteed by the state.

While many post-1945 European constitutions embodied that view, and they are a feature of the European Union (Fabricius, 1992, pp. 153–72), the slide from the definition of a citizen as what a person does, to what that person gets in the dominant liberal-socialist definition that had emerged by the 1950s sometimes led to complacency. For example, the British were among the leaders in establishing the welfare state, one of the architects of that project being T. H. Marshall. In what was without doubt the most influential book on the citizen of the immediate postwar era, he tended to stress that with the establishment of the economic, social and other rights obtained in Great Britain, the battle for the really autonomous citizen who could make the laws under which that citizen lived had been won (Marshall, 1950).

In fact, the facts showed that the battle had still to be won. While the United Nations had readily accepted a standard for democratic citizenship in its Universal Declaration of Human Rights (1948) and the International Covenant on Civil and Political Rights (1966), few countries were prepared to subscribe to that on Economic, Social and Cultural Rights (1966). In addition, within the Council of Europe (1949) and the European Economic Community (1957), the first supra-national organizations marking the emergence of a global society, there is still a resistance to signing the Social Charters. Had Marshall seen the reverses of the welfare system under the policies of 'economic rationalism' of the 1980s, he might not have been so sanguine about what had been attained. Again, and perhaps even more significant than the fact that in the 1960s most of the third generation rights (social rights) remained dead letters in practice on the grounds that they marked creeping Communism, was the fact that many advanced capitalist economies, notably the USA and the old Commonwealth, had constitutions that totally excluded such rights.

All this added up to a need to keep the citizen active and to maintain what had been clear to Bryce when he wrote these words in 1909:

> the highest... duty of a citizen is to fight valiantly for his convictions when he is in a minority. The smaller the minority, the more unpopular it is, and the more violent are the attacks upon it, so much louder is the call to duty to defend one's opinions. To face 'the multitude hasting to do evil' – this is a role and test of genuine virtue and courage. Now this is, or seems to be, a more formidable task the vaster the community becomes. It is harder to make your voice heard against the roar of the ocean than against the whistling squall that sweeps down over a mountain lake. (Bryce, 1909, pp. 6–8)

It was already clear from experience and surveys that the populace felt so divorced from national decision making that, unless coerced, it would not even vote in elections. When it was looked after by the state, it became increasingly passive and absent, leaving it to unaccountable and interested élites to rule. This was characteristic of wealthy and welfare states everywhere by the 1950s (Dalton, 1988; Roche, 1992).

The return to the active citizen, which is the latest stage in this debate (Kymlicka and Norman, 1993), is largely explained by the need for an increasingly passive citizenship to defend what it can of a notion that not only is it central to citizenship to make the laws under which a person lives, but also each person is entitled to certain minimal economic, social and educational standards. What these should be is a matter of continuing debate. Yet what has prompted the latest reformulation of what is needed for citizenship, and indeed thrown even the liberal-socialist definition into crisis by altering the terms of the debate, lies elsewhere.

The Other

Bearing in mind the primary purpose of citizenship – to impose our own rules on a human environment that would otherwise be chaotic and tyrannical – we understand that it continually faces new problems as that world grows bigger and more complex. As we have just seen, the demand for an active democratic citizen right in the French Revolution led to a realization that the economic, social and educational world also had to be controlled to attain that goal. Thus, as has frequently been pointed out, the list of citizen rights is extending and grows each decade.

The citizens who impose their laws on the new and therefore chaotic and whose reason we have discussed so far – that is, citizenship theory – have all been from the Greco-Judaeo-Christian tradition. Indeed, modern citizenship theory comes almost exclusively from Europe and the areas of white settlement. This theory developed just as these regions imposed themselves as the imperial masters of practically all of the rest of the world's inhabitants, the bulk of whom belonged to different civilizations. Just where they fitted in to even the world of the 'open republic' posed a radical problem for citizenship theory as it has been discussed to this point.

All the theorists we have discussed tend not to find the category of 'the people', the 'us', who seek to master a lawless world where men rule, problematic. While most realize that the 'people' who established the modern definition of citizen in the late eighteenth century were in no way united by a common past, common collective memory, common culture or even common language, they tend to see the citizen project against the despot as sharing the commonalty of seeking common procedures of government to guarantee their rights to a private space. They also see this common civic commitment as something so valuable that it was deservedly defended against outside threats. We have already noted the French and American defence of their 'revolutions' against hostile reaction from other nations.

The boundaries between 'us' and the Other were usually drawn where the agreement about civil and political arrangements was also drawn. If others shared or accepted our public values, they were not Other for what were strictly citizenship matters. However, the defence by the warrior-citizens of, for example, the French sovereign people against attack external and internal, even when they shared nothing but that sovereignty, ended in forging a sense of nationality. In a celebrated lecture on 'What is a nation?' in 1882, Renan defined it as the 'daily plebiscite', thus equating nation and open republic. The effect of the shared public life was to create a belief summed up in phrases such as 'the American way of life'.

Most citizens of France did not speak French until the end of the nineteenth century. Like nearly all other European nationals, they learnt it first in the army and the compulsory elementary school (Weber, 1979, Chapter 17; Schnapper, 1994). Thus, even in the new consensual democratic modern nation-state, a process of homogenization took place. It was a softer version of what had taken place under the earlier absolutisms. These had simply extirpated difference and those with different values in brutal campaigns, for example in Scotland, Ireland, France, Germany, Italy and Spain. Since difference arose mainly from earlier communities of an ethnicity different from that of the conquering centralizing monarch, minority ethnic groups of different language and religion had for several centuries been destroyed. Indeed, the spread of French revolutionary ideas could be explained by a minority feeling that such policies had to be stopped. In other words, as Renan said, what was being built rested on ensuring that crushed minorities forgot the history of their own oppression (Renan, 1992, pp. 41–2).

Aided by the development of modern industrial urban life, closer communications and an increased share in national welfare, some of the core European countries, whence our theories of citizenship come, had by 1914 been fairly successful in completing this process. They were only reminded by pockets such as Alsace-Lorraine, the Alto Adige, Ireland and the Basque country that the process was difficult to perfect. It was these metropolitan countries, where the Other had been reduced to insignificant proportions by 1914, that became the great imperial powers after 1870. The Other in the metropolis was already simply something to be re-educated to accept what had become the acme of French civilization – democracy and human rights, the empowering procedures of citizens – or the priceless treasure of the common law and the Westminster system.

In one way, the new colonial peoples were merely the latest example of what had already been dealt with at home, but their sheer scale and number made the problem of the Other qualitatively different by the late nineteenth century. How could this new source of chaos be brought into the realm of law? There were two distinct and countervailing trends that demand discussion, as they affected the response both practically and theoretically.

Old Worlds

The worlds of Islam, Confucius, Africa and the Slavs had been known since earliest history. Although sometimes barely present to European consciousness, when after the fifteenth century Europeans again 'discovered' them as they searched for Prester John and fabulous treasures, they were first overawed by the relative insignificance of their own states. By the sixteenth century, it was no longer possible to doubt Marco Polo's tales, which had been derided when he first told them. Such voyagers to the Middle East and India as Bernier, Chardin and Challe, and to China as the Père du Halde, suggested that the vast kingdoms they saw had started to decline. When the Declaration of the Rights of Man was drawn up, however, these empires were still regarded as enormously important, and as states with whom one made treaties and treated with the greatest of respect. The first conquering forays in India in the eighteenth century scarcely belied this overall picture.

Not only had the Muslims been the traditional enemies of Christendom since the Crusades, but they had also in recent memory controlled parts of the European Mediterranean and besieged Vienna. They were respected and feared as enemies. Relations with the Sublime Porte, or the Ottoman Empire, had been regulated by exchange and treaty. They were recognized as radical Others, with their own values and social and political structures.

In 1748–50, the Baron de Montesquieu had characterized these structures as oriental despotism. The subjects of the Ottomans were nullities, with no rights whatsoever, all power being centralized in the hands of the monarch, who ruled through a standing army. This view was based on a close study of the accounts of the voyagers of the two previous centuries, who had often stressed the arbitrariness and cruel caprice of the rulers. Montesquieu, who is viewed as the founder of both modern history and political science, explained the politico-legal structures of such worlds as being necessary to and reflecting their social cohesion. The lack of will of the people was, as he saw it, in marked distinction to that of Europeans. He often explained the conditions in the East or Africa by climate in an attempt at a comparative classification of political systems (Montesquieu, 1964).

Montesquieu's notion of oriental despotism was developed and refined into a ranking of different systems in an historical hierarchy marked by the increasing mastery of humans over their natural and social environment. The Old World's inhabitants were thus seen from the point of view of the citizen. By the time of the French Revolution, the views of the revolutionary enlightened figures of Europe had been classified at the top, those of the Others being seen as more backward and reprehensible. We see this in Condorcet and in Hegel (Condorcet, 1988; Hegel, 1949). Great horror was always expressed at the suffering that resulted from such powerlessness in the Islamic subjects. It was not unjustified (compare Ibn Battuta, 1982), but it was decidedly partial. It was easy to explain the lack of will of all these peoples by indolence caused by too great a heat or some innate characteristic; this was often done. Claudel wrote in a school primer:

> The Chinese develops more slowly, thinks, learns and acts more slowly than does the European. It is far easier for them than for us to remain in a state of indifference and inertia... From the point of view of physical strength and production [his] value is lower than that of the European. The Chinese spends longer at his work, but he lounges about much more, he sleeps, he chats with his friends, he drinks a cup of hot water, he smokes a little pipe, he is rarely capable of putting his back into whatever he is doing. (cited by Sachs, 1976, p. 6)

The work of Montesquieu, although misused to establish European superiority, had, however, already undermined such surety by indicating how functional that life was to that society and why a different attitude to power existed. In time, this would be reformulated as the 'rationality of the real'. The more advanced thinkers of the late eighteenth century were already realizing that western reason could not comprehend these other societies properly. Rousseau wrote in 1755: 'For the three or four hundred years that the people of Europe have been swarming all over the world and constantly publishing new accounts of their troubles and dealings, I am convinced that we have known no other men than Europeans' (Rousseau, 1971, 218n, p. 253). This first recognition of the limitedness of reason's capacity to master the totality became stronger. Its corollary, an increasing privileging of common sense and popular wisdom, of which there were many variants, had already started in the middle of the eighteenth century.

Thus, when the Europeans either conquered or occupied these Old Worlds, mainly in the nineteenth century, the privilege they accorded the will was already undermined by their loss of faith in a total knowledge. This did not become obvious until the second decade of the twentieth century, but it was working to vitiate all their plans. The first position adopted – obvious in British policy in India – was to convert the conquered to the virtues of democracy and the rule of law. The history of the British Empire became that of the evolution of all its peoples to self-government, by which we may understand 'conversion into citizens'. This could only come about by putting backbone into them, that will to control the objective world through the imposition of law. The nineteenth century became the century of the warrior-citizen, a militant promotion of citizenship as it had evolved in Europe. Any opposition was crushed by a people fearful of the threat to its confidence in the reasonableness of its own values by any others. Everywhere, the Europeans attempted to obliterate difference in culture, to make 'them' like 'us'. This was presented as a reward, much as it had in the Roman Empire, the reward of the protection of law against the outsiders: *civis romanus sum* was a late nineteenth-century motto favoured in early civics classes throughout the British Empire.

But even in this greatest of empires, the project of obliteration of difference in the public realm was only half a success. It was a project undertaken as European theorists themselves recognized that the neo-Kantian citizen needed economic, social and educational wellbeing to be active and wilful. The vast number of people living in absolute poverty in the new empires made the attainment of such rights very difficult. Even the attempt to create an élite educated in the language of the imperial power was not a solution while poverty and discrimination remained. Such élites ended up leading rebellions of the local cultures against the imperialists, even if they started by a claim to the equality that was the starting point for citizens who made the laws for themselves.

Put simply, by 1945, the liberal-socialist project to make citizens of the 'colonies' had proved a total failure. The national liberation movements that dated back nearly a hundred years meant continuing chaos in the political sphere. Citizenship could be and was presented as a western value that was imposed carelessly on people who found it unliveable because of their different cultures. Indeed, the updated explanation for oriental despotism, in which Marxism was complicit, was that it resulted from the terrible droughts that beset certain civilizations and required a powerful central state to create great hydraulic schemes (Wittfogel, 1957). Freedom was itself western, and the wisdom of these Old Worlds taught those in them that it was better to find a niche and status in a world too arbitrary and capricious to be subject to law. It was contact with New Worlds that precipitated a crystallization of these contradictions into new theories of citizenship.

New Worlds

What this contact made clear was the absolute centrality and paramountcy of the category of the Other to any notion of citizenship bent on democratic control of the arbitrary. The Other had been dealt with in Old Worlds by failed attempts to obliterate it in the way in which difference had been obliterated in Europe itself. This had revealed that the Other was too vast to be mastered in thought and obliterated. Put crudely, the Europeans discovered that there were too many peoples for a few dominant militant warrior-citizen people to destroy them. Moreover, the logic of destruction was itself dangerous, as the Fascist experience made clear in 1922–45.

Again, what the Europeans had done when they first met absolute Other with the discovery of America in 1492 was to attempt to exterminate it (Las Casas, 1992). The greatest Holocaust in history, with 70 million Indians killed in 50 years, took place (Todorov, 1984, p. 133). It was justified on the grounds that the Indians were barbarous subhumans because 'we' could not understand them (there being no shared language or history) and they would not accept western values or standards. Hernán Cortés and his wilful conquerors were scarcely citizens in the modern sense, except as defenders of western civilization against those who threatened it. However, the conquest of the Americas changed the western claim to moral or ethical superiority maintained *vis-à-vis* the Old Worlds, since no matter how awful the Mayan and Aztec civilizations, this time the Europeans were greater in their slaughter than those with whom they compared themselves. This was recognized, and in the earliest tracts of international law, by de Vitoria and Suarez, an ethical demand was made that the Other be respected and that the right to conversion be circumscribed until the reason of the Others had been learnt (see, for example, Suarez, 1964; Grisel, 1976).

While scarcely the dominant discourse, this history and its views were first recognized by the Rousseauian tradition of citizenship, towards which even Kant started to move in the 1790s. Thus, Raynal, a disciple of Rousseau, wrote about the savage barbarism of the Europeans and favourably compared the society of those they conquered as being not 'spoiled by the evil institutions which corrupt us' (Raynal, 1794, Part IV, p. 27). In this tradition, the values of these other, totally new societies where 'noble savages' lived became something not to decry but to emulate rather than deconstruct. Like Las Casas before him, Rousseau recognized that the reasons of each society were not commensurate and that peoples could only think within their own systems of reason (Rousseau, 1989). Thus, a romanticized vision, especially of the Pacific, came to reinforce the increasingly sceptical view held by many that any particular story about how the totality worked was true. Moreover, the belief that the past could be overcome and rejected in an act of will, so that the conditioning realm of culture was of little importance, was increasingly undermined.

Thus, while on the one hand the imperial powers were extirpating those aspects of other cultures hostile to the political civilization of citizenship, the very progress in democracy 'at home' and the extension of rights started to privilege popular wisdom as the standard where such matters were concerned. The era of philosophers' dominance in citizenship studies was already over as it began. Where the fear of barbarous views expressing themselves had led to a denial of low-level democracy both at the centre and in the rest of the world, throughout the nineteenth century, in an endeavour to foster the nation, this view was coupled – for example in Mill – by a recognition that a nation-state was not the only model needed for a community of modern citizens.

We can highlight what was taking place by contrasting Renan's views of 1882 with what was imposing itself by 1945. Renan took Smyrna (seen as part of Oriental despotism) as an example of what should be avoided: it was a multicultural city with no common ethic to defend.

> Take a town like Salonika or Smyrna, and you will find there are five or six communities, each with their own memories and with almost nothing in common between them. Now the essence of a nation is that individuals have many things in common, but have also forgotten many things. No French citizen knows if he is Burgundian, Alani, Taifali or Visigoth; every French citizen must have forgotten Saint Bartholomew's day; the thirteenth-century massacres in the Midi. (Renan, 1992, p. 42)

By 1945, it was clear that most of the world was composed and would continue to be composed of irreducible ethnic difference. To obliterate it would call for killing of such dimension that it could not be envisaged.

Conclusion

The new approaches to citizenship discussed in this book all respond in different ways to the irreducibility of multicultural difference posed by globalization. The problem for citizenship theory up until the 1970s was not so much that it was clear that the world was multicultural, nor even that that reality reminded the few metropolitan states that had become near-homogeneous nations that they too were still made up of different ethnies. It was rather that of a world of civilizations described by Huntington in these dramatic terms:

The people of different civilizations have different views on the relations between God and man, the individual and the group, the citizen and the state, parents and children, husband and wife, as well as differing views of the relative importance of rights and responsibilities, liberty and authority, equality and hierarchy. These differences are the product of centuries. They will not soon disappear. They are far more fundamental than differences among political ideologies and political regimes. Differences do not necessarily mean conflict, and conflict does not necessarily mean violence. Over the centuries, however, differences among civilizations have generated the most prolonged and the most violent conflicts. (Huntington, 1993, p. 25)

We have already shown that this awareness of context as lawlessness is centuries old; the issue was always how to deal with it. The problem for citizenship theory posed by such a context was set by its prior recognition that the citizen has a past that has to be manipulated in its economic, social and educational principles by the state if that citizen is to fulfil the allotted role of a free person, living under laws he or she creates for him- or herself. Citizens are formed by where they come from. Thus, when it is no longer a matter of unity against tyranny, but of deciding on the common good together, the laws (state) must allot more to some rather than others to make them politically equal. At the limit, whole ethnic groups within any society or polity must be treated better than others: there must be a state-enforced inequality of outcomes. We might say that the recognition of the irreducibility of the Other meant a corresponding recognition of the need for affirmative action for the latter's values, like that for people similarly deprived economically because of class. Empowerment required their values to enter the debate about the good so that the vote was of value. However, this meant rearranging all the categories within which citizenship had been considered, especially that of state intervention to promote a social welfare threshold without taking into account community inequalities.

How could this be achieved in a multiethnic state where no positive values are shared? What mechanisms can be established to ensure conviviality and common participation when even the terms of any debate are incommensurable because they exist in different idioms? It should be remembered that it is no longer possible to believe naively in educating different peoples to understand or communicate with each other. None shares a past, yet that past which they cannot capture in thought, since it makes them, decides what is tolerable for them.

Thus, those writers who respond to the problem of multiethnic societies by simply reaffirming that no civic culture is possible without there being a single state education or indoctrination in national feeling, which brings a sense of a single common identity, are attempting the impossible (Schnapper, 1994). It is not possible to break the nexus between the ethnos, or gender, or whatever makes a person's identity, simply by inculcating a sense of national obligation. Moreover, obligations cannot be legislated. This book questions the feasibility of that return to the nation-state even when it is defined as an open republic that anyone can join by choice. In the next chapter, we will look in more detail at the processes of immigration and minority formation that have presented new challenges to many states. We will go on to examine some of the cultural and political responses to this situation in various parts of the world.

3

Immigration, Minority Formation and Racialization

A central aspect of globalization has been the rapid increase in international population mobility: millions of people migrate across national borders, many only temporarily, yet nearly every migration flow leads to some long-term or permanent settlement. This often gives rise to the formation of distinct ethnic *communities*, which may in certain circumstances become ethnic *minorities*. As discussed in Chapter 2, population mobility and minority formation have changed the context of citizenship, compared with the period from the eighteenth to the mid-twentieth century. The tension between the universalistic principles of citizenship and its particularistic bond to a culturally defined national community has become unmanageable.

This chapter will give a brief overview of the migrations of the last half-century and go on to examine the complex processes that have led to community formation and the emergence of ethnic minorities. Processes of social exclusion and racialization affect not only immigrants but also other socially and culturally stigmatized groups, such as indigenous peoples in North America and Australia. As will be discussed below, minority formation and racialization are inextricably linked with the fundamental characteristics of the nation-state.

International migration since 1945

It is impossible here to give a detailed overview of the growing global migrations that have led to increased cultural diversity in many countries. Our own account is to be found in Castles and Miller (1998), and many other good analyses are available (see, for example, *IMR*, 1992; Stahl *et al.*, 1993; Stalker, 1994; Cohen, 1995; UNHCR, 1995; Harris, 1996; *New Community*, 1996; OECD, annual). Here we will merely sketch some broad trends and link them to patterns of minority formation.

Two main phases of global migration can be distinguished since 1945. At first, the postwar economic boom stimulated a large-scale labour migration to the old industrial countries from less-developed areas. Economic growth and labour demand were sustained by consumer capitalism, strong welfare states and Cold War armaments industries. This phase ended with the 1973 'oil crisis'. In a second phase from the mid-1970s, capital investment shifted away from the old centres, and transnational production and distribution reshaped the world economy. Migratory flows at first declined and were partly reversed before growing again. The older immigration countries experienced new types of inflow, while new immigration countries emerged in Southern Europe, the Gulf oil countries, Latin America, Africa and Asia.

Western Europe had to absorb millions of 'displaced persons' after the Second World War. In addition, many former colonists returned from newly independent countries. Despite these inflows, strong economic growth soon led to labour shortages, and employers and governments began to encourage labour migration. Virtually all Western European countries recruited foreign workers from the less-developed periphery – Southern Europe, North Africa, Turkey, Finland and Ireland. Some countries, for example Germany and Switzerland, set up 'guestworker' systems, designed to control workers and prevent permanent settlement. Colonial powers such as Britain, France and the Netherlands admitted workers from their possessions (or former possessions) in Africa, Asia and the Caribbean. Colonized peoples had been granted citizenship as a form of ideological integration. Now this facilitated the entry of much-needed labour, although it also meant that colonial workers could bring in their dependants and settle. By 1970, there were over 12 million immigrants in Western Europe, and processes of ethnic minority formation had become irreversible (Castles, 1984).

The white settler nations of the New World also relied heavily on migrant labour in the post-1945 boom. Australia, New Zealand and Canada had large-scale immigration programmes designed to build up the population and provide labour for growing industries. These countries gave preference to British immigrants but gradually extended the recruitment to Northern and Eastern Europe, and then Southern Europe. Non-European immigration was prevented by racial exclusion laws introduced in the 1880s. There was a widespread feeling that European immigrants could be assimilated, but that non-Europeans would threaten national identity and social cohesion. Immigrants were expected to stay and bring in their families, and policies were designed to make them into citizens (see Collins, 1991). Similarly, Latin American countries such as Argentina, Chile, Brazil and Venezuela encouraged migration from culturally similar countries in Europe, especially Spain, Portugal and Italy.

In contrast, the USA initially had restrictive immigration policies and a relatively low intake. About 250 000 persons per year were admitted in the 1950s – mainly Europeans. Cold War politics also ensured a warm welcome for refugees from Eastern Europe and later from Cuba. However, US employers also recruited a large number of temporary workers, mainly for agriculture, from Mexico and the Caribbean. The turning point in US policies came in 1965 with changes to the Immigration and Nationality Act, which abolished the discriminatory national-origins quota system. Immigration escalated, averaging 450 000 per year in the 1970s. An increasing proportion of the newcomers came from Latin America and Asia, and the family reunion provisions encouraged chain migration and community formation.

The oil crisis precipitated a re-orientation of migration policies. All the labour-importing countries of Western Europe stopped recruitment by 1974. Governments expected the 'guestworkers' to depart, but instead a phase of family reunion and settlement set in. The immigrants' consciousness changed from that of temporary sojourners to long-term residents. Social, cultural and political associations were established, and networks of ethnic businesses and services emerged. Education and welfare authorities slowly began to respond to new needs (see Castles, 1984).

This phase of consolidation was, however, not to last. From the mid-1980s, refugees and asylum-seeker movements became a main type of migration. The collapse of the Soviet bloc led to a reshuffle of ethnic groups in Central and Eastern Europe, and movements were swelled by the exodus from the ruins of former Yugoslavia. The annual asylum-seeker inflows to Western Europe increased from 116 000 in 1981 to 695 000 in 1992. Entrants came from Eastern Europe, Africa, Asia and the Middle East (OECD, 1995, p. 195). Between 1980 and 1995, some 5 million applications for refugee status were submitted in Western Europe (UNHCR, 1995, p. 12). At the same time, the traditional emigration countries of Southern Europe experienced a rapid 'migration transition'. By the late 1980s, Italy, Spain, Portugal and Greece were using labour from Eastern Europe, North Africa and even Asia to bring in their harvests and sweep their streets. Most of the immigrants came spontaneously and without documents.

One consequence of such inflows was an upsurge in racist violence and extreme-right mobilization in France, Germany and elsewhere. Another was the politicization of issues of border control. In Germany, after heated debates, Paragraph 16 of the Basic Law was amended in 1993 to restrict the right to asylum. By 1994, asylum-seeker entries had dropped sharply. Sweden also tightened up entry rules: the number of new asylum-seekers dropped from 84 000 in 1992 to 9000 in 1995 (UN ECE, 1996, p. 4). A series of inter-governmental meetings was held to find ways of controlling migration. The most important of these was the Schengen Agreement, through which Belgium, France, Germany, Italy, Luxembourg, the Netherlands, Portugal and Spain dismantled border controls for people moving between these countries, but set up tougher control measures at the external borders of the 'Schengen area'.

North America and Oceania also experienced strong immigration in this period. Entry to the USA averaged 600 000 per year in the 1980s, and close to 1 million per year in the 1990s. The Canadian intake grew from 89 000 in 1983 to an average of nearly 250 000 per year in 1990s. Australia's permanent immigration level fluctuated according to economic and political consideration, peaking at 145 000 in 1989 and then declining to about 80 000 per year in the 1990s (OECD, 1998, p. 222). Areas of origin changed following the removal of racial discrimination in entry policy in the 1960s and 70s. An increasing share of entrants to all of these countries came from Asia, while the USA and Canada also had large flows from Caribbean and Latin America. New Zealand drew in many Pacific Islanders but also strove to attract skilled and business migrants from East Asia.

The early 1990s saw public panics about being 'swamped' by refugees and illegal migrants from less-developed countries. In Australia, 'boat people' from Cambodia or China were detained in remote areas for years and denied many of the basic rights laid down by international bodies for asylum-seekers. From 1996, the conservative government reduced entries, cut welfare rights for newly arrived immigrants and reduced the family reunion intake. In the USA, anti-immigration groups sought the proclamation of English as the 'official language'. In 1996, Congress passed legislation designed to double the number of guards on the Mexican border and to build a 14-mile triple fence south of San Diego. The law also denied welfare and education to illegal immigrants (*Migration News*, October 1996, p. 10).

At the end of the twentieth century, huge new population movements are also affecting Africa, Asia and Latin America. It is impossible adequately to describe these migrations here. Instead, we present a brief overview of Asian migration as an example.

From the 1950s, migration from Asia to western countries took place in the context of decolonization. Western penetration through trade, aid and investment had created the material means, the cultural capital and the communicative networks necessary for migration. Labour migration from the Indian subcontinent to Britain was soon followed by family reunion and settlement. Movements from Indo-China to France, and from Indonesia and the Caribbean to the Netherlands, had both political and economic motivations. Such post-colonial migrations declined from the 1970s, to be replaced by new types of labour movement, such as the recruitment of Asian maids for middle-class households in North America and Western Europe.

Labour migration from Asia to the Middle East grew rapidly after the oil price rise of 1973, the main labour-sending countries being Bangladesh, India, Pakistan, Sri Lanka, the Philippines, Indonesia, Thailand and South Korea (Martin, 1991; Skeldon, 1992). At first the workers were mainly men, but by the 1980s a large number of women were being recruited for domestic service and other service sector positions. Despite the strict rules designed to prevent long-term stay, trends to settlement are apparent. Today, the majority of the population in Gulf states such as Kuwait are rightless non-citizens.

From the 1980s onwards, there was also an upsurge in migration within Asia. The international movement was often linked to internal migrations, such as the huge rural–urban movements currently taking place in China. Rapid industrial and urban growth in the newly industrializing countries created an enormous demand for labour. Improved living standards in the industrializing areas have generally been quickly followed by a decline in fertility, creating both an economic and a demographic need for immigrants. Men were wanted in construction and heavy manufacturing, while women workers were in heavy demand in the textile and garment industries, as well as in precision assembly processes in the burgeoning electronics industry.

The estimated annual number of documented migrant workers going abroad to work from Asian countries was 2.1 million by 1994. Most still went to the Gulf, but about a quarter moved within Asia (Huguet, 1995, pp. 521–4). It is impossible to estimate the number moving illegally, but it probably exceeds that of documented migrants. Until 1997, there was a strong demand for migrant labour in fast-growing Asian economies, including Japan, South Korea, Taiwan, Singapore and Brunei. Other countries – Hong Kong, Malaysia and Thailand – experienced both emigration and immigration. Countries with a slower economic growth rate have become labour reserves (in the same way that Southern Europe was a generation ago). These include Indonesia, China and the South Asian countries. The Philippines is a particularly significant case, with its high birth rate, relatively good education system and lagging development. There are an estimated 4.2 million Filipino workers in 130 countries (Huguet, 1995, p. 524).

Another growing movement is that of professionals, executives, technicians and other highly skilled personnel. One form that this takes is the 'brain drain' – university-trained people moving from less-developed to highly developed countries – a great economic loss. Another form is what Appleyard (1989, p. 32) calls 'professional transients': executives and professionals sent by their companies to work in overseas branches or joint ventures, or experts sent by international organizations to work in aid programmes. Professional transients are not only agents of economic change, but also bearers of new cultural values that affect the countries in which they work as well as the countries to which they return.

Asia has also experienced large-scale refugee movements. In the 1970s, over 2 million people fled from Indo-China because of the Vietnam War. Six million people (a third of the population) fled Afghanistan following the Soviet military intervention in 1979. There have also been a multitude of smaller movements. In 1995, 8 million of the world's estimated 27 million 'refugees and other persons of concern to the UNHCR' were in Asia (UNHCR, 1995, p. 35).

The Asian economic crisis that started in 1997 caused labour-importing countries to reduce their dependence on foreign workers through non-renewal of contracts and expulsion of undocumented workers. However, the crisis actually exacerbated the income differential between the least-developed countries and the better-off economies. Pressure for emigration from countries such as Indonesia increased sharply, leading to new waves of illegal migration. The potential for growth in population mobility in Asia and other less-developed regions remains enormous.

The controllability of difference

Increasing international population mobility has been a crucial factor in the major economic, political and cultural transformations taking place in the second half of the twentieth century. Virtually every country has experienced emigration or immigration (often both), and many countries have undergone major shifts in their ethnic composition. Despite attempts to reduce migration and control borders, there is no reason to think that international migration will diminish in the foreseeable future.

Taking a longer-term historical view, immigration has been always central to the process of nation-building. The collective memories of North America and Oceania emphasize the experience of new settlers. Western European countries have, in contrast, tended to write immigration out of their histories because it contradicted myths of national homogeneity (Noiriel, 1988), although in fact internal and international migrations played an important part in industrialization and urban development everywhere (Moch, 1992, 1995). The regulation of immigration is a recent phenomenon, dating from the late nineteenth century, while government policies to integrate immigrants or regulate 'community relations' date only from the 1960s. Yet nation-states have always had ideas about how to regulate the situation of immigrants and minorities within their borders. Most approaches have fallen into two categories: *assimilation* and *differential exclusion*. A third approach – *pluralism* or *multiculturalism* – has become significant only quite recently (compare Castles, 1995a).

Assimilation meant encouraging immigrants to learn the national language and take on the social and cultural practices of the receiving community. The underlying belief was that the immigrants' descendants would be indistinguishable from the rest of the population. Assimilationist practices were the rule in nineteenth-century Europe. Britain had no specific policies on the integration of Irish, Jewish and other European immigrants prior to the 1905 Aliens Act, but there was an underlying assumption that those who stayed would eventually be absorbed into the population – like the Celts, Saxons, Danes, Normans, Huguenots and Jews who had come before. France, in contrast, consciously aimed to assimilate immigrants from Italy, Belgium, Poland and other European countries, partly because it wanted their labour, but also because it needed them as soldiers in the struggle against Germany. When new waves of migration started after the Second World War, both France and Britain at first emphasized assimilation, as did several other European immigration countries.

The nineteenth-century US 'melting pot', which was meant to 'Americanize' immigrants from Europe, was crucial for both industrialization and nation-building. Canada and Australia encouraged mainly

British immigration up to 1945 and assumed that the relatively small number of other Europeans would be culturally absorbed. When large-scale non-British immigration started in the 1950s, there were explicit policies of assimilation. Latin American countries encouraged immigrants from Southern European countries, who could readily be absorbed into the Hispanic culture (Adelman, 1995).

Differential exclusion meant accepting immigrants only within strict functional and temporal limits: they were welcome as workers, but not as settlers; as individuals, but not as families or communities; as temporary sojourners, but not as long-term residents. This model was developed in Germany and Switzerland from the 1870s as a way of recruiting and controlling Polish, Italian and other foreign workers during industrialization (Bade, 1995). The Nazis developed such rules into a system for recruiting and exploiting millions of rightless *Fremdarbeiter* (alien workers) during the Second World War. In post-1945 Europe, the differential exclusion model, in the guise of the 'guestworker system', would play a major part in several countries, yet was to fail in its central objective of preventing settlement and minority formation (Castles, 1986).

Both assimilation and differential exclusion shared an important common principle: that immigration should not bring about significant social and cultural change in the receiving society. Political leaders saw ethnocultural diversity as a threat to the integrity of the nation, which could seriously weaken it in the event of war. However, they believed that difference was controllable: the immigrants would either be absorbed into an unchanged national community or sent away as soon as their labour was no longer needed. At a time of slow transport and communication, and of well-defined borders, the long-term persistence of ethnic communities with strong links to their homelands was not considered probable. There was therefore no need to have policies for managing ethnocultural diversity, because such diversity was at most a temporary feature of the country.

At the dawn of the twenty-first century, it is becoming increasingly difficult to uphold the doctrine of the controllability of difference. Burgeoning population mobility, the development of new ethnic minorities and the emergence of multicultural societies have become major factors in social and political transformation. The Other can be neither excluded nor assimilated, and the traditional models no longer offer credible solutions. Nonetheless, many people in western countries cling to the idea that immigration will not bring about major changes in their societies. Similarly, the leaders of new immigration countries in Asia and elsewhere try to follow models that have long since failed in older immigration countries. They argue that conditions are different because of differing traditions and values. It is too early to say for sure that these views are unfounded, but historical experience gives grounds for scepticism.

The emergence of ethnic minorities

The burning issue for immigrant-receiving countries is the extent to which migration leads to permanent settlement and to the formation of new ethnic minorities. But what are ethnic minorities, and how large are they? In this section, we will discuss the sociological meaning of the term 'ethnic minority' and then look at statistical data on groups that may be seen as ethnic minorities.

Defining ethnic minorities

The majority of ethnic minority members in western nations are immigrants or their descendants, but not all immigrants have become minorities, while certain non-immigrant groups have taken on minority status. What is the relationship between ethnic minority status and ethnicity? According to anthropologists, everyone has an ethnicity (or ethnic identity) and belongs to an ethnic group. Yet for sociologists, the matter is less clear cut: dominant or majority groups are generally not aware of their ethnicity unless it is threatened in some palpable way. It is the minority groups who are referred to (usually pejoratively) as 'ethnics'. Majorities tend to see their own values, traditions and mores as 'normal' or as 'the national culture', rather than as an expression of a particular ethnic belonging.

When linked to minority status, ethnicity has two facets. The *self-definition* of a group is based on its members' perception of shared language, traditions, religion, history and experiences. The *other-definition* results from the dominant group's use of its power to impose social definitions on subordinate groups. This includes ideological processes of stereotyping, as well as discriminatory structures and practices in the legal, economic, social and political arenas. The markers constructed by dominant groups to differentiate minorities include 'phenotypical characteristics', that is, skin colour and other physical features thought to denote 'race'. A second set of markers comprises culture, represented by dress, language, religion and customs. A third type of marker is national origin, which is often taken as a predictor of social characteristics: origin in an underdeveloped country is a major factor of exclusion.

Negative other-definition of a minority ethnic group by the dominant group leads to the *racialization* or *ethnicization* of social relations: differences in the social, economic or political position of a group are attributed to its (constructed) racial or ethnic characteristics rather than to historical power relationships. In practice, both the societal position and the consciousness of a minority ethnic group are always the result of complex interactions between self- and other-definition, although the relative weight of the two varies. If a group is marginalized by strongly negative other-definitions (that is, racist structures and practices), it may emphasize its cultural identity as a source of resistance. This can in turn reinforce the dominant group's fear of separatism, leading to even stronger discrimination. In a less discriminatory context (that is, weak other-definition), self-definition is still likely to exist but will probably be weaker and less durable, in the sense of being open to interchange with other sociocultural identities within the society (see Castles, 1996).

Ethnic minorities in western nation-states may thus be seen as groups that:

1. have been marginalized by dominant groups on the basis of socially constructed markers of phenotype (that is, physical appearance or 'race'), origins or culture;
2. have some degree of collective consciousness (or feeling of being a community) based on a belief in shared language, traditions, religion, history and experiences.

This definition is oversimplified because it ignores the issue of multiple memberships and identities (especially the relationship between ethnicity, class and gender), as well as the question of minorities within minorities (for example, Kurds within the Turkish population of Germany). Nonetheless, it is useful for the purposes of this chapter.

Whether a specific group is an ethnic minority has therefore to be assessed according to two sets of factors:

1. indicators of exclusion from equal participation in the economic, social, cultural and political subsystems of society;

2. indicators of collective consciousness, such as language use, cultural practices, associations and political mobilization.

The size of ethnic minority populations

An approximation of the size of ethnic minority populations in western countries may be obtained by looking at statistics on such groups as indigenous peoples and immigrants from less-developed areas. Certain other categories of minority have been of great historical significance but are outside the scope of our study; these include: territorial minorities resulting from the incorporation of distinct groups into a nation-state (for example, the Basques in Spain) and traditional ethnic minorities (such as gypsies and Jews).

Table 3.1 shows the size of foreign or immigrant populations in western countries and their share of total population. By 1995, the foreign population of European Organization for Economic Co-operation and Development countries was 19 million, of whom fewer than 7 million were European Union citizens (OECD, 1997, p. 30). Foreign residents made up 9 per cent of the population in Germany, 19 per cent in Switzerland, 6 per cent in France and 1 per cent in Japan. The USA had 25 million foreign-born residents in 1996 (9 per cent of the total population), Canada had 5 million (17 per cent) and Australia had 4 million (23 per cent). Table 3.1 also shows substantial growth since the early 1980s, especially in countries with hitherto fairly small immigrant populations, such as Austria, the Scandinavian countries, Italy, Spain and Japan.

Such general statistics are, however, blunt instruments for identifying minorities. A more useful approach might be to count immigrants from less-developed non-European countries and disadvantaged parts of Europe as groups likely to have ethnic minority status. The most important non-European areas of origin are Turkey (2.6 million immigrants in Western Europe in 1995) and North Africa (about 2 million), but there are also immigrants from virtually every part of Africa, Asia and Latin America in Western Europe today. Among the poorer European sending countries are the former Yugoslavia (nearly 2 million), the former Soviet bloc countries and Portugal. On this basis, some 12 million people (two-thirds of Western Europe's foreign population) may be seen as possible ethnic minority members (compare Münz, 1996).

Table 3.1   Foreign or immigrant population in selected OECD countries

| | Foreign population[1] | | | |
| | *Thousands* | | *% of total population* | |
	1983	*1995[2]*	*1983*	*1995[2]*
Austria	297	724	3.9	9.0
Belgium	891	910	9.0	9.0
Denmark	104	223	2.0	4.2
Finland	16	69	0.3	1.3
France	3 714	3 597	6.8	6.3
Germany[3]	4 535	7 174	7.4	8.8
Ireland	83	94	2.4	2.7
Italy	381	991	0.7	1.7
Japan	817	1 362	0.7	1.1
Luxembourg	96	138	26.3	33.4
Netherlands	552	728	3.8	5.0
Norway	95	161	2.3	3.7
Portugal	na	168	na	1.7
Spain	210	500	0.5	1.2
Sweden	397	484	4.8	5.2
Switzerland	926	1331	14.4	18.9
UK	1 601	2 060	2.8	3.4
TOTAL	14 715	20 714		

| | Foreign-born population[4] | | | |
| | *Thousands* | | *% of total population* | |
	1981	*1996*	*1981*	*1996*
Australia	3 004	3 908	20.6	22.8
Canada	3 843	4 971	16.1	17.4
USA	14 080	24 600	4.7	9.3

Source: OECD, 1997, 1998.

Notes: na = not available

1. Data for the foreign population are from population registers except for France (census), the UK (labour force survey), and Japan and Switzerland (register of foreigners). These figures refer to foreign citizens and include neither immigrants who have the citizenship of the immigration country nor immigrants who have been naturalized.

2. 1990 for France.

3. Data for 1983 refer to the area of the 'old *Länder*' prior to reunification. 1995 figures cover Germany in its present borders.

4. Census data (1980 for the USA), except the 1996 figure for the USA, which is an official estimate.

To get a full picture of ethnic minority status, it would be necessary to add another category left out of the figures of foreign population: marginalized people of immigrant descent who are citizens of their countries of residence. The 1991 UK Census classified 5.5 per cent of the population (over 3 million people) as belonging to ethnic minorities. Most were UK citizens and had been born in the UK, mainly as the descendants of immigrants from the Indian subcontinent and the Caribbean (OECD, 1995, p. 130). France also had around 1 million French citizens of non-European origin – either naturalized immigrants or people from Overseas Departments and Territories – who mainly have ethnic minority status. Overall, a reasonable guess might be that a total of 6–7 million *citizens of immigrant origin* are in ethnic minority situations in Western Europe. Together with the *non-citizen ethnic minorities*, this makes a total of about 18 million, or just under 5 per cent of the total population of Western Europe.

In North America and Oceania, it would be wrong to count all the immigrants as ethnic minorities, but there are also non-immigrant groups with minority status, most notably indigenous peoples, who are often the most marginalized groups of all. The construction of indigenous peoples as the inferior, savage and threatening Other became the basis of national myths, like that of the US 'Wild West'. Although their number is relatively small, their presence is of enormous significance for debates on citizenship and identity. In the USA, the *birthplace* figures in the 1990 Census showed that only 22 per cent of the foreign-born population came from Europe (compared with 60 per cent in 1970). Older European immigrant groups do not have generally have ethnic minority status (although residential concentration and pockets of poverty still exist). People from Central America and Mexico made up over a quarter of the immigrant population (5.4 million in 1990) and Asian-born people made up another quarter (5 million) (OECD, 1995, p. 130).

According to 1990 Census figures on *ethnic composition*, the US population consisted of 80 per cent whites, 12 per cent African-Americans, 1 per cent Native Americans, 3 per cent Asian and 4 per cent 'other race'. There were also 9 per cent Hispanics, who could be 'of any race' . The two million native Americans are highly separated from mainstream society. The 30 million African-Americans are for the most part socioeconomically disadvantaged (although there is a substantial 'black middle class'). Many of the 7.2 million Asians have high educational and occupational status,. but may still experience racism. The 22 million people of Hispanic origin are highly diverse.

They include descendants of the pre-US-conquest population of California and Texas, as well as US citizens from Puerto Rico, Mexican migrant workers and refugees from Cuba and Haiti. Although there are some high-status groups among Hispanics (for example, the Cuban entrepreneurs of Miami), there are also many people who are economically, socially and politically excluded. On this basis, the ethnic minority population could be as high as 60 million or nearly a quarter of the total population of the USA.

In Canada (as in the USA), 'ethnocultural origin' cuts across classification as immigrant or non-immigrant: in 1991, 1.7 per cent of the population were Aboriginal, 21 per cent were of British origin, 23 per cent French, 31 per cent of 'other' (mainly immigrant) origin and the remainder of 'combined origins' (Stasiulis and Jhappan, 1995, p. 123). The long historical struggle between Canadians of French and British origin still continues, and helps to shape the situation of smaller groups. The French are a minority in Canada but the majority in Quebec, where other minorities (immigrants and the Cree people) sometimes find themselves marginalized in conflicts concerning Quebecois autonomy.

In Australia, the main distinction made within the immigrant population is between immigrants of 'English-speaking background' (ESB), mainly from the UK, New Zealand and the USA, and those of 'non-English-speaking backgrounds' (NESB). First- and second-generation NESB people together make up nearly a quarter of the population. However, some NESB immigrants (for example, Northern Europeans) do as well as the Australian-born on a whole range of indicators. In contrast, many Southern Europeans are socioeconomically disadvantaged. Some Asian groups (such as Vietnamese and Lebanese) suffer both socioeconomic exclusion and informal racism. However, other Asians (for example, Chinese from Hong Kong) possess economic and cultural capital and do well in the labour market, although they may experience racism on the streets. Thus, some groups of NESB people can be seen as ethnic minorities, while others appear to hold that position only in certain contexts.

The most disadvantaged group in Australian society is that of the Aborigines and Torres Strait Islanders, who numbered 353 000 in 1996 (2.1 per cent of the total population). These indigenous people are very different in their demographic, social and economic characteristics from the rest of the Australian population. They are virtually excluded from the mainstream employment and political structures, and suffer severe institutional and informal racism. They are certainly a minority, although they themselves would reject the term 'ethnic minority' since it makes them seem like just one ethnic group among others.

As for Asia, it is very difficult to define ethnic minorities in the many diverse societies, and even harder to quantify them. A few Asian countries, such as Japan and Korea, claim to have highly homogeneous populations, but most Asian countries include a variety of ethnic groups, with differing origins and cultural characteristics. The current political boundaries in South East Asia are largely the result of colonialism and post-colonial struggles. Attempts to build nation-states since independence in the postwar period have been fraught with difficulties. Many Asian countries are today multilingual and multicultural. In some cases, this pluralism does not correspond with political and social divisions, and there are many cases of ethnic conflict and minority formation. Many countries also have groups known as indigenous peoples, hill-tribes or tribal peoples, who are largely excluded from modern society. Such groups often experience discrimination and racism.

In addition, new minorities are arising from recent migrations. However, there is a lack of comprehensive and accurate data on this topic. Japan does provide figures: the foreign population increased from 817 000 in 1983 to 1.4 million in 1995 (1.1 per cent of the total population). About three-quarters are permanent or long-term residents (OECD, 1997, pp. 122–5) – mainly Koreans, who were recruited as workers before and during the Second World War. Many current Korean residents are in the third or fourth generations, but still find it hard to obtain Japanese citizenship, remaining a segregated and discriminated minority (Esman, 1994). Other foreign groups such as Chinese, Brazilians (usually descendants of Japanese emigrants) and Filipinos have grown rapidly in size in recent years. Official estimates put the number of illegal immigrants in Japan in 1995 at 285 000 (OECD, 1997, pp. 122–5, 229).

For other countries, we have to rely mainly on rough estimates: by the mid-1990s, there were thought to be about 3 million Asians employed outside their own countries within the Asian region, and another 3 million employed in other continents (Martin *et al.*, 1996, p. 163). In addition, there are millions of refugees and family members. It is impossible to say how many of these migrants are likely to settle permanently in other countries, but there is no doubt that trends towards permanent settlement are emerging. It is also evident that many immigrants are highly marginalized as a result of labour market discrimination and exclusion from a range of rights enjoyed by citizens.

We may therefore conclude that immigration to Asian countries is beginning to lead to the formation of new ethnic minorities, just as it did in Europe 30 years earlier. It is only a matter of time before the rights of these new ethnic minorities come to be identified as matters of significant political concern.

Minority formation

It is important to understand the processes that combine to exclude certain groups from mainstream society. These mechanisms belong to that aspect of the process of minority formation that we referred to above as *other-definition*, through which a dominant group uses its power to impose certain social positions on subordinate groups. The other aspect of minority formation, *self-definition*, refers to the use of cultural and social practices by a group to develop a consciousness of its collective identity. Other- and self-definition take place simultaneously. However, for analytical purposes, we will concentrate on other-definition here, while self-definition will be examined in Chapter 6.

The process of other-definition includes mechanisms of marginalization based on discriminatory structures and practices in various areas of society. These may be referred to as *institutional and structural exclusion*. Other-definition also includes discursive practices of stereotyping, which we refer to as *racialization* (see the definition above). In social reality, both institutional and discursive practices of exclusion take place together and reinforce each other. Often discursive practices provide the ideological justification for discrimination with regard to the allocation of resources or rights. Similarly, discrimination in resource allocation can create the socioeconomic subordination that appears to justify racist discourses on the innate inferiority of certain groups. Here, we look therefore simultaneously at institutional and discursive practices in the legal, economic, social, spatial and cultural arenas. Political factors in minority formation will be discussed in relation to citizenship rules in Chapters 4 and 5.

Legal factors

The most obvious way of forcing certain ethnic groups into inferior societal positions is direct discrimination with regard to legal status. The denial of civil rights to minorities has a long tradition: systems of institutionalized discrimination such as slavery, indentured labour and apartheid have been a central element of modernity. Today, there are many categories of people who do not enjoy full legal equality.

Foreign workers and their descendants: in the period of mass labour recruitment to Western Europe in the 1960s and 70s, most of the millions of workers from Southern Europe, North Africa and Turkey were denied a wide range of rights with regard to:

● the labour market: restrictions on changing jobs or occupations;
● residence: restrictions on duration of stay, mobility within the immigration country and family reunion;
● social security: exclusion from certain types of benefit such as unemployment pay;
● political participation: restrictions on the right of association and on trade union or party activity.

In the meantime, these groups have mostly achieved an improved legal status through the granting of long-term residence entitlements. However, the initial severe discrimination determined entry points into economic and social systems, and thus had long-term effects on the class position of immigrants and their descendants. In addition, some foreign worker groups remain legally disadvantaged. Contract labour systems still exist or have been reintroduced in several countries. Switzerland still employs seasonal workers in agriculture, construction and the hotel industry – a total of 52 000 in 1995 (OECD, 1997). Seasonal workers have very limited rights and may continue in this status for years through a succession of contracts. Germany started recruiting labour in the early 1990s through bilateral agreements with Central and Eastern European countries. Rudolph (1996) reports that the new arrangement had all the restrictive features of the pre-1973 'guestworker system'. It was a way of increasing labour market flexibility and 'exporting problems'. There were problems of low wages, poor conditions and competition with local labour.

Contract labour systems continue to play a major role outside Europe, especially in the Middle East and the fast-growing Asian economies (Castles, 1995b). Recruitment for Arab oil countries takes place within rigid contract labour frameworks: workers are not allowed to settle or bring in dependants, and are often segregated in barracks. They can be deported for misconduct and often have to work very long hours. Foreign workers have little legal protection, although the authorities of sending countries such as the Philippines do try to safeguard their rights. Women domestic workers who experience exploitation and sexual abuse have little chance of legal redress (Lim and Oishi, 1996).

However, workers moving from one Asian country to another are not much better off. In Singapore, unskilled workers may stay only a few years and are not permitted to bring in their families. They are forbidden to marry Singaporeans, and women have to undergo regular pregnancy tests. Malaysia is heavily dependent on migrant workers from Indonesia and the Philippines. In early 1997, the government announced plans for the mass deportation of illegals. They were blamed for crime, disease and immorality, although relatively few deportations actually took place. However, the Asian economic crisis of 1997–98 led to new attempts to stop undocumented entry and to expel illegal workers. Malaysian authorities set up detention camps and rounded up a large number of immigrant workers. Many were deported, despite fears of persecution at home for members of minority groups such as the Acehinese.

Colonial immigrants who came to Britain, France and the Netherlands from colonies (or former colonies) from the 1940s to the 1960s generally possessed citizenship of the receiving country. They had the right to settle permanently, to seek employment and to bring in family members. Here, economic and social exclusion was the result not of legal status but of discrimination in the employment and housing markets. However, from the 1960s, these countries began to change their laws to deprive new colonial immigrants of citizenship, and even to remove rights (especially that of family reunion) from existing immigrants (Castles and Miller, 1998, Chapter 4). A convergence in rights between new colonial immigrants and foreign workers took place: by the 1980s, there was little difference in legal status. However, most of the earlier colonial immigrants – North and West Africans in France, Indonesians and Surinamese in the Netherlands, and Afro-Caribbeans, Indians, Pakistanis and Bangladeshis in the UK – retained their citizenship rights.

Illegal migrant workers are found everywhere. They are a particularly disadvantaged group, lacking residence rights and legal protection. Reliable figures do not exist, but it is widely believed that the number of illegal immigrants is roughly equivalent to 10 per cent of legal foreign residents, which would mean about 2 million people in Europe. When governments introduce regulations to stop existing migratory flows, they may continue as illegal movements, as happened with regard to Turkish migration to Germany after 1973. Changes in regulations can sometimes push previously legal residents into ille-

gality: the 1993 *Loi Pasqua* deprived many longstanding African immigrants of their residence rights in France, leading to the movement of
the *sans papiers* ('the paperless') in 1996, with hunger strikes and
church occupations. The election of the left coalition Jospin government in 1997 led to hopes of a regularization of the *sans papiers*, but
the new measures announced in 1998 failed to offer secure residence
status to all those concerned, and many still faced deportation.

Southern European countries have large illegal worker populations.
In Greece, most foreigners work illegally; their number was put at
250 000–470 000 in 1995 (6–12 per cent of the labour force). Illegal
workers earn about half the normal wage and have no social security
entitlements. Low-wage foreign labour plays a crucial role in many
industries, such as agriculture, tourism and construction. Of the
764 000 illegal entrants deported between 1991 and 1994, 96 per cent
were Albanians, many of whom repeatedly crossed the border (OECD,
1997, pp. 110–13). Similarly, Italy has made a considerable use of
illegal workers, some of whom were offered legal status through
special regularization programmes in 1990 and 1996.

Japan, South Korea and other Asian countries also have a large
number of illegal workers. These are often tourist visa-holders who
overstay their permits, but there is also a great deal of smuggling of
undocumented workers. The number of illegal migrants may well
exceed the number of legal ones (Lim and Oishi, 1996). Most recruitment of migrant workers to the Gulf and within Asia is organized by
migration agents and labour brokers. Some indulge in illegal practices,
such as tricking women and children into prostitution. Thai agents dupe
young rural women into coming to Japan, ostensibly to work in restaurants or factories, and then hand them over to *Yakuza* gangsters, who
keep them in conditions of near-slavery as prostitutes (Okunishi, 1996,
pp. 229–30). The chances of legal redress are very small – any illegal
worker who complains is likely to be imprisoned, deported or both.

The largest flow of illegal workers is to the USA, where millions of
undocumented Mexican and other Latin American workers have been
employed in agriculture, industry and services since the 1950s. The
1986 Immigration Reform and Control Act was designed to regularize
the status of existing workers and to control future movement.
Although some 3 million persons were regularized, illegal movement
has continued despite sharper control measures on the US–Mexico
border. This indicates the difficulty of stopping migration in the face of
strong informal migration networks and powerful vested interests
(especially of employers) that encourage the movement.

Indeed, illegal migration should not always be seen as migration unwanted by employers and governments. It is often tacitly permitted or even encouraged, just because illegals lack rights and are easy to exploit. Governments can ignore the issue and turn a blind eye, while avoiding the need to provide social services or legal protection. If migrant labour is no longer needed, or a public outcry develops, the government can blame the illegal migrants and carry out mass deportations. Thus, illegal labour migration should often be regarded as a deliberate system that reduces costs for the dominant groups in immigration countries.

Asylum-seekers are a further category of migrants with very limited rights. They have to go through long and complex legal processes to prove that they have left their own countries because of persecution. During these procedures, they are generally housed in spartan camps, often isolated from the local populations. In some cases, asylum-seekers are not permitted to work, and are resented by local people who have to subsidize them through social security payments. Where they are allowed to work, the opportunities are very limited, and the asylum-seekers are seen as potential wage-cutters. At the end of the legal procedures – which may take several years – the great majority of applications are refused. However, many rejected applicants stay on, with an uncertain legal status since there were considerable legal and practical obstacles to their deportation (OECD, 1995, p. 121). They remain in the country of refused asylum, either as illegals or with an ambiguous and insecure status. Asylum-seekers are among the most legally and socially disadvantaged people in western societies.

Indigenous peoples generally now enjoy formal equality of rights with the majority populations in Australia, New Zealand, Canada and the USA. However, this situation is quite recent. During the period of conquest, indigenous peoples were deprived of their most basic rights, their societies and culture were destroyed, and their populations were decimated. Survivors were forced onto reservations and controlled by missionaries and special welfare bureaucracies. They were seen as racially inferior and expected to 'die out'. It was not until the 1960s that indigenous peoples' movements were able to make effective demands for change. For example, Australian Aborigines did not gain full rights as citizens until 1967, and were not even counted in the population censuses up to then. The legal doctrine of *terra nullius*, according to which Aborigines had no recognizable system of land tenure and therefore did not possess the land, was overthrown by a High Court decision in 1992. However, in 1997, the Australian government introduced legislation to once again restrict Aboriginal land rights. The result of centuries of legal exclusion and officially sanctioned oppression is a continuing situation of discrimination, exclusion and lack of economic and political power.

Economic factors

The form of economic incorporation of a specific group into society is clearly decisive for its overall situation. Again generalization is difficult. Some immigrant groups do well economically and therefore have a good chance of equal participation in other areas of society. For example, post-1945 British and Northern European immigrants to Australia, Canada and the USA generally encountered few problems in entering the labour markets at a level appropriate to their skills, and obtained incomes and working conditions comparable to those of the locally born populations. However, the majority of immigrants have been incorporated into the lower levels of segmented labour markets.

The aim of 'guestworker' recruitment by Western European countries up until 1973 was to provide labour for unskilled and semi-skilled jobs at a time of expansion when local workers were upwardly mobile. Colonial immigrants in France, the Netherlands and the UK ended up in similar jobs as a result of both racism in employment practices and a lack of 'human capital' (education, language skills, training and industrial experience). Women migrants generally got the lowest-paid jobs of all in textile and garment factories, or in unskilled services occupations. Labour market segmentation was seen as beneficial at the time by policy makers, because it increased opportunities for nationals and helped to defuse class tensions (Castles and Kosack, 1985). Similarly, postwar Australian employers were looking for low-skilled workers for construction projects, or for new manufacturing industries with hard and unpleasant working conditions (Lever-Tracy and Quinlan, 1988; Collins, 1991). Many migrants into the USA – especially those from south of the border – had similar experiences of entering the labour market at the lowest level.

Once in inferior labour market positions, it is difficult for immigrants and their descendants to move upwards. Opportunities for gaining the language skills, education and vocational training needed for promotion are often inadequate, as neither employers nor public authorities have any interest in providing them. The hard conditions and low incomes of migrant workplaces leave little time for efforts at self-improvement. Discrimination in hiring and promotion is frequent – often deliberately reinforced by legal principles of 'primacy for nationals'. When the cycle of recessions and industrial restructuring started in the 1970s, migrants often bore the brunt, losing unskilled jobs and lacking the cultural capital needed to move into new employment sectors.

A 1993 overview of the labour market situation of immigrant workers in OECD countries found that they had above-average unemployment rates everywhere. In Germany, Belgium, Sweden, Denmark and the Netherlands, the rate was two or three times the national average. A major reason for this was that immigrant workers tended to be concentrated in economic sectors that were declining or undergoing restructuring. The study found that concentration in manufacturing, construction and low-skilled services still persisted, although it was gradually declining. Immigrant employment in sectors such as banking and finance, as well as other services, was relatively low. The lowest participation of all was in public administration, where many jobs were only open to nationals. Second-generation immigrants also experienced labour market segmentation. Although their situation was often better than that of their parents, they still had difficulty in getting high-status jobs and had above-average unemployment rates (OECD, 1995, pp. 30–42).

Since the 1980s, the immigration strategies of most receiving countries have been increasingly geared to attracting highly skilled personnel. The employment of executives and professionals with overseas experience is seen as a vital part of internationalization strategies. Programmes exist in many parts of the world to attract migrant entrepreneurs with capital and managerial skills. At the same time, 'ethnic small businesses' set up by former migrant workers are seen as one of the most dynamic economic factors (Waldinger *et al.*, 1990; Collins *et al.*, 1995).

Yet the widely propagated impression of a general shift from unskilled to skilled migration is mistaken. In fact, immigrant workforces have become increasingly bipolar, with clustering at the upper and lower ends of the labour market. The deregulation of employment markets and the deskilling of certain production processes have created a need for flexible, low-skilled workers in industrial countries, at a time when declining birth rates and the increased educational participation of local people reduces their availability for such work. The luxury consumption wishes of highly paid personnel in the corporate sector creates a need for domestic servants, fashion-garment makers, restaurant workers and providers of a wide range of personal services. There is always low-skilled work available for migrants too desperate or too vulnerable to demand fair wages or reasonable working conditions (Castles and Miller, 1998; Sassen, 1988).

Thus, the economic factors that tend to turn immigrants into ethnic minorities still exist. Not all migrants are marginalized, but certain groups tend to be. They are generally those singled out not only by visible ethnic difference, but by its combination with other factors such as lack of human capital due to poor pre-migration educational opportunities, and a lack of labour market rights as a result of a disadvantaged legal situation.

As for the indigenous peoples of North America and Australia, they have for the most part never been incorporated into mainstream labour markets. Forced to the fringes of society, they have been denied the social conditions, health care and education needed to be effective economic participants. Rampant discrimination has blocked their hiring, except for those in certain specialized occupations, such as stockmen on Australian sheep and cattle stations, or construction workers on high-rise building projects in the USA. Unemployment rates remain dramatically high for indigenous people – surveys in Australia have found rates in excess of 50 per cent. What jobs there are tend to be either low skilled or special niches within government-sponsored employment programmes.

Spatial and social factors

To analyse social phenomena adequately, we have to locate them in space (Massey, 1993, p. 155). Ethnic minorities in western societies are mainly located in cities, and within these in certain neighbourhoods. This focus on the city as the site of encounter between differing cultures is nothing new. It was a key theme of the Chicago School of Sociology in the USA during the 1920s (Park, 1950; Lal, 1986), and the focus of considerable research in Britain in the 1970s (Rex, 1973; Rex and Tomlinson, 1979). In the 1980s, Sassen (1988) argued that 'global cities' had emerged through new forms of the international division of labour and were providing altered conditions for the societal incorporation of ethnic minorities. Conflicts around difference are thus located in specific places, their character varying according to local conditions.

The concentration of minorities in certain regions and cities is well documented. In the USA, 10 per cent of the total population lived in

California in 1990, but a third of the foreign-born lived there, including 40 per cent of all Asian and Latin American immigrants. The foreign-born share in California's population was 22 per cent (Rumbaut, 1996). Two-thirds of foreign-born people in France live in cities with over 100 000 inhabitants, while one third live in the Parisian region (Body-Gendrot, 1993a). Within such areas, minorities tend to dwell in specific neighbourhoods, where they form a sizeable proportion – even a majority – of the population. As for the indigenous peoples of North America and Australia, they have been segregated in reserves, missions or 'fringe-dweller' camps (as they were called in Australia) ever since white settlement. When some of them migrated to cities in search of work, they underwent the same processes of segregation as external migrants.

The initial factors in spatial segregation for immigrants are economic: immigrant workers arriving in Western Europe up to the 1970s sought housing around the factories or building sites where they were employed. Low wages and the need to send home remittances caused them to seek the cheapest possible housing. Clustering was often reinforced by provision of on-arrival housing in camps or hostels by employers or governments. When migrants moved out of these – often because of the arrival of spouses and children – they looked for accommodation in the same area. Later arrivals joined existing immigrant communities, frequently because of informal sector employment opportunities in these areas. Such economic factors were always reinforced by racism: many local people in 'better areas' would not rent or sell houses to immigrants, while others made a business of doing so in areas that had come to be seen as incipient 'ghettoes'.

Minority neighbourhoods quickly developed. Local people often moved out, if they had the resources to do so. Those who remained were usually the most disadvantaged. Living in a minority neighbourhood became a stigma – a sign of low status and social exclusion. Housing conditions – poor to start with – deteriorated further because of a lack of both private and public investment. Social amenities, health facilities and schools were all inadequate for the needs of a young and growing population, and continued to decline as a result of neglect and discrimination.

The fear of 'coloured ghettoes' (in Britain), 'Arab quarters' (in France) or 'Turkish districts' (in Germany) was an early motive in campaigns against immigration. Such notions turned into a self-fulfilling prophecy, a vicious circle of racialization. Susan Smith has shown how, in Britain, residential segregation was presented as the choice of immigrants, who wanted to live together in a 'black inner city'. The development of minority neighbourhoods then appeared as the result of 'natural processes' of racial differentiation, rather than as the consequence of economic disadvantage and social exclusion. Minority areas were portrayed as a threat to morality and public order. Welfare dependency, crime, vice and dangerous religious and political ideologies were seen as cancers that developed in such areas and might spread to threaten the whole society. This laid the ground for a racialization of politics in the 1960s, in which extreme-right groups and sections of the Conservative Party mobilized public opinion around demands to stop immigration and curtail the rights of existing immigrants (Smith, 1993).

The racialization of urban space followed a similar course elsewhere. The spatial segregation of minorities in the USA has a long history, going back to nineteenth-century European influxes and the 'Great Migration' of southern blacks to northern and western cities after 1918. Extreme segregation between white and black still exists, and has been joined by new divisions with regard to Hispanic and Asian populations. Race is a major factor in urban conflicts and local politics (Davis, 1990). Such conflicts often occur between minorities competing for the control of urban space, while the white middle classes have moved to well-guarded outer suburbs. It was Asian small business people, rather than mainstream corporations, who bore the brunt of black anger in the 1992 Los Angeles riots. Similarly, in urban neighbourhoods where blacks have gained local political power, it may now be newer Hispanic immigrants who feel oppressed and disempowered (Johnson *et al.*, 1997).

In France, the state-subsidized Sonacotra hostels for single workers became a flash-point for immigrant mobilization and strikes from 1976 to 1980. As family reunion accelerated after 1975, discriminatory forms of public housing allocation led to a concentration in the low-income periphery or the decayed central areas of Paris, Lyons and Marseilles (Body-Gendrot, 1993a, p. 81). The large public housing projects around major cities became 'quarters of exile' (Dubet and Lapeyronnie, 1992) shared by African immigrants and their descendants together with the most marginalized groups of the French population: unskilled workers, the long-term unemployed, single-parent families and the chronically sick. Anti-immigrant organizations such as the *Front National* have their roots in fears about 'immigrant ghettoes', which are portrayed as centres of criminality and terrorism, that will undermine the French nation. These neighbourhoods are, however, also the cradle for social and political movements of immigrants.

Living in disadvantaged inner-city areas or isolated housing projects reduces the chance of occupational mobility. Low-quality recreational amenities and a lack of social and medical services affects health and quality of life, especially for children. Exposure to environmental stresses such as pollution and heavy traffic, or to social stresses like criminality and drug dealing, further reduces the life chances of minorities. Educational and vocational training opportunities tend to be inadequate and low in quality in such areas, which means that the disadvantage of the immigrant generation tends to be carried over to the second and third generations.

This is the basis for racializing discourses on 'ghettoes' and the 'underclass' (see Chapter 5) in the USA, Britain and other countries. Such discourses label members of minorities not only as disadvantaged, but also as inferior. Their inability to leave the 'ghetto' is seen as the result of a dysfunctional lifestyle and values. At the same time, the 'ghetto' and the 'underclass' are constructed as threats to society – confirmation that the Other remains an alien growth within society.

Segregation and disadvantage lead not only to social problems, but also to political mobilization, which appears threatening to the state and the majority population. In response, ethnic minorities everywhere have become the subject of social policy measures designed not only to provide welfare and cope with the most blatant forms of exclusion, but also to strengthen social control. There is a clear link between ethnic minority movements, such as the 1981 and 1985 youth uprisings in Britain, and the introduction of official programmes to improve urban conditions and educational opportunities, and to combat racism.

Cultural factors

Immigrants often come to western countries with an expectation of economic and social integration into a modern society. Differences between immigrants and local people in language and traditions may seem less significant than the common acceptance of a culture of modernity, as embodied in secular and rational economic and political structures. However, such individual integration is usually only easy for highly skilled immigrants, who are not subjected to processes of labour market segmentation and residential segregation. Most lower-skilled immigrants experience discrimination and exclusion. This often provokes a response in which group culture becomes a resource for survival and resistance.

Ethnic minorities form cultural and social associations, build churches and clubs, and seek to preserve their languages and folklore. Such efforts obviously find the most fertile soil in neighbourhoods where ethnic groups are highly concentrated. The church, mosque or temple becomes a symbolic centre of the community. Traditionalist religious and cultural spokespersons encourage the maintenance of pre-modern marital and social practices. The suspicion of western secular ways is reinforced by the experience that these often form a mask for discrimination and racist beliefs.

This reassertion of culture reinforces the racialization of minorities by strengthening the fears of the local population: the immigrant colleague or neighbour becomes a mysterious, threatening and potentially militant Other. Language, religion, dress and even food become issues of conflict. The majority demand is often for assimilation: 'if immigrants want to belong, they should behave like us'. Such developments go hand in hand with the culturalization of racist ideologies; racism based on ideas of biological superiority and inferiority is replaced by a belief in the inevitability of cultural conflict between differing groups. Ethnic group difference becomes naturalized through the belief that a certain culture is inherently superior in a given set of conditions, for example Dutch culture being most appropriate for conditions in Holland, so that groups with differing practices are sure to remain inferior (Essed, 1991).

The counterpart of the culturalization of racism is a racialization of culture: language, religion and custom come to be regarded as symbolic of immutable difference. Islam – the historic foe of European Christian civilization – returns as the archetypal emblem of Otherness. Culture is used as a predictor for social behaviour and personal beliefs and character, in the way in which race (that is, phenotypical difference) used to be. In a situation where national cultures are being eroded by mass media and other globalizing influences, the blame is shifted onto ethnic minorities, who become the scapegoats for a pervasive cultural insecurity.

This not to imply that cultural differences between ethnic groups are solely the result of processes of racialization. Indigenous peoples and immigrants often have a strong desire to maintain their linguistic and cultural heritage. The point is that racialization greatly reinforces cultural difference and gives it a much greater significance and dura-bility for the groups concerned. Culture thus plays an important role in both other- and self-definition. Cultural difference becomes a label for exclusion and racialization, but it is also a vital part of the process of community formation, through which minorities constitute themselves as social and political actors (see Chapter 6).

Conclusion: the nation-state and racialization

As we discussed in Chapters 1 and 2, the invention of the nation –
which is essentially a *cultural community* – is a vital precondition for
the emergence of the modern democratic republic as a *political community*. In older state forms, sovereignty was embodied in the monarch,
while the division between state and society was legally defined
through the rights and obligations of the subjects. In principle, this
applied to anyone within the territory, so that cultural belonging was
irrelevant, but the historical shift from the monarchy to the secular
republic required a new form of political legitimation and a new way
of defining who belonged to the state. Moreover, the shift to the
modern state took place within the context of urbanization and industrialization, which tended to undermine previous forms of authority and
social integration (Habermas, 1996, pp. 135–7).

The solution was found in the democratic constitutional state, based
on the free will of the people as expressed through active participation
in law-making and governing. The idea of the nation, as a cultural
community based on common descent, language and historical experience, became a vital factor in defining membership of the political
community (albeit with many national and historical variations). The
nation was also crucial to social integration, since it provided the
feeling of solidarity or 'imagined community' (Anderson, 1983) on
which the 'national industrial society' (see Chapter 1) could be based.
Despite the inequality and class divisions of industrial capitalism, the
feeling of belonging to one nation was powerful enough to hold societies together and to secure continuity despite war and crisis.

The universalism of the modern state thus stood in an uneasy
symbiosis with the particularism of the nation. Its model of inclusion
always also meant exclusion. Basing the nation-state on a cultural
community inevitably led to nationalism as a mode of dealing with
external relations. If the citizen was always also a national, then he had
to be a warrior-citizen, one ready to fight and die for the nation. Being
a member of one nation meant looking down upon and even hating
members of others, irrespective of possible common class interests. It
meant supporting the colonization of the rest of the world and
accepting racist ideologies of the inherent inferiority of colonized
peoples. The political mobilization intrinsic in the democratic secular
republic thus inevitably led to a racialization of the Other. Nation, race
and class are closely intertwined (Balibar and Wallerstein, 1991) and
are a central element of the culture of modernity (Goldberg, 1993).

The crucial point in our context is that the nation-state has an inbuilt tendency to create difference and to racialize minorities. This is achieved not only through discourses that ascribe difference to the Other, but also through various forms of political and social action that separate and differentiate members of minorities from the mainstream population. These discursive and material practices create the Other, and then take the ascribed Otherness as a justification for the differential treatment. In turn, the excluded minorities tend to constitute themselves as collectivities – sometimes using the very symbols of exclusion as a focus for resistance. Thus, racialization tends in the long run to lead to social and political mobilization by minorities.

These fundamental contradictions were brought to a head by the rapid growth in international migration since 1945. Nearly all developed countries now have large immigrant populations and increasing levels of ethno-cultural diversity. Most western nations have ethnic minority populations that make up at least 5 per cent, and often much more, of their populations. These minorities are heavily concentrated in major cities, where they strongly influence lifestyle and culture. As for the rest of the world, international population mobility has, since the mid-1970s, become an integral part of globalization, affecting all regions. Settlement and minority formation seems probable in many newly industrializing countries.

Such changes have not been intentional. No government set out to build a multicultural society through immigration. The policies that brought about influxes in many Western European countries were concerned with temporary labour recruitment and were not designed to permit permanent settlement. The immigration policies of the USA, Canada, Australia and New Zealand did favour family reunion and settlement, but here the aim was to strengthen the dominant white European population. Refugee admission policies arose out of the political exigencies of the Cold War and were not designed to increase ethnic diversity.

With hindsight, these policies appear naive. Despite centuries of experience with migration, governments failed to understand its probable long-term consequences. An unquestioned belief in the controllability of difference, either through assimilation or through differential exclusion, was the basis of short-term approaches and an absence of planning. Policies on immigration generally failed to meet their declared objectives – indeed, they often brought about the opposite of what was intended. There was no comprehension in official quarters of the character of migration as a self-sustaining social process. Nor have the economists and other social scientists who advised governments shown much understanding or capability for prediction.

In an era of rapid economic and social change, immigrants and indigenous peoples have become ethnic minorities who are partially excluded from mainstream society. This is not a phenomenon that will be overcome simply by the passage of time: many descendants of immigrants remain marginalized over generations, while indigenous peoples are still outsiders after centuries. Racialization is embedded in the historically formed institutions and discourses that contribute to minority formation. As a result, immigrants, indigenous peoples and other minority groups are subjected to special forms of exclusion in the legal, economic, spatial, social and cultural spheres.

The combination of growing ethnocultural diversity with continuing practices of differentiation and racialization throws up new questions, for which there are no readily available answers. These questions go to the core of concepts of cultural and national identity. How can the Other become a citizen when subjected to a whole gamut of exclusionary practices? Where is the legitimacy of political institutions if they can no longer be based on assumptions of historically developed common values? How can communication across difference be achieved without an attempt at cultural homogenization, which is likely to create resistance and separatism? Such questions may well be fundamentally destabilizing for the nation-state in the era of globalization.

4

Becoming a Citizen

In liberal-democratic theory, citizenship is seen as the institution that provides political cohesion. The status of *citizen* seems inclusive and open to all. Yet, as discussed in previous chapters, this universalistic principle is belied by historical practice, in which citizenship has almost always been bound to the status of being a *national* – an intrinsically particularistic and. exclusionary category. That has meant either the exclusion or the forced assimilation of groups not considered part of the national community. This contradiction has been exacerbated by globalization. The mass migrations of the last half century have played a major part in undermining myths of national homogeneity. A range of structural and cultural factors inherent in western societies have marginalized immigrants, indigenous people and certain other groups, turning them into ethnic minorities. This has negative effects not only for the marginalized groups, but also for the political culture as a whole, as democratic citizenship cannot flourish in a society based on exclusion.

Becoming a citizen is clearly of crucial importance to an immigrant, but gaining formal *access to citizenship* – symbolized by getting the passport of the country of residence – is only one aspect of this. Equally important is the extent to which people belonging to distinct groups of the population actually achieve *substantial citizenship*, that is, equal chances of participation in various areas of society, such as politics, work, welfare systems and cultural relations. This chapter deals with access to citizenship – *becoming a citizen* – while Chapter 5 will examine substantial citizenship – *being a citizen*.

The rules for becoming a citizen in various countries are complex and have undergone a considerable change in recent **years**. Apart from the many national studies, a number of useful comparative overviews have appeared (see, for example, Çinar, 1994; Guimezanes, 1995). It is necessary to differentiate between the situation of immigrants themselves (the 'first generation') and of their descendants (the 'second' and subsequent generations). Conditions for the naturalization of immigrants and for the acquisition of citizenship by their children vary considerably, which often reflects historical differences in processes of nation-state formation. However, citizenship is not always an 'either/or' situation: in response to large-scale settlement, some countries have devised forms of quasi-citizenship that confer some but not all of the rights of citizenship. One important new form of quasi-citizenship is the citizenship of the European Union (EU), introduced through the 1991 Maastricht Treaty.

Laws on citizenship or nationality[1] derive from two competing principles: *ius sanguinis* (literally, law of the blood), which is based on descent from a national of the country concerned, and *ius soli* (literally, law of the soil), which is based on birth in the territory of the country. *Ius sanguinis* is often linked to an ethnic or folk model of the nation-state (the German *Kulturnation*), while *ius soli* generally relates to a nation-state built through the incorporation of diverse groups in a single territory (as in the case of the UK). *Ius sanguinis* has been seen historically as being appropriate for an emigration country (such as Germany, Spain or Greece) that wishes to retain the allegiance of people who have settled elsewhere.[2] A 'law of return' to reintegrate former emigrants may be based on this principle, as in the case of contemporary Germany and its *Aussiedler* (ethnic Germans from Eastern Europe). *Ius soli*, on the other hand, is particularly useful for integrating immigrants of diverse national origins into a new nation, which is why it has been adopted in former British colonies in North America and Oceania, and former Spanish colonies in Latin America.

In practice, all modern states have citizenship rules based on a combination of *ius sanguinis* and *ius soli*, although one or the other may predominate. For example, *ius soli* countries use the *ius sanguinis* principle to confer citizenship on children of their citizens born overseas. A further principle is growing in significance at present: that of *ius domicili* (law of residence), according to which people may gain an entitlement to citizenship through residence in the territory of a country.

Naturalization of the immigrant generation

Naturalization procedures, through which immigrants can become citizens, exist in all countries. However, the rules and practices of these differ considerably; it is generally much easier to get naturalized in *ius soli* countries than in those where citizenship is based mainly on *ius sanguinis*. Naturalization is a *discretionary act* by the state, one usually carried out by the executive in the form of the head of state, a government minister or a bureaucracy. In Canada it is the task of a 'citizenship judge', while in Belgium, Denmark and Luxembourg naturalization is a legislative act (Guimezanes, 1995, pp. 161–2). Apart from certain exceptional circumstances, immigrants have no *entitlement* to naturalization and are mere objects of decisions from above. In some cases, there is a right of appeal, although generally only on procedural grounds. It is thus the state, acting in the name of the existing political community, that decides on the inclusion or exclusion of newcomers.

Each country imposes a series of conditions for naturalization. A period of legal residence is required everywhere: the shortest is 2 years, in Australia; 5 years is the most common, occurring in the USA, Canada, Belgium, France, the Netherlands, Sweden and the UK; 10 years is required in Austria and Germany; and 12 in Switzerland (Çinar, 1994, pp. 51–2). Being lawfully admitted for *permanent* residence is a requirement in Australia, Canada and the USA. Most countries require a certain proficiency in the national language, although the level required and the rigour with which the provision is applied varies considerably. In some Swiss cantons, for example, immigrants have been tested not only in one of the official languages, but also in the local dialect. In Australia and the USA, the language requirement is waived for those over 50 years of age. A knowledge of the language is often taken as an indicator of the capability and desire to become assimilated (as, for example, in France and the Netherlands).

Most countries also demand that applicants for naturalization be 'of good character', which generally means not having been convicted of a crime. This may include not ever having violated immigration rules (as in Germany and France, for example), which could exclude many people where such rules are strict and inflexible. Good character can, however, mean much more: in the USA, people to be rejected include drunkards, polygamists, gamblers and members or former members of the Communist Party. Many countries reject the naturalization of people considered to be a threat to public order and security, which can easily be used against immigrants who have protested against dictators in their country of origin or racism in the immigration country.

Some requirements are highly subjective: Austria demands 'loyalty to the Republic of Austria' and the absence of damaging relations to a foreign country; Germany requires 'commitment to the constitutional order'; and Switzerland calls for familiarity with the Swiss way of life, customs and habits. Other criteria are economically selective: 'adequate means of livelihood' or 'financial solvency' are required in many countries, and German authorities may measure up an applicant's dwelling to see whether it is 'adequate' (Çinar, 1994, pp. 50–3) – a double discrimination for immigrant workers who cannot get decent housing because of low income and racism. Germany also requires that there be a 'public interest' in granting of citizenship to an applicant. This is a 'rubber paragraph' allowing people to be refused on nebulous grounds, but also allowing the state to declare that there is an interest in the naturalization of a whole category of people, as occurred with regard to long-term foreign residents and young foreigners (the second generation) from 1991.

A very important criterion for naturalization is whether an applicant can retain their original nationality, thus becoming a dual citizen. People cling to their original affiliation for both practical and emotional reasons. Renouncing it may block a return upon retirement, or lead to a loss of rights to land ownership. Giving up the original nationality may mean finally burying dreams of going back home and can be damaging to personal identity. Dual citizenship seems an appropriate way of managing the multiple identities that arise from globalization, especially as more and more people actually live in more than one country.

The principle of singular citizenship is in fact being eroded everywhere by mixed marriages, with their binational offspring. This is a result of changes made in the 1970s and 80s to secure equal rights for women in family law and nationality law. In many countries, the nationality of a child born abroad used only to be transmitted through the father. Once mothers obtain the same right to transmit their nationality as fathers, binational marriages automatically lead to dual citizenship. If a binational immigrant couple is resident in a third country where *ius soli* prevails, this may lead to children having three nationalities.

According to Guimezanes (1995, p. 165), Austria, Denmark, Finland, Germany, Japan, Luxembourg, Norway and Sweden require a renunciation of the former nationality, while other OECD countries, including

Australia, Canada, France, the UK and the USA, permit dual citizenship. However, law and actual practice are at odds in some countries: Sweden, for example, generally accepts dual citizenship in practice. According to Çinar (1994, p. 62), 'the availability of dual citizenship has now become a matter of course in Western Europe'. This represents a major shift since 1963, when most European countries signed the Strasbourg Convention on the Reduction of Cases of Multiple Nationality. The abandonment of this principle is quite recent in some cases, dating from 1991 for Italy, the Netherlands and Switzerland (Çinar, 1994, p. 53). The burgeoning of multiple citizenships is a major challenge to the traditional nation-state model.

Dual citizenship has become a major political issue in Germany. The requirement for a renunciation of the former citizenship is seen as a major obstacle to the political integration of immigrants, and hence as a significant factor in the racism and extreme-right mobilization of the early 1990s. The largest minority, the Turks, are generally not permitted by their own government to renounce their former affiliation, although rules introduced in 1998 do now permit dual citizenship. Some other groups, such as Greeks, are also prohibited from renouncing their previous citizenship. Regional authorities, particularly in areas of large-scale settlement like Berlin, have been increasingly willing to relax the rules to allow Turks and Greeks to acquire German citizenship. Dual citizenship is anyway on the increase through binational marriages and because *Aussiedler* who acquire German citizenship by right do not have to give up their previous citizenship. There are estimated to be 1.2 million dual citizens in Germany (Çinar, 1994, p. 54), which makes the official line look rather absurd.

For many years there has been an active campaign for improved access to citizenship for immigrants and their descendants, including the right to dual citizenship. Changes introduced through the 1990 reform to the Foreigners Law and through the 1993 Asylum Compromise did improve naturalization rights as well as the access to citizenship for descendants of immigrants, but still rejected the principle of dual citizenship. The Social Democrat–Green Coalition which came to power in October 1998 announced that it would introduce a law permitting dual citizenship for immigrants. This proposal met strong opposition from conservative parties, which organized a public campaign to prevent it. The compromise measure passed by the German parliament in the spring of 1999 represented a considerable change in citizenship rules. The previous law gave adult foreigners legally resident in Germany for at least 15 years a claim to citizenship provided they gave up their previous citizenship; had not been convicted of a major felony; and were able to support themselves and their families. The new law (which came into force on 1 January 2000) reduced the period of legal residence required for a claim to citizenship to eight years. The same conditions apply, plus the additional requirements of proficiency in the German language and a declaration of allegiance to the Basic Law. However, the new law still generally prohibits dual citizenship, although with a list of exceptions in cases where renunciation of the previous citizenship would cause hardship or unreasonable difficulties (*www.germany-info.org/content/np_3c.html*). The new law also makes major changes for children of immigrants (see below).

The legal requirements for naturalization seem quite similar in various countries, but this should not be allowed to obscure the fact that actual practices are very different. Some countries, such as Germany and Switzerland, impose long waiting periods and complex bureaucratic practices, making it clear to applicants that naturalization is an act of grace by the state. At the other end of the spectrum, classical immigration countries encourage newcomers to become citizens and treat any decline in their propensity to do so as a serious problem. The Australian government declared a Year of Citizenship in 1989, while Canada actively promotes naturalization.

In the USA, Vice President Gore launched a 'Citizenship USA' drive in April 1995 to encourage the estimated 8 million eligible immigrants to be naturalized. An estimated 1.2 million persons were naturalized in financial year 1996 – more than twice as many as in the previous year. By October 1996, some 327 000 persons had acquired US citizenship in Los Angeles alone, including 60 000 in mass ceremonies in August 1996 (*Migration News*, October, 1996). In Texas, 10 000 new citizens were sworn in at once through mass ceremonies at the Dallas Cowboys' football stadium and 6000 at the Houston convention centre (*Guardian Weekly*, 22 September, 1996). Republicans claimed that 'Citizenship USA' was designed to mobilize new voters for Bill Clinton in the 1996 Presidential Election. What is significant in our context is the element of ceremony and celebration about becoming American (or Australian or Canadian). This act of naturalization is part of the national myth, while to be German (or Austrian or Swiss) really means to have been born so, and naturalization is still a shamefaced exception.

Such differences are reflected in the statistics. As Table 4.1 indicates, Australia had a very high rate of naturalization (that is, the number of naturalizations per 1000 foreign residents) in both 1988 and 1995. It has not been possible to calculate rates for the USA and Canada, because of a lack of data on the foreign resident population. However, the very large numbers of naturalizations make it reasonable to assume high rates in these countries too. It is interesting to note the growth from 1988 to 1995 in several European countries. Sweden and the Netherlands now have rates of naturalization comparable to Australia's. This represents changes in rules (such as the acceptance of dual citizenship) and conscious efforts to encourage immigrants to become citizens. Nonetheless, Table 4.1 shows that rates remain very low in Germany, Japan and Switzerland, while Belgium, the UK and France take an intermediate position. Other data indicate fairly low 1993 naturalization rates in Austria (23 per 1000), Denmark (28 per 1000), Italy (7 per 1000) and Spain (21 per 1000) (Guimezanes, 1995, p. 158). However, in the case of Italy and Spain, the recentness of immigration is likely to be the cause.

Table 4.1   Naturalizations in selected countries 1988 and 1995

Country	Number of naturalizations 1988	Naturalization rate 1988	Number of naturalizations 1995	Naturalization rate 1995
Australia	81 218	57	114 757	74
Belgium	8 366	10	26 109	29
Canada	58 810	na	227 720	na
France	46 351	13	59 988	17
Germany (FR)	16 660	4	31 888	5
Japan	5 767	6	14 104	10
Netherlands	9 110	14	71 440	98
Sweden	17 966	43	31 993	60
Switzerland	11 356	11	16 795	12
UK	64 600	35	40 500	19
USA	242 063	na	445 853	na

Sources: Australian Census 1996 preliminary figures; OECD, 1997, Table III.1, Tables A.1, B3, and C5.

Notes: The naturalization rate is defined as the number of naturalizations per thousand foreign residents.

The calculated naturalization rate for Australia is based on an estimate for the foreign resident population, assuming that 60 per cent of overseas-born persons are Australian citizens. The naturalization rate for France is calculated using the foreign resident population figure for 1990. The German naturalization figure excludes naturalization based on legal entitlement, which applies mainly to 'ethnic Germans' from Eastern Europe. The comparison has only indicative value, as definitions and procedures vary from country to country.

na = not available.

Although the desire of immigrant groups like the Turks to become naturalized has increased, rates vary sharply between immigration countries. In 1991, the naturalization rate for Turks in Sweden was 5.1 per cent, compared with 0.2 per cent in Germany. It was 5.4 per cent in the Netherlands in 1992. Similar variations exist for former Yugoslavs (Çinar, 1994, p. 66). Differences in the annual naturalization rate are reflected in long-term trends. About two-thirds of immigrants who have been in Australia over two years are Australian citizens. Non-citizens remain so of their own choice, either because they plan to leave at some point or because they see no advantage in becoming Australian. This applies particularly to settlers from Britain and New Zealand, while the overwhelming majority of immigrants from Eastern and Southern Europe and from Asia have become citizens. About half the foreign-born populations of both France and Sweden have been naturalized (Çinar, 1994, p. 65). In contrast, the overwhelming majority of immigrants in Germany, Austria and Switzerland remain foreigners. Despite all the recent debates and changes, fundamental differences remain between different types of immigration country.

Acquisition of citizenship by later generations

The transmission of citizenship to the second generation (the children of the original immigrants) and subsequent generations is the key issue for the future. National variations parallel those found with regard to naturalization. In principle, *ius soli* countries confer citizenship on all children born in their territory. *Ius sanguinis* countries confer citizenship only on the children of existing citizens, so that the children of foreign immigrants remain foreign even if they have spent all their lives in the country concerned. However, most countries actually apply models based on a mixture of the two principles. There have been substantial changes in regulations over the last two decades. Entitlement to citizenship increasingly grows out of long-term residence in the country: the *ius domicili*.

Ius soli is applied most thoroughly in Australia, Canada, New Zealand, the USA, the UK and Ireland. In the USA, a child born to immigrant parents in the territory of the USA becomes a US citizen even if the parents are visitors or illegal residents. However, anti-immigration groups and sections of the Republican Party have called for an end to this practice of 'birthright citizenship' (*Migration News*, October, 1996). In Australia, Canada and the UK, the child obtains

citizenship if at least one of the parents is a citizen or a legal permanent resident. However, these countries have regulations to confer citizenship on children who did not acquire it at birth if they remain in the
country until a certain age (10 in the UK and Australia). Thus, the
overwhelming majority of children of immigrants do acquire citizenship. Such countries apply the *ius sanguinis* principle only in order to
confer citizenship on children born to their citizens while abroad
(Çinar, 1994, pp. 58–60; Guimezanes, 1995, p. 159).

A combination of *ius soli* and *ius domicili* has emerged in France,
Italy, Belgium and the Netherlands. All these countries have rules that
grant citizenship to children born to foreign parents in the territory,
providing they have been resident for a certain period, make a declaration of their wish for citizenship and fulfil certain other conditions.
Until 1993, France conferred citizenship upon children born to foreign
parents in the country provided they had lived there for at least five
years before reaching the age of 18. Acquisition was automatic unless
the young person specifically rejected it. The 1993 *Loi Pasqua* changed
this rule. Young foreigners born in France had to declare their wish for
citizenship at the age of 18, and it could be rejected on grounds of
criminal conviction or a prior deportation order. Another change
concerned the right of foreign parents to apply for the naturalization of
their children born in France before the age of majority, even if they
themselves did not wish to be naturalized. This was abolished in 1993,
creating an insecure situation for a large number of young immigrants,
who could be forced to leave France if their parents departed (volun-
tarily or otherwise) (Çinar, 1994, p. 60). However, these measures were
largely reversed in 1998 by the new Socialist government.

France, Belgium and Netherlands also apply the so-called 'double
ius soli', according to which children born to foreign parents at least
one of whom was also born in the country acquire citizenship at birth.
This means that members of the 'third generation' automatically
become citizens unless they specifically renounce this right upon
reaching the age of majority (Çinar, 1994, p. 61).

Ius sanguinis is still the dominant legal principle in most European
countries as well as in Japan (Guimezanes, 1995, p. 159). Here, citizenship depends mainly on descent. However, of the major Western
European immigration countries, only Austria and Switzerland still
apply the principle strictly: children born in these countries to foreign
parents have no entitlement to citizenship even if they have lived there
all their lives. In 1994, a referendum was put to the Swiss people that
would have entitled young foreigners to citizenship, subject to resi-

dence and schooling in the country. The voters rejected this reform (Çinar, 1994, pp. 68–9). However, Switzerland does count the years spent in the country between the ages of 10 and 20 as double for the purpose of calculating the 12-year qualifying period for naturalization. Austria requires the renunciation of the previous citizenship, while Switzerland does not.

Other *ius sanguinis* countries have taken cautious steps towards introducing elements of *ius domicili*. This means giving an *option* of facilitated naturalization to young people of immigrant origin. Foreigners who have been resident in Sweden for five years before reaching the age of 16 and who have lived there since that age can become citizens by declaration between the ages of 21 and 23. Dual citizenship is permitted. The 1990 German Foreigners Law gave an entitlement to naturalization to young foreigners who applied between the ages of 16 and 23, had been resident in the country for at least eight years, had completed six years of schooling in Germany, and had not incurred any serious convictions. However, the value of this reform was seriously undermined by the requirement for renunciation of the previous citizenship, even though (as mentioned above) many exceptions are made. Similar rules also exist in Belgium (Çinar, 1994, p. 61; Guimezanes, 1995, p. 178).

The new citizenship legislation approved by the German parliament in 1999 substantially improved access to citizenship for descendants of immigrants. As of 1 January 2000, children born in Germany to foreign parents acquire German citizenship at birth if at least one parent has lived legally in Germany for a minimum of eight years. Children who acquire German citizenship in this way are allowed to hold dual citizenship until they reach maturity; they are required to choose between their German and foreign citizenship by the age of 23. Children born to foreign parents before the new law who are under the age of 10 can claim German citizenship by virtue of birth in Germany. They have to make this claim within one year of the promulgation of the law, and also have to choose between German and foreign citizenship by the age of 23 (*www.germany-info.org/content/np_3c.html*). The 1999 law is the most significant change in citizenship rules in the history of the German Federal Republic. It goes a long way to abolishing the principle of ethnic descent hitherto intrinsic to the German concept of the nation. However, the rejection of dual citizenship is likely to reduce the practical effects of the reform.

In general, it appears that the distinction between *ius soli* and *ius sanguinis* countries still remains significant; the clear entitlement to citizenship for the second and subsequent generations in the former type provides a basis for social, political and cultural incorporation. Most *ius sanguinis* immigration countries have realized that the exclusion from citizenship is problematic, leading to social marginalization, political exclusion, conflict and racism. A number of them have made significant reforms, especially through facilitated naturalization on the basis of *ius domicili*. Yet this generally stops short of being a clear right, so situations of insecurity and exclusion still exist. It remains to be seen how the recent German changes will influence other countries.

Quasi-citizens, denizens and margizens

Immigrants who have been legally resident in a country for many years usually obtain a special status, granted by the authorities according to criteria such as length of stay, labour market participation and social integration. This status is formalized through privileged residence permits such as 'settlement permits' (*Niederlassungsbewilligungen*) in Switzerland or 'residence entitlements' (*Aufenthaltberechtigungen*) in Germany. The rights granted vary from country to country, but usually include some or all of the following:

- long-term or permanent security of residence status;
- protection from deportation (except in exceptional circumstances, such as conviction for a severe offence);
- the rights to work, seek employment and run a business;
- entitlements to social security benefits and health services;
- access to education and training.

The furthest going measure is the granting of voting rights in local elections to resident non-citizens, starting with Sweden in 1975 and followed by the Netherlands in 1986. Other countries have extended lesser political rights to resident foreigners, for example the right of association and the right of assembly. In several European countries, foreigners' advisory councils have been set up at the municipal level.

Such arrangements create a new legal status, which is more than that of a foreigner but less than that of a citizen. Tomas Hammar has suggested the term *denizen* for people 'who are foreign citizens with a legal and permanent resident status' (Hammar, 1990, p. 15). The term *quasi-citizen* may also be used. The pivotal right is clearly that of permanent residence, for once a person is entitled to remain in a country, he or she cannot be completely ignored. Social rights, such as the right to work and entitlement to social benefits, education and health services, flow from this right to be present, as the institutionalized exclusion of a section of the population is inconsistent with the principles of a modern democratic state.

Hammar estimated that some 7.5 million persons – more than half the foreign resident population of Western Europe – were denizens by 1987 (Hammar, 1990, pp. 22–3).[3] This figure has doubtless increased since then, although it is hard to procure exact data. By 1992, 52 per cent of Germany's foreign residents had been there for more than 10 years, 26 per cent of these having been resident for over 20 years (OECD, 1995, p. 88). The great majority of these people would by now have permanent residence rights and should be seen as part of the population. Similarly, in Switzerland, most foreigners now have *Niederlassungsbewilligungen*. Many of these denizens were actually born in their countries of residence.

A further factor in the emergence of quasi-citizenship is in the development of international human rights standards by bodies like the United Nations, the International Labour Organization and the World Trade Organization. A whole range of civil rights and social rights are guaranteed for citizens and non-citizens alike in the states that adopt and implement these international norms. As was discussed in Chapter 1, Soysal (1994) argues that immigrants in Western Europe actually enjoy most of the rights of citizenship through a form of 'universal personhood'. As Storey (1994) demonstrates in the case of Britain, however, the legal protection provided by international conventions can be severely deficient where states do not incorporate norms into their national law despite ratifying the conventions. Even when legal foreign residents do enjoy a fair degree of legal protection, this falls short of full citizenship, since quasi-citizens enjoy neither political rights nor a complete equality of social rights. How international legal norms can help to create transnational citizenship will be examined in Chapter 7.

It is important to emphasize that there are millions of long-term foreign citizens who are not denizens or quasi-citizens because they lack secure residence status. These include illegal workers, unauthorized family entrants, asylum-seekers, refused asylum-seekers who have not (yet) been deported, former legal residents who have lost this status (as happened to many immigrants in France in 1996), the long-term unemployed who may be subject to deportation in some countries, and people classed as temporary workers who are in fact permanently integrated into the workforce. Martiniello (1994, p. 42) suggests the term *margizens* for these people, who are truly living on the margins of prosperous western societies.

Even margizens are not totally without rights: they enjoy the civil rights and legal protection given to everyone in a democratic society, but in a precarious way because they may be deported if the authorities find it expedient. They even have some social rights, for example, asylum-seekers are usually provided with accommodation and social security payments. In the USA, illegal residents had, until recently, rights to basic social and medical services, and to education for their children. In 1994, a Californian referendum adopted Proposition 187 – a measure that would have denied such services to illegals – but the courts blocked its implementation on the grounds that it violated constitutional rights of equal treatment. In September 1996, the US Congress passed a law designed to deny education and welfare to illegal immigrants, and drastically to cut the welfare entitlements of legal immigrants. Restrictions on immigrants' entitlements have been introduced in many states. The recent upsurge in applications for US citizenship may in part be a reaction to the denial of social rights to non-citizens.

Quasi-citizenship arises mainly in countries with restrictive policies on naturalization and the conferral of citizenship on the second generation. It is a problematic constellation. On the one hand, it reflects a much-improved legal status compared with that of the original 'guest-workers' in the *ius sanguinis* countries. On the other hand, it is still an inferior status, tantamount to a permanent division between first- and second-class citizens. In the 1980s, immigrant and anti-racist groups called for improvements to quasi-citizenship, for example through the introduction of local voting rights for foreign residents or, where these already existed, their extension to provincial and national elections. The German Green Party introduced a Bill for a Settlement Law (*Niederlassungsgesetz*) into the Federal Parliament in 1985. This would have given foreign residents virtually all the rights of citizenship, but without the formal act of becoming a citizen.

In the meantime, struggles around immigration law, political rights and racist violence in the early 1990s have led immigrant organizations and the left to abandon demands for quasi-citizenship. In Germany, attempts to secure local voting rights were blocked by the Constitutional Court. In Sweden and the Netherlands, many people opposed the granting of provincial and national voting rights to non-citizens on constitutional grounds. The response to post-reunification racist violence in Germany was a strong demand for dual citizenship for immigrants. In France, debates around the 1993 changes to the Nationality Code led to calls for political rights for minorities. Campaigns by *beurs* (second-generation immigrants of North African origin) asserted that they were 'citizens by participation' without necessarily being nationals. The notion of a 'new citizenship' was viewed as the answer to a crisis in democracy. Members of the second generation demanded a more participatory citizenship in a multicultural society, based on residence rather than nationality or descent (Wihtol de Wenden, 1995).

The demand for stronger forms of quasi-citizenship appears as a passing phase in the migratory process. The objective of immigrant organizations is now full participation in a reconstituted multicultural democracy that can accept difference. This includes the right to dual citizenship, as the best reflection of immigrants' binational experience and identity. Nonetheless, millions of quasi-citizens remain and will do so for the foreseeable future. The millions of margizens will also continue to present a dilemma: they are not going to go away, yet governments are reluctant to find ways of integrating them. Such groups provide major challenges for the politics of citizenship.

Citizenship of the European Union (EU)

A special form of citizenship has recently been created within the EU and could conceivably develop in future in other regional economic and political organizations such as the North American Free Trade Area or the Association of South East Asian Nations. This topic will be discussed in detail in Chapter 7. Here we will look at EU citizenship in terms of formal incorporation of non-citizens.

The Maastricht Treaty of 1991 lists the following individual rights as constituting EU citizenship (Martiniello, 1994, p. 31):

- freedom of movement and residence on the territory of member states;
- the right to vote and to stand for office in local elections and European Parliament elections in the state of residence;
- the right to diplomatic protection by the diplomats of any EU state in a third country;
- the right to petition the European Parliament and the possibility of appealing to an ombudsman.

This set of civil and political rights is limited compared with the rights enjoyed by citizens of a democratic nation-state. EU citizens living in another member state do not have the right to vote in the national elections of that state. Their civil and social rights are incomplete: people dependent on social security do not have a right to settle in another member country, and access to civil service employment is still generally restricted to nationals (Martiniello, 1994, p. 41). It therefore seems appropriate to treat EU citizenship as a case of quasi-citizenship: it does confer significant rights on the nationals of one member state living in another, but these fall short of full citizenship, especially with regard to political participation. The limited character is made even clearer by the fact that EU citizenship is always bound to being a citizen of a member state; an EU passport is actually still a passport of one of the 15 constituent countries.

An important reason for the limitations of EU citizenship appears to lie in the origins of the EU as an economic community concerned, as Dahrendorf (1994, p. 17) puts it, with 'provisions rather than entitlements'. In other words, the objectives of integration have been to improve economic performance rather than to create political rights. Similarly, Habermas (1994b, p. 28) points out that the European Community brings the 'tension between capitalism and democracy to the fore'. There is a 'vertical divide between the systemic integration of economy and administration at the supra-national level – and political integration that thus far works only at the level of the nation-state'.

The unwillingness of national élites to shift the main focus of rights to a supra-national entity may also be linked to the role of historical cultural identities in securing political cohesion at the national level. As Martiniello (1994, p. 35) points out, EU citizenship is at present 'a sort of complementary supra-citizenship which confirms the existence of the cultural and political identities corresponding to the member states of the European Union'. EU citizenship does not separate citizenship from national belonging; instead, it creates a two-level model in which supra-national rights (at the EU level) are dependent on national belonging (at the member-state level).

At the same time, there are attempts to create a European cultural identity. This, according to Martiniello (1994, pp. 38–9), has two variants: the 'traditionalist option' based on myths of a common Judaeo-Christian and humanist experience, and the 'modernist option' based on the programme of constructing a 'common European cultural space' through plurilingualism, education, secularism, modern communication techniques and so on. Both options are, however, created in distinction to an external Other, which is constructed as culturally, politically and technologically inferior. Within Europe, this Other is represented by 'extra-communitarian' immigrants, especially those from non-Christian areas, which mostly means Muslims. The emerging European identity specifically excludes millions of immigrants, which helps to explain why EU citizenship does not take account of the situation of long-term foreign residents from outside the Union.

There is, however, another way of looking at European citizenship, which focuses not on political rights, but on the social entitlements that have been created for intra-EU migrants through the construction of a common economic space. The 'Five Freedoms of the Common Market' – the free exchange of goods, the free movement of labour, the freedom of entrepreneurial domicile, the freedom of service provision and the freedom of currency movement – were laid down in the 1957 Treaty of Rome for economic reasons. These freedoms, particularly that of the free movement of labour, lead to the notion of the *industrial citizen* or *citizen-as-worker*. In response, a whole range of social policies and entitlements for intra-European Community (EC) migrants and their families were laid down through European Community (EC) Regulations and Directives (Meehan, 1993a, pp. 78–100). Not only do intra-EU migrants have equal rights to social benefits and services in their country of residence, but there has also been a trend towards harmonization and improvement in national provision, sometimes against the wishes of reluctant member states (notably Britain).

Meehan argues that this development affects public space in the sense that EC/EU rulings promote 'a common civil society'. She questions the division between political, legal and social rights on the grounds that these are interdependent, and that social rights are increasingly seen as being a necessary condition of equal citizenship. Meehan concludes that 'the enforcement of social rights has "spilled-over" into previously exclusive national competencies and that, in many ways, Community individual legal and social rights are virtually the same thing' (Meehan, 1993a, p. 146). The consequence of this argument is that rights accorded to *citizens-as-workers* are likely in the long run to develop into the rights typical of *citizens-as-human-beings*. Thus, European citizenship, despite its present limitations, appears as a stage on the way to a form of supra-national citizenship (compare Meehan, 1993a, pp. 146–60).

In a similar vein, Habermas argues that such developments will occur not automatically but instead as a result of struggles between social movements and powerful supra-state bureaucracies, which seek to reduce politics to a matter of rational administration. The European single market may provide a space for political mobilization and the emergence of 'communication networks of European-wide public spheres'. A common political culture could articulate with differing national traditions of art, literature, historiography, philosophy and so on, in the context of increasingly multicultural societies (Habermas, 1994b, pp. 30–4).

Conclusion

Rules for formal access to citizenship are highly complicated, vary between countries and are in a state of flux. Nonetheless, some general trends can be discerned. Half a century of large-scale immigration to western nations is leading to a grudging realization that people of diverse ethnocultural backgrounds are there for good, and that there is no real alternative to incorporating them as citizens. This recognition has been easier for some countries than others.

Classical immigration countries such as the USA, Canada and Australia have been able to continue their tradition of incorporating newcomers as citizens, although they have had to drop practices of racial selectivity and find new ways of dealing with cultural difference. Immigrants are encouraged to become citizens with automatic citizenship for their children. These countries seem highly inclusive. However, it may be argued that the real decision on citizenship is made when immigration applications are rejected or accepted, rather than later on when settlers apply for naturalization. The selectivity of immigrants according to economic, social and humanitarian criteria may be based on (possibly unconscious) political and cultural biases.

European countries, with their strong historical links between imagined cultural community and political belonging, have found it more difficult to change their access criteria. Nonetheless, naturalization rules have been gradually relaxed to grant citizenship to longstanding foreign residents.

Many observers speak of a cross-national convergence of rules, but a comparison of actual practices and outcomes shows that major difference still exist. Naturalization rates are still very low in the *ius sanguinis* countries that used to recruit guestworkers: Germany, Austria and Switzerland. Countries with models combining elements of *ius soli* and *ius sanguinis* – France, Belgium and the UK – have intermediate rates. Sweden and the Netherlands have done most to change rules to include immigrants and now have a naturalization rate close to that of Australia or Canada.

Measures are also being introduced to facilitate access to citizenship for the second and subsequent generations through the extension of *ius soli* or through various combinations of *ius soli*, *ius sanguinis* and *ius domicili*. Immigrants' children are automatically citizens in the USA, Australia, Canada and the UK. The overwhelming majority become citizens on reaching adulthood in France, Sweden, the Netherlands, Belgium and Italy. Rules are still restrictive in Austria and Switzerland, so that many young people remain foreigners in their country of birth and upbringing. Important changes have just been introduced in Germany, and their effects cannot yet be assessed. Another general trend is that towards dual or multiple citizenship. Although many governments reject this because of fears of 'divided loyalties', there are now millions of people with two or more passports. This contributes to the erosion of notions of exclusive national belonging.

Several states have created systems of quasi-citizenship, through which long-term residents are granted some but not all of the rights of citizenship. Such measures do improve the legal and psychological security of settlers but seem fundamentally unstable because they create a two-class system of citizenship that is inconsistent with democratic principles. However, once immigrants have civil and social rights, they are in a better position to demand political rights. Citizenship of the EU also appears to be a problematic form of quasi-citizenship. It is linked to the citizenship of a member state and confers only limited political rights, albeit quite considerable social rights. EU citizenship does nothing for the millions of 'extra-communitarians' and is seen by some as one aspect of the construction of an exclusionary European identity. However, like other types of quasi-citizenship, EU citizenship could be an important stepping-stone towards full membership. The question is whether this will be membership of an exclusionary nation-state or of a new type of transnational democratic entity.

Issues of formal access to citizenship for immigrants are thus far from resolved. A large number of people still have ambiguous and disadvantaged legal positions. In some countries, a generation of young people are reaching maturity without clear and equal rights in their country of birth. Populations can be divided up into full citizens, denizens and margizens. Such legal differentiation perpetuates and exacerbates social divisions and racism against minorities.

Notes

1. Legal and political documents often use the terms 'citizenship' and 'nationality' as synonyms. This differs from the political sociology usage applied in previous chapters, according to which citizenship refers to political inclusion as a relationship between individual and state, while nationality refers to national belonging in the sense of membership of a cultural community. According to Guimezanes (1995, p. 157), the countries of the European mainland and Japan use the term 'nationality', while Common Law countries (Britain, the USA, Canada and so on) use 'citizenship'. In fact, the practice in most countries is inconsistent and contradictory.
2. Another way of achieving this was to declare colonies to be part of an empire, under the same sovereign as the country of origin, thus allowing emigrants to retain their citizenship. However, this too could lead to citizenship for the colonized populations, which was to have important consequences for France, Britain and the Netherlands in the period of decolonization.
3. Hammar excluded the UK from his calculation, because the imperial model of citizenship there meant that most immigrants were full citizens (at least in formal terms).

5

Being a Citizen

In Chapter 4, we examined the contested and rapidly changing rules of access to citizenship in western countries, but there is no clear cut-off between the process of *becoming* a citizen and the condition of *being* a citizen. Nor is there an absolute distinction between *being* and *not being* a citizen. Like so many other divisions in the contemporary world, these are blurred boundaries. The construction of in-between categories, like denizens and margizens, is a reflection of the real ambiguity of citizenship status. Citizenship is not an either/or situation. This applies to all citizens because of the discontinuities and fluidity of different aspects of citizenship. It applies even more strongly to immigrants and other minorities as a result of their exclusion from certain rights or their precarious legal status. In this chapter, we will examine the different sets of rights that make up the substance of modern citizenship, and examine the links between them. We will discuss the extent to which marginalized groups – especially immigrants, indigenous peoples and ethnic minorities – possess these rights, not only in formal terms, but also in practice.[1]

The interdependence of rights

Until recently, citizenship essentially meant political membership in a particular nation-state recognized in international law (Habermas, 1994b, p. 24). Within this political definition, there was room for divergent approaches. One tradition conceived the citizen as an economic citizen or *burgher*, whose civil rights towards the state were connected with the protection of private property and the creation of legal security for commerce. The German *Staatsburger* of the Second Empire (1871–1918) had civil rights within the *Rechtstaat* (the state based on the rule of law) but little political say. This type of citizenship could easily turn into a doctrine of the obligations of the individual towards the state. As discussed in Chapter 2, more democratic traditions conceived of the citizen as a political subject, the *citoyen* of the French Revolution, the person who participated in government. The community of political citizens was the basis of popular sovereignty.

Both of these traditions shared two characteristics. First, the possession of political rights did not in itself confer an entitlement to social rights. The right to work or to receive medical or social services could not be derived from being a citizen. Second, the status of citizen was not necessarily inclusive of all members of society. It could be based on qualifications, such as property ownership, gender, religion or ethnicity. Those who were not citizens were often seen as being represented by those were: the husband represented the wife, the master the servant and so on. This narrow concept of the citizen still exists and has indeed experienced a recent resurgence in liberal theories that call for a reduction of the social role of the state. The 'active citizen' of new right theorists such as Lawrence Mead (1986) is the person who fulfils his or her obligations to the community (by having a job, paying taxes and obeying the laws), rather than making demands on the state (see Dahrendorf, 1994, p. 12).

The terms of the debate were changed in the post-1945 period through T. H. Marshall's sociological analysis of citizenship. Marshall pointed to the contradiction between formal political equality and the persistence of economic and social inequality in capitalist society. Members of the working class had become enfranchised in Britain, but impoverishment and insecurity could prevent full participation in the community. Marshall distinguished three types of citizenship rights, which had developed in an historical progression. The first type was *civil rights*, which emerged in the eighteenth century as 'negative rights': individual freedom from unlawful infringement on private property, personal liberty and justice by the state. These were joined from the nineteenth century by 'positive' *political rights* through which the active citizen could take part in opinion formation and political decision making. In the twentieth century, *social rights* developed, through which citizens were guaranteed a certain basic standard of economic and social wellbeing, either through the right to work or through welfare provision. These social rights were vital to permit members of the working class genuine participation in society as citizens (Marshall, 1950, 1964).

Marshall's theory was a reflection of the broadening of social rights through the emerging welfare state in postwar Britain. His work has been frequently criticized, on a variety of grounds (see Turner, 1992, pp. 36–41). It focuses exclusively on the British experience, and its appropriateness to other countries is questionable. The evolutionary development of the three types of rights seems almost teleological, with the implication that the emergence of social citizenship marks 'the end of the history of citizenship' (van Steenbergen, 1994, p. 3). Yet the neo-liberal roll-back of the welfare state led by Thatcher and Reagan has shown the fragility of social citizenship. Turner (1992, pp. 38–9) argues that Marshall failed to develop the economic sociology of the state necessary to explain how the resources for welfare were to be generated. He also failed to emphasize the role of violence – both war and class struggle – in bringing about social citizenship. Finally, Marshall's work is predicated on the autonomous nation-state, which can freely decide on the redistribution of income. This makes the relevance of his model questionable in an era of globalization.

Yet Marshall's model has been highly influential in US and British social theory, and is used in European debates too, where, especially in Scandinavia, it complements other social-democratic theories of the welfare state. A key aspect of Marshall's work is the idea of the *interdependence* of different types of right: that is impossible to have full civil and political rights without a certain standard of social rights. A corollary of this is that social rights may be just as important as political rights as an indicator of citizenship, and that Marshall's historical order could be reversed: social rights could lead to political rights, as discussed with regard to the European Union (EU) in Chapter 4.

Here we will discuss the quality of citizenship enjoyed by minorities, both immigrant and indigenous, using Marshall's three categories. We will then examine two further areas – gender rights and cultural rights – and argue that these are essential aspects of citizenship in multicultural societies.

Civil rights

Civil rights include:

- the freedom and inviolability of the person;
- freedom of expression;
- freedom of religion;

- protection from unlawful acts by the state, such as imprisonment or forced labour;
- equality before the law;
- the prohibition of discrimination on grounds of gender, origins, race, language or beliefs.

Such rights are laid down in state constitutions (such as the German Basic Law), in bills of rights (as in the USA, Canada and France), and through common and statute law and its interpretation by the courts (as in the UK or Australia). These guarantees are the expression of historical struggles against the arbitrary power of monarchs and tyrants. In principle, they are for everyone present in the country, whatever their citizenship or residence status. Even visitors passing through a democratic country enjoy protection. However, things are not always as clearcut in practice: minorities often do not enjoy genuine equality before the law.

Although indigenous peoples in the USA, Canada and Australia today have formal equality of rights, this status is fairly recent, dating back to the success of civil rights movements in the 1960s. The same goes for African-Americans in the USA and for New Commonwealth Immigrants in Britain. All of these groups are legally full citizens, but rights that are guaranteed by law may be violated in the practice of powerful institutions such as the police, prisons and the courts. For example, in Australia the Human Rights and Equal Opportunities Commission's *Report of the National Inquiry into Racist Violence* (HREOC, 1991, pp. 61–135) documented widespread violence and discrimination against Aboriginal people by police and other public officers. The Royal Commission into Aboriginal Deaths in Custody found a rate of incarceration of Aboriginal people 29 times higher than that of the rest of the population. There was clear evidence of institutional racism, which reflected strongly racist attitudes towards indigenous peoples.

Racist violence can in itself be a constraint on civil rights as it reduces people's chances of an equal participation in society. In the USA, federal authorities sometimes prosecute perpetrators of racist violence for violations of civil rights when state authorities fail to act. The Anti-Defamation League of B'nai B'rith (ADL, annual) regularly documents the activities of 'hate organizations', of which the largest is still the Ku Klux Klan. Neo-Nazi and 'militia' groups also carry out systematic campaigns of violence and intimidation against African-Americans, Asian-Americans and other minorities. In 1990, the US

Congress passed the Hate Crimes Statistics Act to provide a system of national monitoring of racist violence. Institutional racism plays a major part in 'hate crimes', either through the failure of the police to counter racist attacks, or by their own participation in them. Indeed, the Los Angeles riots of 1992 erupted in response to police violence against an Afro-American. Police forces in the USA and other countries have introduced special training and management schemes to counter institutional racism, but the success of these is very mixed (Shaw *et al.*, 1987).

Most European countries have experienced the dual problem of growing racist violence and inadequate institutional responses. In 1985, the European Parliament's Committee of Inquiry into Fascism and Racism in Europe came to the conclusion that 'immigrant communities... are daily subject to displays of distrust and hostility, to continuous discrimination... and in many cases, to racial violence, including murder' (European Parliament, 1985, p. 101). The situation deteriorated further, as the end of the Cold War coincided with a serious recession in most European countries. A comparative study found that: 'By the early 1990s, many groups of people have had to face racist violence and harassment as a threatening part of everyday life' (Björgo and Witte, 1993a, p. 1). These groups included immigrants and asylum-seekers, as well as longstanding minorities such as Jews and Roma.

State agencies often play an active role in the erosion of minority members' civil rights. The urban riots of the 1980s in Britain were triggered by heavy-handed police action against black youths. In France, the anti-racist group *SOS-Racisme* has documented widespread racist violence by the police against North Africans and blacks. In early April 1993, a series of police killings of immigrants led to violent confrontations. However, most acts of racist violence come from extreme-right and neo-Nazi groups. The main institutional problem here lies in the failure of the state to effectively contain such groups through legislation and police measures. Most countries have introduced laws to combat racist violence and incitement. In some cases, there are special agencies, like the British Commission for Racial Equality, to monitor the implementation of anti-racist measures. There is, however, little evidence that such responses have been adequate or effective. Perhaps the lack of zeal is attributable to the willingness of many political leaders to blame immigrants for social evils and to call for restrictive immigration policies.

The civil rights situation is even more precarious for the millions of immigrants without a clear entitlement to be in a country, such as illegal entrants, asylum-seekers and people with short-term residence permits. They too enjoy certain basic rights to legal protection, but find these hard to enjoy in practice. Police and other authorities often ignore formal rules when dealing with groups lacking the resources to take legal action. Weak legal status may also apply to immigrants with long-term residence or even to citizens of immigrant origin.

Political rights

Political rights refer above all to the rights required to participate actively in democratic processes of government:

- the right to vote and to stand for office at the various levels of government;
- freedom of assembly and of association;
- freedom of information.

In formal terms, there appears to be a fairly clear division between citizens (whether by birth or by naturalization), who enjoy political rights, and resident non-citizens, who do not. However, as we saw in Chapter 4, things have become less simple as a result of measures designed to achieve the integration of long-term settlers. In principle, quasi-citizens enjoy all the political rights except the first (and most important) category. In Sweden and the Netherlands, long-term foreign residents even have the right to vote and stand for office, but only at the level of local government.

However, the formal possession of political rights does not guarantee genuine political participation for members of minorities that have a marginal economic and social situation. Minority status in a literal, quantitative sense may also exclude certain groups from effective political participation: in Australia, indigenous people make up only 2 per cent of the population, and there are few constituencies where they have a genuine chance of securing representation. Their only chance of making their voice heard is through special representative bodies. In recognition of this, the Aboriginal and Torres Strait Islander Commission was set up in 1990 as a national body directly elected by indigenous people. However, its prerogatives are limited and insecure, as was shown in 1996 when the Liberal-National government took steps to curtail its autonomy in financial matters.

Criteria of exclusion based on socioeconomic position and on minority status may be mutually reinforcing: in the USA, impoverished African-Americans are highly unlikely to vote or even to be registered as voters. Indeed, the USA shows most dramatically the contradiction between participative democracy and social exclusion: large numbers of the poor and of ethnic minorities are not registered as voters. This favours conservative parties. Even in presidential elections, only about half the population votes, while the proportion is far lower in congressional and state elections. The 1996 'motor voter' law aimed to redress the situation by attaching voter registration forms to applications for driver's licences. Republicans saw this as an attempt to increase the Democratic vote (*Migration News*, October, 1996).

Freedom of information is of crucial importance in complex modern societies, where claims for popular participation can be brushed aside through the assertion of technological imperatives comprehensible only to experts. The concentration of media control in huge corporations makes access to balanced and unbiased information problematic for everyone. The resources required to obtain adequate information are least likely to be available to disadvantaged social groups. In addition, ethnic minorities may be excluded from information by language problems. Thus, the demand for political rights can lead to the demand for *cultural rights* – for example, multilingualism, resources for learning the official language and adequate education.

There are two main issues with regard to minorities and political rights. The first is the formal denial of political rights, which affects the millions of immigrants who are non-citizens. The second issue is the formal possession of political rights but the actual inability to enjoy them. This situation applies to the growing proportion of the population of western nations who are so economically and socially disadvantaged that they cannot fully participate in society, groups often referred to as the *underclass* or the *excluded*. This will be a theme of the next section, but its political implications should be noted here.

Members of ethnic minorities have a high probability of belonging to socially excluded groups, as the result of a combination of class factors and racialization. Most (although not all) people in such situations have formal political rights but lack real opportunities of participation in established political structures. Their voice is largely absent in parties and parliaments, despite all the rhetoric of politicians on combating unemployment and exclusion. Social exclusion often means a situation of political powerlessness.

Social rights

Social rights became an essential part of citizenship in the 'social Keynesian' model that was so successful in the boom period of capitalism from 1945 to the mid-1970s. Full employment in an expanding national industrial economy was linked to a welfare state, which provided a safety net for those temporarily or permanently unable to work. Marshall's principle of the need for a minimum economic and social standard to secure political participation was an expression of this model. Social rights were also a crucial part of what American sociologist Talcott Parsons called 'full membership in the societal community', which he in turn saw as a precondition for political integration (Parsons, 1965).

Social rights may include the following:

- the right to work;
- equality of opportunity (in education, the labour market and so on);
- an entitlement to health services, welfare benefits and social services in the event of unemployment or inability to work;
- an entitlement to a certain standard of education.

Social rights are hard to define precisely. Civil rights are 'freedom from' certain types of transgression, especially by the state. Political rights are entitlements to vote, stand for office or express political views. Social rights are, in contrast, much vaguer. What is the 'minimum standard'? Who decides and how? Clearly, it cannot imply complete equality in a capitalist society, where inequality of wealth and income is seen as vital to economic efficiency. Many social rights are provided by the state and are thus closely linked to social policy (Barbelet, 1988, p. 65), yet inclusion in the private sector of the economy also plays an important part. After all, economic well-being comes, for most people, through at least one member of their household having a job. Perhaps the core of the notion of social rights is that of decoupling *achievement* from *entitlement*: everyone should be entitled to the minimum standard seen as appropriate for a given society, whether or not they are able to make an economic contribution.

Social rights are continually contested. The achievement of social justice in various areas is the result of struggles by social movements (above all the labour movement) against powerful groups (such as owners of capital) that seek to maintain their own privileges. Social rights are constantly in danger of being rolled back, as the recent erosion of the right to work and cut-backs in welfare transfers in most western nations have shown.

Social rights of minorities in the post-1945 boom

The period of dominance of the social Keynesian model ran roughly from the 1940s to the early 1970s. It was linked to efforts to secure working-class loyalty during the Second World War and then the Cold War. It was based on the global economic hegemony of the old industrial nations (above all the USA), financial stability being guaranteed by the Breton Woods monetary agreement. Its industrial core was the Fordist mass production system, which required a large number of worker-consumers.

Prior to this, large sections of the population lived in conditions of *absolute poverty*, their incomes being inadequate to meet basic survival needs and to provide for old age, sickness or other crises. This included 'the working poor': large sections of the working class with low wages and insecure employment. The postwar trend to full employment and improved welfare meant higher living standards for the great majority of the population. Some pockets of absolute poverty always remained, but the main issue was now *relative poverty*: that of people who lacked the resources needed to participate in the activities and lifestyles considered customary in a modern industrial society (Townsend, 1979). It was the task of the welfare state to provide income support, housing, health services and education to guarantee social citizenship for all.

Indigenous peoples in the USA, Canada and Australia were largely excluded from mainstream employment and welfare systems in this period. Labour-market incorporation was very limited, and unemployment rates were high. Some special forms of employment were seen as being suitable for indigenous peoples (such as work on the cattle-stations in Australia), but in such cases they were paid far below the prevailing wage rate. Many indigenous people were subjected to special welfare regimes. Their work was seen as peripheral to the economy, and their income came largely in the form of in-kind welfare or minimal income transfers (see Yarwood and Knowling, 1982, pp. 259–68).

This was also the period of the large-scale recruitment of immigrant workers for the expanding factories of the industrial core economies. The social citizenship of minorities depended above all on their inclusion in the employment and welfare systems. The actual degree and forms of inclusion varied considerably. The overall pattern for most immigrant groups was that of inclusion at low levels in labour markets segmented according to ethnic origins and gender. This was linked to processes of spatial segregation based on both economic factors and the racialization of immigrants. Minorities became concentrated in certain neighbourhoods, marked by poor housing, social facilities and educational opportunities. Upward social mobility out of such disadvantaged occupational and residential locations was very limited for the immigrant generation. Opportunities were, however, somewhat better for their children. Many achieved better educational credentials and jobs than their parents' generation, but on average they remained disadvantaged compared with the majority populations.

Although most highly developed countries had growing welfare sectors in this period, their underlying principles and coverage varied considerably (Esping-Anderson, 1990), with much more comprehensive entitlements in continental Europe (especially Scandinavia) than in the UK, the USA, Canada and Australia. The degree of incorporation of immigrants into the differing national systems varied. In Australia, most immigrants had full rights to social, health and other services on arrival (although with a qualifying period for some groups). In the USA too, most social services were available to all legal residents (and often also to illegal ones). In European countries, immigrant workers gained access to most occupationally based social benefits, such as unemployment, health, and pension insurance. There were, however, important restrictions, especially in 'guestworker' countries. Workers on limited residence permits could be deported in the event of long-term unemployment. Public housing was often barred to foreigners (as is still the case in Austria today).

Many countries had special welfare services or agencies for immigrants. Australia had 'on-arrival' services, including camps or hostels, help in finding employment and basic English courses. In Germany, advice and assistance for foreign workers was provided through special agencies run by charitable organizations (such as the Catholic *Caritas* and social-democratic *Arbeiterwohlfahrt*) with government funding. In France, a special *Fonds d'Action Sociale* was set up to fund worker hostels and other services. Such special regimes were ambivalent in character: they provided services that responded to the special needs of immigrants, but they also kept immigrants separate from the mainstream population, and helped to maintain the myth that they were only temporary residents.

Overall, one can sum up the social situation of most minority members up to the 1970s as one of differential and partial inclusion at the lower levels of occupational and welfare state systems. Some groups had special situations: indigenous peoples were usually incorporated into welfare systems but only minimally into employment, while illegal immigrants were included in employment but not in welfare. The most important form of social exclusion at this time was the restriction of the right of family reunion, which applied in most European immigration countries in one way or another.

Social rights of minorities in the era of globalization and restructuring

Since the 1970s, globalization and economic restructuring have had major effects on social citizenship in industrial countries:

- The decline of stable employment for routine blue- and white-collar workers, particularly a loss of the expectation of full-time employment for men at a wage level sufficient to keep a family.
- A trend towards increasing income inequality.
- Growing spatial differentiation within cities, with emerging areas of concentrated disadvantage.
- Increasing heterogeneity and instability of households, leading to an erosion of the protective role of the nuclear family.
- Severe financial and political constraints on the capability of welfare states to respond to social needs, at a time when these are growing rapidly (compare Mingione, 1996a, p. 15; Morris, 1996, p. 160).

These factors affect the whole population. To understand the consequences for minorities, it is necessary to examine the extent to which ethnic minority status and racialization lead to increased vulnerability at a time of rapid change.

Since the 1970s, many manufacturing workers have become redundant, while others have experienced insecurity and deskilling. New employment opportunities in services and manufacturing are characterized by a bimodal skill profile, with a demand for both highly skilled specialists and low-skilled routine workers. The latter are often women, employed on a part-time basis at a low wage. This has frequently meant the casualization of employment, or the development of informal types of employment such as out-work and subcontracting. Numerous young labour market entrants cannot find formal-sector employment. Real wages have fallen for many workers, so that two or more incomes are needed to provide a reasonable standard of living for a household. The creation of new jobs has not kept pace with the growth in the labour force, leading to chronic unemployment. The USA has achieved relatively low unemployment rates by cutting wages to the point that the 'working poor' have reappeared: many workers now earn so little that they remain below the poverty line. European countries have unemployment rates of 10–12 per cent. There has been a dramatic growth in the numbers of the long-term unemployed and 'discouraged workers' who leave the workforce.

These trends have different effects on various labour market segments. The types of employment (especially in manufacturing) that were previously the main sites of incorporation for immigrants have been those most affected by restructuring, with a considerable loss of jobs and changes in employment patterns. New immigrants are more diverse in skill level than in the past; those with high-level recognized credentials have good prospects of finding appropriate jobs, but low-skilled workers have little chance of getting formal-sector employment. Many therefore find themselves unemployed, or have to work in insecure and marginal workplaces. Immigrants everywhere have a higher unemployment rate than local workers. Second-generation immigrants with poor educational qualifications have little chance of steady employment.

Such patterns are well illustrated by Seifert's (1996) analysis of occupational and social integration in Germany. Using the results of a large longitudinal survey, he found that the proportion of immigrant workers in unskilled or semi-skilled occupations declined from 70 per cent in 1984 to 60 per cent in 1994. However, the proportion of Germans in such jobs declined from 16 per cent to only 12 per cent. As for the second generation, the proportion in unskilled and semi-skilled work declined from 47 per cent in 1984 to 34 per cent in 1994 – an improvement, but still unfavourable compared with just 6 per cent of the same age cohort of Germans. The picture is similar with regard to sectoral distribution: immigrants are not as concentrated in manufacturing as they used to be, but they are still considerably overrepresented in manufacturing compared with Germans. Seifert finds that foreign employees earn less on average than Germans. However, this is not the result of wage discrimination – as workers doing the same jobs have comparable earnings – but of differing employment patterns (Seifert, 1996, pp. 423–7).

Faist's (1993) study of the entry of young Turkish nationals into German labour markets in the 1980s helps to explain what has happened. He reported an increase in access to vocational training over the period. However, ethnic inequality persisted: while two-thirds of German youths aged 15–24 had completed or were enrolled in apprenticeships, less than one-third of Turkish youths had done so. Moreover, Turkish apprentices were heavily overrepresented in craft occupations (for example as hairdressers, bakers or motor mechanics) not likely to offer good future perspectives. They were underrepresented in industrial occupations and almost completely absent from advanced services (banking, insurance and public administration). Many Turkish youths were enrolled in special programmes for the unemployed or disadvantaged. Such programmes were meant to improve basic work skills, but most companies in fact refused to hire youths who had taken them. The situation was particularly bad for young Turkish women: a third were not in the labour force, and nearly a quarter were in programmes for the disadvantaged.

Certain groups tend to remain in a disadvantaged labour market position, this position often being passed on to subsequent generations. In some cases, the second generation are actually worse off than their parents, as a result of the decline in availability of entry-level jobs in industry, so that young ethnic minority members face a future of casual work and frequent joblessness. Some groups and individuals break out of this situation, but many are caught in a vicious circle: initial incorporation into low-skilled work and residential areas with poor educational opportunities is reinforced by processes of racialization. Young job-seekers may be rejected because the combination of poor educational credentials, ethnic appearance and living in certain neighbourhoods has become a stigma, denoting marginality and unreliability (Häussermann and Kazapov, 1996, p. 361; Wacquant, 1996, p. 237).

Labour market segmentation and residential segregation tend to isolate minorities from the rest of the population. The German survey analysed by Seifert indicates a 'sharp decline in interethnic friendships' from 1990 to 1994. He takes this as evidence of the 'increasing distance between the foreign and the German population'. The survey also found that the proportion of immigrants intending to settle permanently in Germany increased from 30 per cent in 1984 to 46 per cent in 1994, yet only 16 per cent of all immigrants identified themselves as German in 1994. The figure for the second generation was 26 per cent. Identification remained overwhelmingly with their own ethnic group (Seifert, 1996, pp. 427–8). Such findings are not surprising, since these were the years following German reunification, when there was an upsurge of racism against immigrants.

A study of ethnic minorities in London and Amsterdam by Cross (1995) shows the links between employment and spatial factors. Greater London contained 58 per cent of Britain's black population and 35 per cent of those of South Asian origin in 1991. Ethnic minorities made up 20 per cent of the population of Greater London, compared with only 9 per cent 10 years ago. A quarter of Amsterdam's population belonged to ethnic minorities (Surinamese, Antilleans, Turks and Moroccans) in 1991. Most ethnic minority groups in the two cities showed a high degree of concentration in certain locations. They also had an employment pattern very different from that of the majority population, with a concentration in manual occupations, and a high rate of unemployment. Black men in London had an average unemployment rate of 27 per cent, compared with 12 per cent for white men. Matters were even worse in Amsterdam, where over half of all Turks and over 40 per cent of other minorities were unemployed in 1991. Cross concludes that both cities 'face a crisis of *class exclusion* associated with the rapid rise of the long-term jobless' (original emphasis). Of all the minority groups, only South Asians in London could be seen in the less dramatic terms of *class segmentation*. The excluded are mainly dependent on welfare payments (Cross, 1995, pp. 72–3).

Social exclusion is concentrated in specific urban areas, generally run-down inner-city areas or isolated and decaying peripheries. In France, for example, the large public housing projects on the periphery of Paris, Lyons, Marseilles and other cities (known as the *banlieue*) have become 'quarters of exile' (Dubet and Lapeyronnie, 1992). Ethnic segregation affecting particularly the Turkish population has become a major issue in German cities such as Berlin and Frankfurt. In Britain, problems of urban decay and racial segregation have been the focus of research and government programmes on the 'inner city' since the 1970s. Exclusion and racialization have become key themes in the sociology of the city in all western nations (Davis, 1990; Cross and Keith, 1993; Mingione, 1996b).

There is clearly a close relationship between segmentation and social exclusion. The factors that lead to an unequal distribution of minorities in occupational, residential, educational and social strata make them particularly vulnerable to processes leading to exclusion from mainstream economic and social relationships. Mingione (1996a, p. 33) characterizes such situations as the 'chronic cumulation of disadvantages which triggers malign circuits and leads to social exclusion or the formation of an underclass'. These 'malign circuits of exclusion' are to be found particularly where there is a very high concentration of disadvantaged minorities in poor ghettos (as in the USA). The malign circuits consist of the cumulative effects of 'violence, low level of education, poor quality of services, absence of work opportunities, discrimination and so on' (Mingione, 1996a, p. 32). In contrast, in areas with a lower degree of spatial concentration of disadvantage and less marked ethnic or racial closure (such as Milan), individual 'downward drift' may occur as a result of specific crises (unemployment, illness, drug dependency or relationship problems), but this does not lead to the exclusion of whole minority populations.

Wilson (1987) has designated the 'truly disadvantaged' African-Americans living in urban ghettoes as the underclass. He argues that poverty in inner-city areas has been sharply concentrated through growing joblessness combined with the outmigration of working-class and middle-class blacks. The underclass becomes socially isolated and highly vulnerable at times of economic change. This underclass concept has been followed by some European social scientists, but most prefer to speak of exclusion, arguing that the term 'underclass' is not appropriate in the European context because of two qualitative differences: the particularly strong racism in the USA resulting from the legacy of slavery, and the effects of welfare state measures in Europe in alleviating extreme disadvantage (Faist, 1993, pp. 327–9).

Indeed, many US scholars also reject the underclass label because it implies negative subjective characteristics of the disadvantaged, reminiscent of the 'culture of poverty' debate of the 1960s. The underclass has become a New Right cliché, denoting a group that rejects the values of mainstream society, especially the work ethic and the family, and which is characterized by welfare dependency, immorality, drug use and criminality (Morris, 1996, p. 161). In a revival of the nineteenth-century notion of the 'undeserving poor,' the underclass is seen as being responsible for its own poverty. The gendered discourse of the new moral panic constructs black women as sexually wanton single mothers who deliberately exploit welfare systems. Young black men are seen as primitive and violent, controllable only through incarceration.

There is a marked contrast between the situation in the USA and that in Europe and Australia. Wacquant compared the Paris neighbourhood of La Corneuve and the black ghetto of Chicago's South Side. In South Side, exclusion was based on race, and reinforced by class and the state. In La Corneuve, exclusion was based mainly on class and was mitigated by state welfare policies (Wacquant, 1996, p. 237). The result was much higher levels of racial homogeneity, separate group consciousness, isolation and violence in South Side compared with La Corneuve. Similarly, Marcuse (1996) found that rates of spatial segregation on the basis of income, education or occupational status were much lower in Australia than in the USA. The same went for spatial segregation by race or ethnicity. Marcuse also found no parallels in Australia for the concentration of unemployment, crime, drug use, homelessness, poverty, extreme racism and lack of effective welfare measures that affect US minorities, especially African-Americans.

The question is whether the intensification of racialization and the cuts to welfare states typical of the 1980s and 90s could drive European cities down the US path. The growth in urban violence – both on the individual level, and through gangs and neo-Nazi groups – is one indicator of this possibility. Body-Gendrot (1993b, p. 9) has argued that the ideology of social solidarity, although still dominant in Europe, is beginning to show cracks. Insecurity, austerity and the crisis of national societies lead to a search for safety valves. Delinquency, drug abuse and sporadic violence against the police in the UK and France show similarities with the US experience. The frustrations of young people of immigrant origin, deriving from unemployment, marginalization and racism, could turn into rage and political violence. Wilson himself has compared the European situation with that of the USA, speaking of a 'growing convergence' between Western Europe and the USA, not only with regard to the growth of ghetto neighbourhoods, but also in public attitudes that blame the excluded themselves for their plight (Wilson, 1994, pp. 60–3).

What conclusions can we draw from this discussion on the social citizenship of minorities? Two main categories may be distinguished. First, the majority of immigrants and their descendants do not live in ghettos, nor do they find employment in workplaces completely separate from those of the majority populations. Yet their position is frequently precarious: the combination of only partial incorporation into mainstream economic and social systems with continuing processes of racialization makes them vulnerable to social exclusion. This category may be referred to as *social segmentation*. People in this category have an insecure position, and their social citizenship is not guaranteed.

Second, there are minority groups particularly susceptible to marginalization as a result of weak legal position, severe racial stigmatization, a lack of human capital resulting from past discrimination, and specific historical conditions of conflict. These groups include indigenous peoples in North America and Australia, Afro-Americans in the USA, Afro-Caribbeans and South Asians in Britain, and asylum-seekers in Europe. Groups on the verge of such situations include Muslim immigrants in most countries, some (but not all) Hispanics in the USA, and certain Asian groups (especially those of refugee origin). Members of such groups are very likely to suffer *social exclusion*, and therefore do not enjoy social citizenship.

These are not the only groups who may suffer social exclusion and end up in 'quarters of exile'. In increasingly polarized societies with declining welfare states, such a fate can befall anybody, as a result of economic change or personal crisis. However, the probability of individual 'downward drift' is low for members of the majority population. The probability of exclusion is much higher for members of the groups subject to social segmentation, and is extremely high for the most disadvantaged and racialized groups (compare Mingione, 1996c, pp. 379–83). As Mingione (1996a, p. 12) argues, their disadvantage is so severe as to weaken the social bond and to question the strength of citizenship as an integrating force in contemporary society.

Welfare and stigmatization

There is a doubly ambivalent relationship between social citizenship for minorities and government social policies. First, strong welfare states may actually be conducive to closure to the initial entry of immigrants and their access to citizenship. In situations of fiscal constraint, opponents of immigration emphasize the social costs of admitting newcomers to the country. Governments tend to seek ways of reducing these costs by keeping people in situations of disadvantage through a denial of naturalization. The 'guestworker' policies of the past can be seen as a way of gaining workers while keeping down social costs. Openness to illegal Mexican workers in the USA was based on their cheapness, owing to lack of social rights. Today 'welfare-chauvinism' in western countries is a way of defending social institutions against outsiders from the poor South (Lutz *et al.*, 1995; Bommes, 1994).

Second, social policies for minorities are caught in a tension between inclusion and marginalization. Special social regimes often have the effect of separating and marginalising minorities. Faist found that it was not direct discrimination that disadvantaged Turkish youth in Germany in the 1980s, but rather the character of the public policies and informal networks that determined hiring patterns in various sectors of the labour market. Public policies did not specifically exclude Turks, but they failed to guarantee access to quality training as a social right, thus allowing the persistence of mechanisms of structural discrimination. Special training programmes for minority youth proved to be a mechanism of exclusion. Faist argues that 'participation in these dead-end programmes turned immigrant school-leavers into foreigners, a stigmatized minority' (Faist, 1993, p. 321).

In the US context, Wilson writes that welfare programmes such as food stamps and Medicaid do provide some relief but have failed to reduce the poverty rate for the non-elderly. Programmes for the poor neither address class inequities, nor help to bring recipients into mainstream economic and social life. Instead, 'they tend to stigmatize and separate them' (Wilson, 1994, pp. 56–7). Weil has put forward similar arguments with regard to social policies concerned with urban youth in France. He argues that such measures have not improved integration but rather have linked social problems to immigration and encouraged the formation of ethnic minorities (Weil, 1991, pp. 176–9).

Such arguments are well founded, but they do not justify blanket condemnations of special social policies for minorities. It is important to examine the ideological and political context in which social policies develop. Paternalistic welfare systems for indigenous peoples in Australia and elsewhere were introduced in the first half of the twentieth century as a deliberate form of social control, in the context of an openly racist and exclusionary world-view. The same could be said of the special social and educational regimes for 'guestworkers' in Germany and similar countries in the 1960s. Their aim was to prevent integration into society, in order to maintain the capability for return to the country of origin (Castles, 1984, pp. 159–89). But in the context of pluralist models of society, in which collective identities and cultures are respected, there is a strong case for social policies for minorities. Since such groups often suffer particular forms of disadvantage and have distinct needs, special forms of protection and services are crucial. Recent multicultural policies in Australia and Canada have been based on this nexus between cultural rights and social justice. Unequal treatment (in the sense of affirmative action) may be a precondition for full social citizenship.

Gender rights

To achieve full citizenship for minorities, it is necessary to go beyond Marshall's triad of civil, political and social rights. Oppression and exclusion linked to gender and culture have always been important, yet they have played little part in classical theories of citizenship. Since the 1960s, the women's movement and feminism have made gender into a key theme of political discourse, while ethnic minority movements have focused on cultural exclusion.

Until recently, women were excluded from formal citizenship. In liberal theory, they were seen as part of the private sphere (Pateman, 1988) and as the property of their husbands, who represented them in the public sphere (Gregory, 1987, p. 13). Universal suffrage is a fairly new institution: women won the vote in 1902 in Australia, 1918 in Britain, 1920 in the USA and 1944 in France. Even then, however, women were not legally independent persons: in Britain, it was not until 1929 that the Judicial Committee of the Privy Council declared that the word 'person' in common law actually included women (Gregory, 1987, p. 14). Marriage laws allowed a husband to control the body, property and freedom of his wife. Although legal discrimination had disappeared in most places by the 1970s, the legacy of subordination remains: women have worse jobs, lower incomes and lower rates of participation in decision-making processes, and are still seen as being primarily responsible for the domestic sphere (Meehan, 1993a, pp. 101–20; Vogel, 1994, p. 85). 'Extension of equal citizenship rights has not led to social justice and equality' (Young, 1989, p. 250).

Ethnic minority women are marginalized through both sexism and racism. These are not simply additive processes. Rather, the racialization of minority women takes specific forms within the reproduction of gendered social relations. Anthias and Yuval-Davis (1989) have analysed the complex links between gender relations and the construction of the nation. Women are not only the biological reproducers of an ethnic group, but also the 'cultural carriers' who have the key role in passing on the language and cultural symbols to the young. In nationalist discourses, women often serve as the symbolic embodiment of national unity and distinctiveness. They nurture and support the warrior-citizens (invariably seen as male). In defeat and suffering, the nation is portrayed as a woman in danger (implicitly of penetration or rape by the Other), or as the mother who has lost her sons in battle. Women embody the nation, while men represent it politically and militarily (Lutz *et al.*, 1995, pp. 9–10). This implies the 'natural' non-citizenship of women.

The control of female sexuality and reproduction is crucial to nationalism. If women are signifiers of community, access to their bodies is a key aspect of ethnic closure (Wobbe, 1995). Especially in countries with *ius sanguinis* and an ethnic model of nationhood, the purity of the nation depends on the transmittal of 'pure blood' through the mother. This explains why most European nations until recently permitted the transmission of nationality only through the father. For example, a German woman who married a foreigner could not pass on German citizenship to her children until the 1970s (Klug, 1989, p. 22).

Images of sexual violence are also important in boundary drawing. Caribbean men in Britain, Turkish men in Germany and African-American men in the USA are portrayed in racist propaganda as potential rapists, from whom white women must be protected. Rape was part of the process of 'ethnic cleansing' during the break up of former Yugoslavia. Discourses on rape focus not just on violence towards women, but also on the violation of the dominant community and of the territory that it owns (Wobbe, 1995, pp. 88–9). Women from the dominant group who have relationships with minority men are depicted as weak and treacherous. Minority women are, in contrast, seen as exotic and available, yet – in extreme racist views – as threatening because 'miscegenation' might 'weaken the superior race'. Racist discourses include a direct incitement to rape of minority women, as Wobbe (1995, pp. 94–9) shows through her analysis of the songs of right-wing German rock-bands.

The role of gender in ethnic closure is evident in immigration rules, which are still often based on the assumption that men are the principal immigrants, while women and children are mere dependants. In the 1970s, women from the Indian subcontinent coming to join their husbands or fiancés in Britain were subjected to 'virginity tests' at Heathrow Airport (Lutz *et al.*, 1995, p. 12). The authorities also sought to prevent Afro-Caribbean and Asian women bringing in husbands from overseas, on the grounds that women entered as dependants in the first place, and that the 'natural place of residence' of the family is the abode of the husband (Klug, 1989, pp. 27–9). In many countries, legal factors increase women's vulnerability: women who separate from their partners as a result of violence or incompatibility may lose their residence status and be forced to leave the country (Essed, 1991).

In the labour market, gender is still the main factor of differentiation: women have a lower average occupational status and income than men. In an analysis of the Australian labour market, Collins (1991, pp. 80–6) concluded that migrant women formed a distinct segment, concentrated in the least desirable occupations, such as repetitive factory work and lower-skilled positions in the personal and community services sectors. Professional employment is often linked to traditional caring roles: for example the main professional occupation for Afro-Caribbean women in Britain is nursing (Lutz *et al.*, 1995, p. 12). Minority women have experienced casualization of employment and increasing unemployment (which does not usually appear in the statistics because of their status as 'dependants').

Phizacklea (1990, pp. 72–93) examined the sexual and racial division of labour in the fashion industry in Britain and other European countries. She found that the industry had been able to survive, despite the new global division of labour, through the development of 'subcontracting webs': large retail companies were able to put pressure for lower prices on small firms controlled by male ethnic entrepreneurs, whose market position was constrained by racial discrimination. They were in turn able to use patriarchal power relations and the vulnerable legal position of women immigrants to enforce extremely low wages and poor working conditions in sweatshops and outwork. Collins *et al.* (1995) have presented a similar picture of the links between racialization and gender in ethnic small business in Australia. The self-exploitation of women was vital to many businesses, yet was accepted as being preferable to the even more exploitative experience of minority women in the mainstream labour market.

Economists attribute this situation to a lack of human capital, but minority women's frequent lack of education and vocational training is in itself a reflection of patriarchal attitudes in both sending and receiving societies. The emphasis on the domestic role of women may persist in the new country, especially where discrimination leads to group closure and a reassertion of traditional values. Yet most migrant women are forced by economic circumstances to seek paid employment, leading to the dual burden of household and low-skilled work (Alcorso, 1993). Highly skilled migrant women often find that they cannot get their qualifications recognized. In many cases, skilled migrant women toil at menial jobs, while their husbands undertake further education. Ethnic minority women often belong to the 'working poor', with incomes and welfare entitlements so limited that they do not have the means for effective societal participation.

The concentration of ethnic minorities in disadvantaged areas with poor child-care facilities and other social amenities affects women more than men. So does violence on the streets, which may confine women to their homes. Just as women become signifiers of the nation,

ethnic minority women may become signifiers of the ethnic community. A return to traditional values in response to racism, as in the re-
Islamization of some immigrant groups in Europe, generally means
constrained social roles for women. This may be symbolized by
wearing religious dress, which in turn becomes a symbol to be attacked
by progressive secularists and nationalists alike. Protecting minority
women from the real threat of extreme-right violence legitimizes the
male control of women's mobility and behaviour.

Minority women share with minority men the disadvantages brought
about by partial exclusion from the civil, political and social rights that
make up citizenship. However, the women suffer other types of exclusion and disadvantage that are not simply add-ons to those suffered by
men (Vasta, 1993). Minority women's exclusion from citizenship is
brought about through discourses and practices in which gender, racialization and class are interlocked (see Collins, P. H., 1991, pp. 234–5).
This has important political consequences. Minority women cannot
become full citizens simply by achieving formal equality, because this
will not in itself overcome the sexism and racism that are deeply rooted
in western societies. Rather minority women need specific sets of
rights, which recognize the historical forms in which their oppression
and exclusion have been constructed.

Cultural rights

Culture is another area excluded from mainstream theories of citizenship. In liberal theory, the political sphere is one of universalism, while
cultural specificity is to be restricted to the private sphere. This requires
a separation between a person's political rights and obligations, and his
or her membership of groups based on ethnicity, religion, social class
or regional location. But this conflicts with the reality of nation-state
formation, in which becoming a citizen has depended on membership
of the dominant cultural community. Members of other cultural groups
(whether internal minorities or immigrants) have had to adopt the
majority culture in order to enjoy full citizenship. In many cases, pressure to assimilate has been experienced by minorities as oppression.

Since the 1960s, minority movements have demanded the right to
recognition as distinct cultural collectivities within the nation-state. In
the USA, the African-American and Native American movements
concentrated on cultural rights and their relationship to political and
economic power. An 'ethnic revival' of longstanding European immi-

grant groups asserted the importance of their homeland cultures for identity and self-esteem. Since then, culture has become a rallying cry in many places. Within Europe, old territorial minorities such as the Basques, Catalans, Corsicans and Scots have demanded cultural rights and some degree of regional autonomy. Indigenous peoples in Australia, Canada and New Zealand have asserted that cultural rights are vital for their survival as distinct groups in modern society.

The maintenance of language and culture is seen as a need and a right by most minority groups. Many immigrants' associations are concerned with language and culture: they teach the mother tongue to the second generation, organize festivals and carry out rituals. Language and culture not only serve as means of communication, but also take on a symbolic meaning that is central to ethnic group cohesion. In most cases, language maintenance applies in the first two to three generations, after which there is a rapid decline. The significance of cultural symbols and rituals may last much longer.

However, many members of the dominant group see cultural difference as a threat to national identity. Migrant languages and cultures become symbols of Otherness and markers for discrimination; giving them up is seen as essential for integration and success. A failure to do so is regarded as indicative of a desire for separatism. Hostility to different languages and cultures is rationalized with the assertion that the official language is essential for economic success, and that migrant cultures are inadequate for a modern secular society. The alternative view is that cultural maintenance helps to create a secure basis that assists group integration into the wider society, while bilingualism brings benefits in terms of learning and intellectual development.

Policies and attitudes on cultural and linguistic maintenance vary considerably. Canada's policy of bilingualism is based on two 'official languages': English and French. Multicultural policies have led to the recognition of immigrant languages and government support for their maintenance. Switzerland has a multilingual policy for its founding languages but does not recognize immigrant languages. Australia and Sweden both accept the principle of linguistic and cultural maintenance, providing a wide range of language services (interpreting, translating and mother-tongue classes) and support for ethnic community cultural organizations. Both countries have multicultural education policies. However, since the mid-1990s, multicultural programmes have been eroded in most of these countries, and there seems to be a shift away from policies of cultural recognition.

In the USA, monolingualism is being eroded by the growth of Hispanic communities: in cities like Los Angeles and Miami, the number of Spanish speakers is overtaking that of English speakers. This led to a backlash in the 1980s, in the form of 'the US English movement', which called for a constitutional amendment to declare English the official language. Several states passed referenda to introduce this measure, but it proved hard to implement, and public agencies and private companies continued to provide multilingual services. Monolingualism is also the basic principle in France, Britain, Germany and the Netherlands. Nonetheless, these countries have been forced to introduce language services in order to take account of migrant needs in communicating with courts, bureaucracies and health services. The multilingual character of inner-city school classes has also led to special measures for the integration of immigrant children. Here one can speak of '*de facto* multiculturalism', despite the general rejection of pluralism in some of these countries.

Culture has a complex role in relations between ethnic groups. Cultural difference has traditionally been seen as a threat to the integrity of nation-states, especially when minorities are concentrated in specific areas or enclaves. Today, new forms of orientalism are constructing Islam in particular and non-European cultures in general as threats to secularity and modernity. In contrast, advocates of pluralism argue that language and culture play a key role in the formation of individual and collective identity. Traditional principles of assimilation into dominant cultures are unviable because lifestyles in modern cities have become increasingly transcultural, especially for young people (Ålund, 1991). Accepting difference and developing intercultural communication are vital in contemporary multi-ethnic societies.

Increasing ethnocultural diversity, together with globalization, therefore makes cultural rights an essential part of citizenship. Such rights include:

● full access to the majority language and culture;
● the right to the maintenance of minority languages and cultures;
● the right to different customs and lifestyles (within a general framework of law which is not culturally biased);
● educational equality;
● the right to intercultural and international communication.

Conclusion

Globalization, the increased mobility of people and the burgeoning of new forms of communication make myths of homogeneity unsustainable. Cultural diversity has become a central aspect of virtually all modern societies. Assimilation is no longer an option because of the rapidity and multidirectionality of mobility and communication. More and more people have dual or multiple citizenship. Other people lack formal citizenship in their country of residence, yet have many of the rights of citizenship on the basis of long-term residents' rights and international law. Still others are formal citizens, yet lack important rights that are supposed to accompany this status. Many people are excluded from full participation through unemployment, poverty, sexism or racism. Answers to the question 'Who is a citizen?' are becoming increasingly difficult.

It remains vital to insist on the need for easy access to formal citizenship for minorities. This principle is still far from being achieved, especially in countries where immigrants cannot readily become citizens. Formal membership generally confers civil and political rights, yet it may be hard for socially marginalized groups to make use of these in practice. Access to formal citizenship is thus merely a first step on the way to full membership. Social exclusion threatens many people in increasingly polarized societies with declining welfare states. However, the probability of individual or collective exclusion is higher for members of ethnic minorities, and highest of all for minority women.

The social exclusion of minorities weakens the social bond and questions the strength of citizenship as an integrating force in contemporary society. The exclusion of ethnic minorities from citizenship is brought about through discourses and practices in which gender, race, class and culture are interlocked. This has important consequences. Excluded groups cannot become full citizens simply by achieving formal equality, because this will not in itself overcome discriminatory discourses and practices that are deeply rooted in western societies. Rather minority groups need specific sets of rights and forms of representation, which recognize the historical forms in which their oppression and exclusion have been constructed (see Young, 1989).

However, this leads to difficult new questions about how to define group membership, and how to devise mechanisms for group representation that combine differentiated rights with full participation in mainstream institutions and relationships. Top-down social policies clearly cannot achieve full rights for minorities. Indeed, special welfare regimes may be an important element in the stigmatization and separation of minorities. The issue is instead one of establishing conditions under which democratic social and political movements of minorities can develop. This means working to establish political frameworks and information resources that will stimulate democratic participation at all the sites of societal decision making. In a process of redemocratization of post-national societies, it may become evident that the interests of minorities are not very different from those of the rest of the population. Or, to put it differently, most people now belong to groups treated as minorities by globalizing capital. Struggles for minority rights are, in the final analysis, struggles for democracy and equality.

Note

1. Parts of an earlier version of this chapter are published as Castles (1999).

6

Ethnic Mobilization and New Political Subjects

Social and political mobilization on the basis of ethnic belonging can mean the formation of separate organizational or institutional structures by minorities – that is, community formation. It can also mean action within mainstream structures by groups based on common ethnic identification. Ethnic mobilization is often a reaction to the social, cultural and political exclusion experienced by immigrants, indigenous peoples and other minorities. Mobilization may exacerbate such divisions by reinforcing fears of separatism and fundamentalism, leading to a backlash by elements of the majority population. Alternatively, ethnic mobilization may help to create the conditions for the societal participation of minorities, while at the same time precipitating significant changes in political structures and practices in the process. Thus, ethnic mobilization may be an important factor in the incorporation of minorities as citizens, while at the same time changing what it means to be a citizen.

Although ethnic mobilization and community formation are the result of actions that may not be based on political intentions, they may well have profound political consequences. Ethnic or minority *communities* have the following features:

- They are mainly concentrated in specific locations, although usually without clear or absolute boundaries.
- Such communities in western countries rarely have exclusive occupancy of their neighbourhoods: they generally share them with other groups (both of the majority population and other minorities) who have similar social characteristics. The major exceptions are certain highly segregated African–American neighbourhoods of the USA, which are the result of longstanding and extreme forms of racialization.

129

- Minority communities are based at least in part on common origins and cultural identity, and may sometimes transcend locality in the sense that members of a certain ethnic group may feel a sense of community with co-ethnics in other locations.
- Localized ethnic communities tend to be transitory phenomena arising in the initial period of settlement and lasting only a few generations. A feeling of common ethnic belonging may last longer than the localized community, but without any territorial basis.

Community formation involves a number of interlinked processes. These start on an individual or family level with what may be termed 'home-building', which may be extended into the more collective activity of 'place-making'. Other (more or less simultaneous) processes include the development of ethnic economic infrastructures, the setting up of religious institutions and various types of association, and the emergence of group-specific forms of political mobilization. All these processes take place in a context of processes of inclusion into or exclusion from the wider social relations of the society concerned. The generational shift within the ethnic groups is also a crucial factor. This is not just a demographic shift, but also a cultural one, as descendants of immigrants have different experiences of education, labour market entry and inter-group relations from their parents.

Home-building and place-making

The notion of *home* plays an important role for most people: home is where one feels a sense of belonging and security, and where one can decide on acceptable values and forms of behaviour – Fehér and Heller (1994, pp. 143–7) have proposed the concept of 'house rules' for this. Home also implies closure: only those who belong can come in, and a home-owner can shut the door on outsiders. However, home does not just refer to a house, but by analogy to a wider social space – even a country. The notion of home is part of the discourse of the nation-state, having emotive connotations of solidarity with those inside and the exclusion of those outside. Migration means leaving home and taking up residence in someone else's home. This implies a clash between the 'house rules' of the new place and the practices that immigrants bring with them. The newcomers seek to construct a place that they can again call home, and follow their own preferences. This involves negotiations with neighbours.

Hage (1997, p. 102) defines *home-building* as 'the building of a feeling of being at home' using 'affective building blocks' based on four key feelings: 'security, familiarity, community and a sense of possibility'. The last of these four is particularly important as it implies that a home is not something closed off from society, but rather a place offering shelter that allows its residents to move out in search of such opportunities as work, education, social mobility and emotional growth. In his study of Lebanese immigrants in the west of Sydney, Hage argues that introduction of material goods (especially food) and cultural symbols from the homeland is not a nostalgic attempt to symbolically return home. Rather the function is to create a new sense of home as a base from which to perceive and grasp the Australian opportunities (Hage, 1997, p. 108).

The use of homeland languages in the household, the import or production of 'ethnic food', the desire to own one's own house, to decorate the home in traditional ways and to follow homeland patterns of familial roles all seem almost universal among immigrants. In principle, such practices within the private sphere should not be the concern of the majority population or the state. However, things are not always so simple. For example, the use of homeland languages at home was condemned by the Australian authorities in the 1960s because it was seen as hindering the educational assimilation of children. Homeland eating practices may cause conflict if they involve unfamiliar smells (for example, curry odours) or practices seen as abhorrent (for example, *halal* methods of slaughter – particularly within the household). The eating of ethnic food may have to take place away from the 'dominant gaze', while the children of immigrants may feel highly embarrassed when their lunch-boxes contain the 'wrong' ingredients (salami and egg-plant rather than Vegemite and cheese in Australia). On the other hand, ethnic food has proved one of the main points of contact between neighbours in multicultural societies, and has become a significant factor in cultural change.

Place-making can be seen as a spatial extension of home-building through which ethnic groups partially reshape their neighbourhoods to correspond more closely to their needs and values. It is a collective process that only becomes possible as a result of ethnic clustering. Place-making is (unlike home-building) a highly visible process, through signs on shops and restaurants, ethnic markets and a different use of public space (for example, Turkish families picnicking in Berlin parks). This may shock the majority group and confirm their views that the aliens are taking over. Racist campaigns against minorities almost invariably use the ethnic neighbourhood (labelled an 'enclave' or 'ghetto') as a key aspect of propaganda. The idea that foreigners control part of the national space evokes emotive reactions because it goes to the heart of the myth of nation.

Place-making is linked to the partial control of local markets, above all the housing, labour and retail markets, by minorities. When members of minorities own houses and shops, and set up businesses mainly employing co-ethnics, they are in a position to reshape urban space. Place-making has therefore been more rapid in countries where such markets are free and accessible (like the USA) than in countries where access is restricted. In Germany, working-class access to home ownership is restricted through the typical form of urban housing (apartment blocks rather than individual houses) and the credit system. Access to business ownership was for many years highly restricted for non-European Community immigrants. These barriers became more porous in the 1980s, leading to results similar to those in the USA and elsewhere.

Pascoe (1992) describes the place-making process with regard to Italian migrants, showing how Italian regionalism is reflected in patterns of settlement in the USA, Britain and Australia. He argues that place-making consists of three sets of strategies concerned with 'naming, rituals and institutions'. Naming refers to the practice of giving homeland names to places in the new country. It also applies to business signs in homeland languages – as, for example, in Chinatowns all over the world. Rituals refer to public events that affirm the belonging and the cohesion of the group, such as the 'blessing of the fleet' that regularly takes place wherever Italians own fishing boats. Institutions include welfare associations, clubs, churches and so on that both demonstrate the presence of a community and provide the services it needs.

Home-building and place-making are important parts of community formation. If the home is a place to go out from into the wider society, it is also a place to return to for protection from discrimination or violence. The black communities of Britain served as the bases for anti-racist movements in the 1970s and 80s, even if the rage of such movements often led to considerable destruction within the community. Minority communities were the springboard not only for individual mobility, but also for movements for emancipation and equality. Thus, as Keith and Pile (1993, p. 5) argue, minority neighbourhoods can be seen as locations of struggle, communities of resistance and political spaces.

Ethnic economies

Minority enterprises have become a major economic factor in North America, Western Europe and Australia (Light and Bonacich, 1988; Waldinger *et al.*, 1990). In former 'guestworker' recruiting countries, the shift to small business came as a surprise: foreign workers were meant to provide low-skilled labour for German employers, rather than to compete with them. Even in permanent settlement countries, the extent of the shift was unexpected. Although minority entrepreneurs are to be found in all sectors, they tend to be concentrated in certain locations and certain economic branches, which come to be seen as 'ethnic niches'. These are typically sectors that require relatively little entry capital and a limited level of training for managers and workers. However, such sectors (which include taxi-driving, retail stores, catering firms and clothing manufacture) are also marked by high competition and uncertain returns.

Many immigrants see setting up a business as the only way out of jobs in the mainstream economy that offer poor pay, unpleasant conditions and few opportunities for advancement. Owning a shop or other small business in the ethnic neighbourhood offers a dream of autonomy and prestige – which may be quite illusory, since the reality of such enterprises is often long hours of drudgery and a high degree of insecurity (Collins *et al.*, 1995). On the other hand, many ethnic enterprises do survive, and a certain number make the vital transition from the ethnic niche to servicing a mainstream clientele.

Ethnic businesses tend to be set up in areas of minority concentration, because these provide ready markets for homeland foods, publications and other products. Ethnic professionals – such as medical practitioners, travel agents, lawyers and estate agents – may provide ethno-specific services, or they may attract co-ethnics through the use of minority languages and sensitivity to cultural needs. In turn, the presence of such businesses attracts further members of the minority group to settle in the area or to visit it. In the extreme case, an enclave economy may develop, in which the production and consumption of a large proportion of goods and services all take place within one group – the Cuban enclave in Miami is a well-known example. In other cases, certain ethnic groups may come to dominate business in a neighbourhood, even though the population remains ethnically mixed. Examples of this are the large Chinatown that has developed in the Thirteenth Arrondissement of Paris, or the Vietnamese and Chinese business area of Cabramatta in Sydney.

Ethnic entrepreneurs and professionals are the core of an ethnic middle class, which often takes on leadership roles in minority associations. They have the resources and skills needed to organize projects such as the building of places of worship, ethnic schools or clubs. Ethnic middle classes use the symbols of homeland culture as a focus for mobilization, because in this way they can gain support from the more numerous minority members who have a working-class position. Ethnic middle classes tend to be socially and culturally conservative, as their influence rests mainly on their claim to traditional authority, which allows them to present themselves as 'natural leaders'. They are often concerned to ward off the influences of mainstream secular cultures, which they see as having harmful effects on women and youth.

Ethnic middle classes may be agents of both ethnic mobilization and of social control. In situations of repression from the outside, these leaders may be effective in organizing group resistance. Where multicultural policies exist, state agencies may seek to coopt such 'natural leaders' by offering them recognition and rewards. However, this puts the ethnic middle class in an ambivalent position, which may lead to a loss of support within their communities. As contradictions of class and gender develop, their situation is likely to be contested by alternative leaderships, especially from the second generation.

Religion, nationalism and identity

One of the first collective actions of a new immigrant group is often to set up a place of worship. A modest prayer-room or meeting place in borrowed premises may in time grow into a mosque, temple or church, built through much hard work and sacrifice, and representing the centre of a community. In turn, religious buildings may become symbols of Otherness for the majority population. In Western Europe, the emergence of Islam has been the most visible sign of cultural change. By the mid-1990s, there were perhaps 8–10 million Muslims in Europe, of whom some 3 million were in France, 2 million in Germany and 1 million in the UK. The rise of Islam – now the second religion of France and the third of Germany – has been the trigger for fears of separatism, conflict and loss of national identity. Such fears are rooted in historical conflicts between Christian and Muslim civilizations, as well as being a reaction to the self-assertiveness of the new 'domestic Islam' (Husbands, 1995).

The spectre of fundamentalism has become a mechanism of closure, but is it true that immigrants generally have traditionalist outlooks? For many, the motivation for migration to western countries was an expectation of participation in a modern society. Differences between immigrants and local people in language and traditions may seem less significant than the common acceptance of a culture of modernity. However, individual integration has generally proved attainable only for a minority of highly-skilled immigrants. The exclusion and racism experienced by the majority of immigrants often provoke a response in which religion and other traditional cultural forms become the resources for survival and resistance.

Religion should not be seen in isolation, but as a core aspect of culture around which other expressive forms – linguistic maintenance, the formation of associations and folkloric practices – may be focused. The consolidation of religion is based on three factors: first, the value of religion as a resource for settlement and community formation; second, the use of religion by the authorities of both sending and receiving countries as a mechanism of social control; and third, the role of religion in rebuilding identity and developing resistance in situations of exclusion and racism.

The first factor is to be found almost everywhere. The Catholic Church has played a major role in providing help and orientation for Poles, Southern Europeans and Latin Americans wherever they have gone in the world. As a transnational body, the Catholic Church was able to provide 'a familiar place' and 'institutions where assistance could be sought during the settlement process'. Immigrants needed services in their own languages, and called for priests from their homelands. These played a vital role in community formation and helped to bring about cultural change in the Church of the immigration country. In Australia, for example, the Capuchin and Scalabrini orders had a strong impact on a church hitherto dominated by an Irish hierarchy that found it hard to respond to the religious and social needs of Italian migrants (Alcorso *et al.*, 1992, pp. 107–12).

The presence of varying Christian faiths among immigrants in western countries is usually not seen as a problem (although the immigration of Catholics has been perceived as a threat to historical political balances in such countries as Belgium and Germany). Even Islam was not seen as a problem until recently. In fact, governments of both sending and receiving countries encouraged religious practices, and facilitated the provision of priests or imams for migrant communities. This occurred because religion was seen as a useful way of disciplining 'unruly young men' in the early stages of migrations. It was also a way of providing social assistance in a cheap and culturally appropriate way. In the later stages of settlement, priests, imams or heads of religious associations were often seen as 'natural community leaders' by authorities in search of partners for social measures. The conservatism of many religious leaders was seen as being useful in combating the influence of left-wing parties and trade unions.

In the guestworker-recruiting period, the German government delegated social assistance functions to non-governmental organizations: *Caritas* for immigrants from Catholic areas, the Protestant *Diakonische Werk* for Greeks, and the social democratic welfare agency *Arbeiterwohlfahrt* for Turks and other Muslims. Religious instruction in German schools is provided separately for the two dominant Catholic and Evangelical churches. In accordance with this model – and to combat the influence of private Koran schools – the educational authorities recruited religious teachers from Turkey, often with the help of the Turkish authorities (Kastoryano, 1996, pp. 139–40). Support for Islam was consistent with the German myth of temporary stay: maintaining homeland culture and religion would make it easier for migrants to reintegrate into their countries of origin. In France, the government and employers encouraged the creation of mosques and prayer-rooms in workplaces in the 1960s and 70s as a way of combating left-wing trade unions (Kepel and Leveau, 1987).

Sending-country governments played a complementary role. Consulates of Southern European countries worked closely with Catholic or Orthodox clergy and encouraged the establishment of religious associations. The Turkish government cooperated with German authorities in recruiting imams for German schools – even though such instruction is banned in Turkish schools. Mosques and Islamic associations in Western Europe have also received substantial funding from the governments of Saudi Arabia, Libya and other oil-rich states. Such countries clearly follow their own political objectives in seeking to influence Muslims in Western Europe. This is increasingly perceived as problematic by the public and authorities, but it is important to remember that considerable initial impetus was given to Islam by the receiving country governments for their own ends: they helped to create the Islamic communities that they now fear.

The third aspect of religion – its role in rebuilding identity and developing resistance – is the most significant for politics. Religion is the 'hard kernel' of identity (Kastoryano, 1996, p. 104), through which migrants can compensate for the loss of social orientation caused by displacement to another society. Where settlement is experienced in terms of economic marginalization, social isolation and racism, religious solidarity becomes a key form of resistance. Islam has played a major role in consolidating North African communities in France and Turkish communities in Germany. Where Islam had been just one part of a mainly secular culture before migration, it now became 'culture in its totality' in the diaspora situation. Islam provided a source of self-esteem and a hope of protecting children from a culture of moral laxity, violence and drug-taking, as experienced in the run-down areas where immigrants had to live. Islam became a source of ethnic pride and community solidarity. It also gave a sense of belonging in a transnational 'imagined community' based on religion, which compensated for isolation in the society of residence (Kastoryano, 1996, pp. 106–11).

The 're-Islamization' of migrant communities should therefore be seen not just as a religious phenomenon, but also as a specific way of inventing group culture and of constructing ethnicity in a situation of disempowerment. In a comparison of France and Germany, Kastoryano (1996) shows the complexity of the interplay between religion and other aspects of group identity. The French Republican model of individual assimilation and the rejection of collective difference has found it hard to come to terms with the emergence of North African communities. Hence the strong reaction against the use of religious symbols in the *foulard* affair in 1989 and again in 1995, when school authorities banned young girls from school for wearing Islamic headscarves. Yet the consolidation of these communities since the 1970s is in part a result of government policies designed to find leaders or associations to act as mediators between the state and the minorities. Government support encouraged the growth of secular community organizations. Such secular organizations are weaker than Islamic ones, yet both help to construct the community: the secular associations organize social measures, while the religious ones take responsibility for identity (Kastoryano, 1996, pp. 124–5).

In Germany, in contrast, the very fact that immigrants were not meant to become part of German society made authorities more relaxed about accepting them as organized collectives. German school authorities were not concerned about Turkish girls wearing headscarves, because their non-assimilation was seen as a welcome sign that they were not part of German society. However, as it became clear that the Turks were going to become a permanent non-citizen population, religion was seen as a way of achieving greater social cohesion among

Turks to facilitate communication with the state. However, Kastoryano (1996, pp. 141–56) argues that this was impossible because of the high degree of fragmentation of the Turkish population on religious lines (the division between the Sunnis and Alevites), ethnic lines (the division between the Turks and Kurds) and political lines (right–left polarization). The result is that there are hundreds of competing Turkish associations of different complexions. Thus, Turks in Germany are not held together as a community by common values and goals. Instead, the feeling of ethnicity is based on common origins and the experience of being a minority defined through exclusion, disadvantage and racism.

This points again to the multidimensional character of the linkages between racialization, ethnic identity and mobilization. Religion is one important form of expression for ethnic identity; in some cases, it may take a secondary role compared with other symbols of ethnic belonging. For certain groups – such as Croats, Serbs, Greeks and Armenians – nationalism is the key rallying factor. Nationalism involves a symbolic repertoire including language, shared history, folklore, sense of place and ways of life. Religion does play a part in such cases, but its role is simply as a part of national culture.

Ethnic consciousness

What has been said so far indicates processes of community formation and ethnic consolidation, which are – in part at least – responses to experiences of exclusion and racialization in western societies. Different forms of ethnic consciousness are emerging. However, each case is complicated and often contradictory in its own right. Moreover, the measurement of ethnic consciousness presents great problems. The key question is whether such patterns of community formation are likely to be permanent, or whether they are transitory stages in a long-term process of intergenerational change. In other words, are the processes leading to the separation of ethnic minorities from the mainstream population likely to be so strong and enduring that they become structurally separate groups? (see Zhou, 1997).

In principle, four variants of ethnic consciousness are conceivable:

- *assimilation*, in which minorities are absorbed into the dominant culture and identity;
- *separatist consciousness*, in which minorities feel that they are permanently excluded from mainstream culture and identity;

- *diasporic consciousness*, in which immigrant minorities identify mainly with their ancestral homeland and with people of the same ethnic origin, both in the homeland and in other countries (see Cohen, 1997);
- *transcultural consciousness*, in which minorities interact with specific groups in the population of the receiving country, and together develop new forms of culture and identity (see Basch *et al.*, 1994).

The notion of transcultural experience focuses above all on the descendants of immigrants (the 'second generation') growing up in the cities of highly developed countries. Their experience at school, in peer groups and in the neighbourhoods is rarely monocultural. Nor is it one of assimilation into the dominant ethnic group, as most members of minorities grow up in ethnically mixed areas. Young people may spend much of their leisure time with peers of the same ethnic background, but it is also common for them to hang out in mixed groups. This leads to the development of new forms of communication and expression, in which a youth culture influenced by both local and global sources interacts with a wide range of class and ethnic elements. The result is new slangs, musical styles, ways of dressing and behaving – in short, new lifestyles. The development of syncretic cultures (Gilroy, 1987) and new identities has become a major theme of research in sociology and cultural studies, generating a large literature that cannot be explored here.

The point is that modes of exclusion in western societies are rarely absolute or rigid. In statistical terms, there are distinctions between ethnic groups according to a range of economic and social indicators, but (with rare exceptions) there are no rigid boundaries that cannot be crossed. As Burnley (1994, p. 87) has shown for Australia, the dominant ethnic group is often 'the ethnic mix'. Exclusion or discrimination is no less real because of this, but it does mean that there is a diversity of experiences and reactions among minority members. In older studies based on assimilation theory, the second generation were typically seen as 'marginal' people who were socially handicapped by 'being between two cultures'. Today, from a more multicultural perspective, young people of immigrant origin are seen as having dual (or multiple) linguistic and cultural competencies. They have learnt to negotiate different cultures, to switch between varying codes and to utilize elements of the differing lifestyles. For some, such choices can be a source of stress and conflict (for example, with more traditional parents), but for others – and for society in general – they can be a source of enrichment (Ålund, 1991).

In the light of such complex experiences, formal adherence to religious symbols has to be seen in a different light. Alarmists have equated Islam with fundamentalism, yet the 8–10 million Muslims in Europe are not necessarily practising Muslims, just as the majority of people classified as Christians rarely enter a church. In a large-scale survey of immigrants in France, Tribalat (1995, pp. 91–109) found that half the Algerian-born respondents stated either that they were not religious or that they did not practise their religion. The level of religious observance was higher among Muslims from Turkey and black Africa. Women tended to be somewhat more religious than men. However, religious observance among children of immigrants born in France was much lower: 68 per cent of young men and 58 per cent of young women of Algerian origin stated either that they were not religious or that they did not practise their religion. As Tribalat argues, this goes against prevailing ideas of religious homogeneity and the re-Islamization of youth.

Tribalat, however, found a much higher degree of observance of religious rules on eating practices: the great majority of immigrants from Muslim countries claimed to observe the Ramadan month of fasting and to conform to prohibitions on the consumption of alcohol and pork. This applied also to descendants of immigrants born in France. This leads to the hypothesis that religion is mainly significant as a set of cultural practices, rather than in the sense of a strict observance of beliefs. Religious observance and respect for food rules were highest in areas of immigrant concentration, indicating the significance of religion in situations of exclusion. Tribalat also found that a large number of immigrants planned to have their bodies returned to their native soil for burial. This applies even to Southern Europeans: 10 per cent of Spaniards and a third of Portuguese plan to re-migrate after death. For Muslims, the figure is about half, except for Turks, of whom two-thirds wish to re-migrate posthumously (Tribalat, 1995, pp. 109–11).

Such data indicate that there is no simple either/or situation with regard to cultural practices and identity. A discussion of other social and cultural issues would indicate a similar complexity. Studies in countries as different as Australia and France show a dramatic growth in ethnic intermarriage in the second generation. However, patterns vary considerably between differing groups and are influenced by class: higher socioeconomic status is linked to a greater propensity to marry someone of a different ethnic background (Tribalat, 1995, Chapter 4; Castles *et al.*, 1998, Chapter 2).

It appears that all the variants of ethnic consciousness may co-exist in any one country at the same time. Which variant predominates depends mainly on the extent to which ethnic divisions are linked to other forms of social differentiation. Where ethnicity and class are strongly correlated – that is, where most members of certain ethnic groups are locked into an inferior class position over long periods – separatism or diasporic identity are most likely to emerge. In countries without significant barriers to socioeconomic integration and mobility, assimilation may take place. However, in general this only happens for immigrant groups that are either culturally close to the ethnic majority or that have a high level of human capital (or both). Finally, transcultural identities are most likely to develop where there are uneven patterns of exclusion/inclusion, and with differential patterns of discrimination against various groups. This latter situation is, we would argue, the most common case in contemporary western countries.

Ethnic politics

Ethnicity has become one of the key factors in contemporary politics. This goes against the expectations of nearly all the major modern schools of thought from political liberalism to functionalist sociology, and from Marxism to social democracy. All these theories were based on ideas of growing rationality and secularism in politics (Glazer and Moynihan, 1975), but in recent times it has become evident that issues of identity and culture are taking on new political meaning. As Esman argues:

> Indeed, since the end of the Cold War, ethnic conflict has emerged as the principal source of destabilisation and organised violence around the world, producing massacres, destruction of whole communities, and pathetic streams of refugees. (Esman, 1994, p. 2)

International migration and ethnic difference are now seen as major security issues. According to Teitelbaum and Weiner (1995, p. 11), 'International migration has risen rapidly to the top of the agenda for both foreign and domestic US policy.' A whole genre of literature on the perceived threats to the international order from ethnic conflict is emerging (see, for example, Huntington, 1993; Moynihan, 1993). Moreover, there has been a spate of intergovernmental conferences and agreements on controlling migration and refugee movements (Castles and Miller, 1998, Chapter 4). On the domestic level too, immigration and ethnicity have become major political factors: 'Indeed, in ways that were wholly unexpected a few years ago, every aspect of political life has been touched by the issue of immigration' (Baldwin-Edwards and Schain, 1994, p. 1). This can lead to major shifts in mainstream politics, with the emergence of extreme-right parties and neo-Nazi movements.[1]

The different forms of ethnic consciousness play a major part in shaping patterns of minority political participation and mobilization. To fully understand the links between ethnicity and politics, it would be necessary to study a large number of specific examples. This task cannot be attempted here; all we can do is discuss some types of political mobilization that have emerged.[2] It is important to note that there is no rigid distinction between the types outlined below. Although they correspond to some extent with stages in the process of the societal incorporation of minorities, they may also exist side by side, even within the same ethnic community.

Homeland politics

In the early stages of immigration, the expectation of return combined with a lack of political rights makes homeland politics seem more relevant than the affairs of the immigration country. The authorities of immigrant workers' countries of origin frequently attempt to maintain political loyalty by setting up cultural, social and political associations. One of the best known is the *Amicale des Algeriens en Europe* (AAE), the overseas branch of the ruling Algerian National Liberation Front. The AAE virtually monopolized the representation of Algerian workers in France and other European countries in the 1960s and 70s (Castles and Miller, 1998, Chapter 10). Such officially sponsored bodies are instruments of social control, but also serve to articulate migrants' interests towards both homeland and immigration country governments.

On the other hand, migrants' resentment at having to leave their country for economic or political reasons may give rise to political associations and parties that work for change in the homeland. In the 1960s and 70s, virtually every Southern European political party had its subsidiaries among compatriots in Western European countries. In some cases, such organizations cooperated with political parties in the immigration country, the German Social Democratic Party, for example, supporting foreign-worker groups fighting the dictatorships in Greece, Spain and Portugal. There was, however, also a fear that the immigrants would infect local workers with their militancy. Security authorities saw immigrants as potential subversives; special police services (such as the German *Ausländerpolizei*) were set up for the surveillance and control of immigrants. Immigrant political groups were sometimes seen as a foreign policy threat when they agitated against foreign allies. For example, Iranian groups opposed to the Shah experienced considerable repression in Germany in the 1960s.

With a longer duration of residence, immigrants' concerns generally shift to obtaining social and political equality in the country of residence, yet homeland politics can resurface among people who have become citizens of the immigration country, or even those who were born there. Support for the various warring groups in the former Yugoslavia by well-established settlers in Australia is an example. If such issues lead to conflict and even violence, immigrants may be seen as a domestic political problem, as well as an unwelcome influence on foreign policy. Such an interest in homeland politics can persist over generations, and there are cases of nations being created by the political activities of diasporas (Cohen, 1997).

Immigrants in the labour movement

Up to the 1970s, the great majority of labour migrants became manual workers in manufacturing and construction. Even today, immigrant workers remain concentrated in manual occupations. In some cases, unions were unwilling to represent immigrant workers, especially in the early phases of immigration. This led to attempts to create alternative immigrant unions. However, such efforts have rarely been successful – by reinforcing existing divisions, separate unions weakened worker representation. In any case, most trade unions, in time, realized the vital importance of organizing immigrants. This sometimes led to special foreign language sections, or the use of bilingual organizers and shop-stewards. The huge German *Industriegewerkschaft Metall* (Metal Workers Union), for example, has special officials, newspapers and language services for its many immigrant members.

Where immigrants mainly occupy manual positions while local workers have skilled or supervisory positions, interest conflicts may emerge. Prior to the strike movements of the 1970s and 80s in the French car industry, foreign workers had become heavily concentrated in production line jobs. There were 'ethnic workgangs' with common origins and religion. These were often the result of employer practices:

workers were split up by language to facilitate supervision, as well as bring about national divisions. Some employers encouraged the construction of Islamic prayer-rooms in the workplace, in the hope of weakening trade union influence. The result, however, was a growth of solidarity based on ethnicity, and isolation from French workers. The militant strikes at Renault, Citroën and Talbot led to considerable violence between immigrant and French workers, who were members of different unions. The strikes also affected French public opinion on immigration, and helped to create the climate for the rise of the *Front National* (Castles and Miller, 1998, Chapter 7). Similar disputes have taken place in several countries, with varying outcomes (Castles and Kosack, 1973; Lever-Tracy and Quinlan, 1988).

Immigrants bring with them different experiences and traditions that may present considerable challenges to labour organizations. On the one hand, workers of rural origin may not be familiar with labour organization, or may be ideologically opposed to them. On the other hand, immigrants – especially from countries with traditions of struggle against colonialism and dictatorship – may be much more radical in their demands and methods. Labour organizations try with varying success to impose their way of doing things on the newcomers, but they themselves often have to change in the process, especially if immigrants get into leadership positions.

Racist movements

Movements opposed to immigration and to minority rights have developed just about everywhere. Although not ethnic minority movements, these should also be seen as an element in the political change brought about by growing cultural diversity. Anti-minority movements vary considerably in character. They include groups pressing for restrictive policies within mainstream political parties (such as the British Conservative Party since the 1960s); specifically anti-minority parties such as the French *Front National*, the German *Republikaner* and *Deutsche Volksunion* or Pauline Hanson's One Nation Party in Australia; and violent extremist groups such as the Ku Klux Klan in the USA or neo-Nazi organizations in most European countries (Layton-Henry, 1992; Björgo and Witte, 1993b; Hargeaves and Leaman, 1995).

The growth of racist movements in the past 30 years is not simply a reaction to immigration. Although the historical culture of racism affects all social groups, there is considerable evidence that active and violent racism is particularly to be found among those sections of the working class most exposed to rapid change. The catalysts for the support of extremist views and organizations are often declining living standards and growing insecurity resulting from globalization and economic restructuring. The economic and social crisis brought about by these changes is often experienced at the personal level as a crisis of culture and identity. Immigrants, who are different in appearance and behaviour, become the visible symbols of this crisis.

In such situations, racism against minorities takes on a central role: it helps to recreate a threatened community. Racism is often a form of white ethnic solidarity, in the face of the apparent cultural strength of immigrant groups. If local workers lose their jobs, and find their social security and environment declining, they can blame the alien influences that are undermining the nation: hating immigrants helps to maintain an illusion of national unity and pride. Racism becomes a form of 'identity movement', which can help to strengthen group and personal identity in a situation of crisis (Balibar and Wallerstein, 1991; Wieviorka, 1995; Castles, 1996).

Anti-racist movements

Movements to combat racism have also emerged in all immigration countries. These are generally loose coalitions with several components. One is the minority populations themselves, which seek ways of protecting themselves against discrimination and violence in their daily lives. Their activities range from cultural and political organizations, through to self-defence groups designed to ward off racist violence. Minority youth play a major part in anti-racist action, and this has given rise to many violent confrontations. Since the early 1980s, Britain has had successive waves of riots in inner-city areas by black youth protesting against heavy-handed policing and extreme-right violence. In France, there have been militant youth movements in the large peripheral housing estates where people of immigrant origin are concentrated. In Germany, Turkish youth formed self-defence groups to protect their neighbourhoods against skinhead attacks in the early 1990s.

Anti-racist movements also include such groups as trade unions, churches, and left-wing parties and organizations. Anti-racist politics has become an important part of left discourses in every country. Although we tend to take this for granted today, it is important to remember that labour organizations and the left were often supporters of racist policies in the past. For example, the White Australia policy was seen as vital for protecting working-class interests as late as the 1950s by Australian trade unions and Labor politicians. Just as racism has become a core part of right-wing ideologies, the left now sees anti-racism as being crucial for social justice and democracy. This means that anti-racist movements have become important sites of cross-cultural communication.

Identity movements

If racist movements can sometimes be seen as the identity movements of 'poor whites' (that is, members of the majority population adversely affected by change), ethnic separatist movements can have analogous roots. Minority groups that experience social and economic exclusion and racial discrimination may give up their hopes of equal participation in society and instead seek to reconstruct their identity in enclaves. The development of Rastafarianism among Afro-Caribbean youth in Britain in the 1970s was the result of the experience of racism and the lack of real chances for social and economic participation. The assertion of a separate diasporic identity based on mythical symbols and distinctive cultural practices (such as reggae music) was an attempt to create an autonomous social space in a hostile society. Where discrimination is less pronounced (or declines over time), cultural separatism is only a transitory phenomenon. Many Greek and Italian immigrants in Australia joined ethnic organizations and tried to recreate traditional practices, but such an emphasis on the pre-migration culture fell off rapidly in the second generation.

Where immigrants cling to (or reconstruct) pre-migration identities, this can have important political consequences. The failed promises of universalism give rise to separatist politics, which in turn comes to be seen as a major threat to secularism and modernity. The current situation of young people of Algerian origin in France is one such case. This group experiences considerable racism and exclusion, despite the official ideology of equal rights and assimilation. Kastoryano (1996) argues that North African-origin youth in France and Turkish-origin youth in Germany are increasingly turning to Islamic organization, because of the failure of secular organizations to achieve genuine political participation. At the same time, the bloody civil war between an authoritarian secular government and Islamic fundamentalists in

Algeria has spilled over to France, leading to an even greater discrimination against people of North African origin.

Identity movements can, however, have paradoxical effects. The reassertion of minority cultures may help to reshape mainstream life patterns. European youth culture has been profoundly affected by Mediterranean, Afro-Caribbean and black American music and styles. The result is often considerable changes in values and behavioural patterns. This in turn affects political ideas and activity. The multicultural inner-city areas become places where not only lifestyles, but also political ideas are remade. The meeting of identity movements and anti-racist groups gives rise to a new politics that can affect society as a whole.

Mobilization for societal participation

Minority struggles against discrimination and for equal rights have profound political effects. In settler colonies, such as the USA, Canada, Australia and New Zealand, indigenous peoples' struggles for land rights, self-determination and cultural recognition have gained momentum since the 1970s. Although (with the exception of New Zealand), indigenous peoples make up only a small proportion of the population, their political demands have a disproportionate effect because they question the foundational myths of these nation-states. The image of the open frontier and of vast areas of vacant land played an important role in the development of national identity. Indigenous peoples' demands for recognition of their prior ownership and their claims for a restitution of their rights are thus seen as a threat to the existing order. In New Zealand, Maoris make up over 10 per cent of the population, and have made substantial gains with regard to land rights and political representation.

Immigrant mobilization around demands for greater equality of rights goes back to the earliest stages of settlement, and is often to be found even when the main political concern is with homeland politics. Immigrants' lack of political rights forces them to act outside the normal political framework. In European countries, demonstrations and hunger strikes against deportation go back to the 1960s. The most fundamental immigrant demand is for the right to secure residence status, since this is the precondition for all other rights. Many groups still lack that right, as was shown in France in 1996 by the movement of the *sans papiers*, when immigrants threatened by deportation through changes in immigration law occupied churches and carried out hunger strikes.

Once immigrants become more established, their political focus tends to shift. Wihtol de Wenden (1995) has observed three phases in France. In the first, immigrants tended to focus on homeland issues, in the second the main concern was with the politics of community and identity, while in the third the emphasis moved to demands for equal participation in the wider society. This change is to some extent the result of a generational shift, since the young people who grow up in the immigration country are keenly sensitive to discrimination and the denial of equal rights. Mobilization for greater participation takes various forms. The most obvious is movements that organize at the national level and carry out campaigns with directly political objectives, for example *SOS-Racisme* and *France Plus* in France, or the Federation of Ethnic Communities' Councils in Australia.

A second level, which is sometimes less visible, is the work of the many smaller community organizations that work for social rights. Community groups may demand ethno-specific services for certain groups, or call for improvements in mainstream services. The community sector has been an important factor in achieving change, but its effects are hard to assess. At the local level, there is no clear division between political pressure and direct social action, so that community organizations are often part of broader social movements (especially anti-racist movements). They may be closely linked to left-wing organizations, as well as to religious groups. Many of the community workers are women, and there has been a close relationship between feminist and community politics in most countries. The national or regional organizations that link community groups often have more directly political aims. There is, however, also no clear boundary between community groups and the state: many community activists are (or become) employees of social bureaucracies (Vasta, 1997).

National-level political movements are mainly concerned with the civil and political dimensions of citizenship: they claim full rights of political belonging for minorities. The community sector is, in contrast, concerned with the social dimension of citizenship: it demands participation in the welfare state. Both types of movement, however, have to address issues of culture. At the national political level, the inclusion of minorities without cultural assimilation requires a struggle against nationalist notions of belonging – for the right to be a citizen without being a national. At the community level, inclusion as social citizens means demanding the recognition of different cultural values and needs.

State strategies and cooption

However, there is another side to minority mobilization: governments may seek to coopt minority movements and their leaderships, and build them into state strategies of surveillance and control. The frequent success of such strategies arises from the intrinsic ambivalence of community action. In the short term, minority leaders and community workers seek to improve their community's position by securing improved social entitlements and services; in the long run, they seek more fundamental changes. In many cases, minority organizations are offered government grants to provide services to their communities, and thus become dependent on official goodwill. This may involve conformity with officially set policies, which effectively means abandoning the goal of fundamental change. Similarly, community activists may be offered positions within welfare bureaucracies. Such jobs give the opportunity of representing the interests of their community, but within rules and structures set from above.

Australian multiculturalism is an example of this dilemma (as will be discussed in Chapter 7). Multicultural policies have led to the inclusion of many community activists in government bureaucracies and consultative processes. This has delivered real gains for ethnic communities in the form of improved welfare services and the recognition of cultural difference. However, multiculturalism has failed to change the cultural biases built into key political, economic and cultural institutions. Arguably, it has weakened the political thrust for change developed by ethnic organizations in the 1970s.

Another example is the French anti-racist movement *SOS-Racisme*, which was able to bring about a mass mobilization of minority youth against racism in the early 1980s. The decision of the movement's leadership to work closely with the Socialist Party seems to have divided the supporters of the movement and reduced its potential for achieving real change.

Minority groups therefore need to consider whether they can achieve more through mobilization outside the normal political structures than through seeking inclusion in them. Dryzek (1996) argues that inclusion in the state only brings benefits when minority demands correspond at least to some extent with basic state imperatives. Where this is not the case, minorities tend to lose out through cooption. In Dryzek's view, they would do better to further their goals through mobilization in civil society (understood as that area of social interaction not encompassed by the state, the economy and private life). Oppositional politics and self-organization in civil society may wring reforms and concessions from democratic states more effectively than may a direct participation in state organs.

Against this position, it may be argued that restricting minority politics to social movements outside the state is tantamount to giving up the claim to full democratic participation. Other authors (such as Young, 1990) argue instead for special representative mechanisms to ensure that minority voices can make themselves heard in mainstream politics. However, minority groups (especially relatively small ones) are always likely to find it hard to gain adequate representation through electoral systems. They may need a mixture of civil society mobilization and mainstream political involvement to make sure that their needs and values are not ignored.

Minorities in mainstream politics

This complex topic – which can only be touched on here – includes such issues as minority participation in political parties, the activities of minority lobby groups, the role of the 'ethnic vote' in influencing party and government policies, and the extent to which minority members are elected to parliaments and other representative bodies. It obviously makes a big difference whether minorities have citizenship and the right to vote. In the USA, Canada, Australia, New Zealand and Britain, most minority members can vote. Some other European countries, notably France, Sweden and the Netherlands, have naturalization policies that make access to voting rights relatively easy for immigrants. In addition, Sweden and the Netherlands have granted local voting rights to resident non-citizens. Other Western European countries, such as Germany, Switzerland and Austria, still bar most immigrants and their children from formal citizenship and political participation, although this may be about to change in the case of Germany (see Chapter 4).

There is a long history of political parties seeking to utilize ethnic solidarity. In the USA, the Democratic Party used community leaders to control the Irish and Italian vote in the early twentieth century. In return, ethnic bosses expected concessions for themselves and their communities. Today, African-American, Hispanic and Asian blocs may play a major role in local and national politics, and the parties negotiate with their leaders to gain support. However, there are factors that attenuate this: many poor people in the USA are not registered as voters and hardly take part in the political process; a given ethnic community may have competing leadership groups; and finally, a party that courts minorities may risk losing votes from the white majority.

In Australia, efforts to recruit immigrants to parties started in the 1950s, although with little initial success. Later, the Australian Labor Party (ALP) set up Greek and other ethnic branches, and these had a significant role in Labor's 1972 electoral victory. In return, the ALP pursued social policies designed to improve the situation of immigrant workers. The conservative parties soon followed suit, so that multiculturalism became a bipartisan policy, at least until 1996, when the Liberal–National coalition parties seemed to be shifting back to an anti-minority policy. In Britain, the Labour Party has courted the black vote, although the Conservatives seem to have had some success in attracting ethnic entrepreneurs.

Ethnic lobby groups can wield considerable power, especially when an ethnic group is relatively united on an issue. US policy on Cuba is strongly influenced by conservative Cuban leaders, whose influence may be sufficient to decide a state or federal election. Ethnic lobby groups also play an important role through representation on government consultative bodies. This is very important in countries with corporatist structures designed to include social groups in certain decision-making processes, such as Australia, Sweden and Germany. In this area, access to formal citizenship is not decisive: non-citizen groups tend to be included in consultative procedures as an effective way of managing difference. This helps to explain why a sort of '*de facto* multiculturalism' may develop in certain sectors (such as welfare and education), even in countries where this goes against official principles.

If members of a certain group tend to live in specific neighbourhoods, political parties cannot ignore their voting power. Spatial concentration is often linked to a common class position, which in turn reinforces the likelihood that members of a group will vote in a similar way. Conversely, immigrant groups that are widely dispersed and have varying social positions are unlikely to be seen as a significant political factor. An exception is found in groups of common origins or religion that may act as a bloc on certain issues, for example Catholics on issues of family law, or Jews on the interests of Israel. An interesting case was the 1996 referendum over the separation of Quebec from the Canadian Federation. Both Cree Indians and immigrants overwhelmingly voted against separation, for fear of being culturally submerged in a francophone state. This had a significant effect on the outcome, prompting angry anti-immigrant speeches by Quebecois leaders.

Political scientists are divided over whether there is an 'ethnic vote', and over how significant this is as a political factor. For example, in Australia there do not appear to be blocs of votes that can be controlled or manipulated by ethnic power brokers, yet the majority of Southern European voters seem to have consistently supported the ALP in the 1980s, while voters from Northern Europe and English-speaking countries are more conservative (McAllister, 1988). Moreover, politicians behave as if there were an ethnic vote by holding meetings in community clubs and courting the support of ethnic leaders. In countries where immigrants cannot gain the right to vote, it much easier for politicians to pander to populist prejudices.

One way for parties to gain ethnic community support is to choose a prominent member of the community as a candidate. This tends to happen first in local politics, where the effects of ethnic residential concentration are most strongly felt (Ball and Solomos, 1990). However, an increase in the minority membership of regional and national parliaments can be observed in Australia, the USA, Canada and Britain. Despite this, indigenous people remain very poorly represented, while immigrants are still considerably underrepresented compared with their share in the population. New Zealand is a special case, since a number of parliamentary seats are reserved for Maoris. At the 1996 election, Maoris were also elected on the lists of most mainstream parties, giving Maoris considerable representation for the first time.

The presence of minority members in parliaments raises several questions. If they are elected as party candidates by voters of all ethnic backgrounds, can they be seen as representatives of their own group? Does the political acculturation required to gain selection by a political party erode their effectiveness as minority representatives? There are no simple answers to these questions. The experience of migration, settlement and exclusion is likely to influence the attitudes and behaviour of political representatives. Recent research in Australia indicates that ethnic members of parliament are more responsive towards ethnic constituents, as measured by the extent and type of intervention they make in parliament. However, non-ethnic members also respond to the needs of minorities, if these make up a high proportion of their constituency. Minority members may have different ideas on the relationships between representatives and electors, compared with the majority groups. Participation in political parties may not be seen in terms of the beliefs of individual citizens, but rather as a community activity, based on social networks within a group. Similarly, some members of minorities may see political relationships in terms of patronage and mutual interest (Zappalà, 1997).

Minorities may also have different views on how democracy should function. The adversarial model of party politics typical of western democracy may be repugnant to people from cultures based on principles of consensus and deference. Some immigrants may want more direct involvement in decision making, through the principle of subsidiarity (the devolution of decisions to the lowest possible level), than is customary in some political systems. Ideas on acceptable modes of political mobilization, communication and participation may vary. Overall, people from different cultural backgrounds may hold differing concepts of desirable social goals and how society is to achieve these. The result may be a significant shift in political culture.

Conclusion

This chapter has discussed some of the complex processes through which minorities constitute themselves as new social and political actors in western societies. The processes we described – home-making and place-making, the development of ethnic economies, the re-creation of religious and cultural identities, and ethnic social and political mobilization – take place everywhere, although in widely varying contexts. Community formation under conditions of full or partial exclusion from various aspects of societal participation leads to the development of new forms of consciousness and identity, which in turn become major factors influencing political goals and forms of action.

The position of minorities within democratic nation-states today is marked by a fundamental contradiction: a failure to make them into full citizens undermines the inclusive principle of democracy and leads to divided societies, but political inclusion without cultural assimilation may undermine cultural and national identity, which is a crucial factor of integration in nation-states. This problem has always existed but could in the past generally be managed, because processes of incorporation of new groups were slow enough to give time to forget the history of difference and cultural homogenization. The new context is the telescoping of space and time through globalization and the development of new forms of communication. Minorities can no longer be assimilated because of the speed and volume of migration, the continual nature of population mobility, the cultural and social diversity of the migrants, the ease with which they can remain in contact with the society of origin, and the situation of rapid economic and cultural change.

The notion of the immigrant who comes to stay and can be assimilated as an individual into a relatively homogeneous society is no longer viable. This leaves three possible alternatives: separatist consciousness, in which minorities do not feel that they are part of the society in which they live; diasporic consciousness, in which immigrant minorities identify mainly with people of the same ethnic origin whatever country they inhabit; and transcultural consciousness, in which minorities develop new forms of culture and identity together with various subgroups of the population.

Which of these alternatives will prevail depends on the institutional structures and the behaviour of the majority population, as well as on the aspirations and actions of the minority members. The least desirable option – separatism – is above all a reaction to exclusion and discrimination. Indeed, policies of assimilation, however well meaning, are likely to give rise to separatism. Diasporic identity is a form of separatist consciousness, which can be the result of both experiences of persecution and cyclical forms of migration. Transcultural consciousness is the most promising perspective for a peaceful and creative society, but it does require a considerable willingness to change on the part of the majority population.

Social peace and democracy are unthinkable without political strategies that link cultural recognition with social rights for minorities, and that seek to give them a legitimate voice in the polity. The old principle of individual incorporation as citizens has no chance of success, in the wake of half a century of differentiation and racialization. The challenge is to develop procedures and institutions that are acceptable to all the varying groups now making up society. This does not mean trying to be culturally neutral, for all political institutions in fact reflect cultural values and traditions. Rather it is matter of developing ways of negotiating about identity and difference, so that all members of civil society can feel a sense of political belonging. These are the themes of the remainder of this book.

Notes

1. For just a few examples from the vast and growing literature on ethnicity, race and politics, see (for Britain) Layton-Henry, 1992; Solomos and Back,

1995; (for France) Wihtol de Wenden, 1988; (for Germany) Cohn-Bendit and Schmid, 1992; (for Australia) Jupp and Kabala, 1993; (for the USA) Carnoy, 1994; (for Canada) Breton *et al.*, 1990; and (for Europe in general): Wrench and Solomos, 1993; Baldwin-Edwards and Schain, 1994; Rex and Drury, 1994; Wieviorka, 1994; Hargreaves and Leaman, 1995.
2. A useful overview is provided in Chapter 10, 'Immigrant Politics', in Castles and Miller (1998). This, it should be added, is the work of Mark Miller.

7

The End of National Belonging

When globalization processes (see Chapter 1), new migration patterns (Chapter 3) and the actions of new political subjects (Chapter 6) impact on the historical traditions of citizenship described in Chapter 2, radical changes ensue. The context for a citizenship based on belonging to a single nation is being eroded. A version of citizenship is developing that is at least as novel as the citizenship of a modern nation-state was when compared with the citizenship of an ancient city-state (Constant, 1990; Davidson, 1996a). Its emergence is uneven. Most societies and polities have still not got beyond the citizenship of the nation-state, which we can expect to remain a dominant form into the twenty-first century. The new level of citizenship is emerging in the same way as that of the nation-state did in the earlier context of city-states. Long before the constellation of city-states that made up Spain, Italy and Germany was superseded by the contemporary nation-state form already present in England and France, the new types of state had started to influence the old ones to alter their practices of citizenship. Above all, the democratic quality of city-states was replaced by an absolutism that paralleled that in the new nation-states.

What then is the nature of the new context for citizenship? This chapter seeks to trace the emergence of the new and expanded forms of citizenship that are evolving in response to globalization. These have a practical, *ad hoc* and contested character, but are empirically real. Since the new forms represent a transition from the citizenship of the nation-state, they are marked by contradictions. These are most evident when attempts are made to reconcile the nation-state framework with new types of multicultural citizenship, as we will discuss in the cases of the USA and Australia. Then, we will examine the most innovative experiment: the new transnational citizenship of regional entities such as the European Union (EU).

The changing character of migration

As our preceding analysis has made clear, the increasingly rapid international movement of people in the past 50 years has resulted in the emergence of multiethnic societies of a new type within nation-state borders practically everywhere. Even those places which 10 years ago boasted of the homogeneity of their population – for example, Japan or Korea – are increasingly being forced to come to terms with the reality of ethnic minority workforces. These must be distinguished from indigenous minorities who have been present for as long as – or even antedate – the majority ethnic group. On the other hand, the experiences of immigrants and indigenous peoples have impacted greatly on each other, especially since 1980. What must be emphasized is not only the volume of migration, but also its new qualities, which makes it quite different from earlier mass migrations. It is the rapidity of this migration and its great variety that are forcing the creation of a new layer of citizenship above that of the nation – the citizen who does not belong.

Most of the English- and Spanish-speaking world consists of so-called settler societies – although they always contained indigenous people before the settlers arrived. Until recently, such countries were made up mainly of people who came from just one or two source states. The main motive for leaving one's birthplace was the search for work and a better livelihood elsewhere. In much of the 'white' world, and especially the settler colonies of the British Empire, there was a shortage of labour in the nineteenth century. The colonial state actively searched for immigrants and encouraged them to come and settle. This pattern also prevailed – with its ups and downs – in the twentieth century's boom periods up to 1914 and after 1945. On this level, newcomers were welcome as they filled labour shortages and stimulated economic growth, profit and even, in some places, improved standards of living. As we saw in Chapter 3, an economic downturn such as the oil crisis of the 1970s could result in a rapid reversal of the pattern.

The massive assisted migrant programmes were understood by the majority population in the society of destination as being more than the purchase of labour power. They were seen as entailing – sooner or later – a transfer of allegiance from the place of birth to the new country, and the gradual adoption of a new national identity, especially for the children of the migrants, but also for the migrants themselves. This expectation followed from the fact that this was a world of nation-states and the core value was the attainment of nation-statehood by those areas which had not achieved it before. Little more than that could be expected for distant places in an era when ships and telegraph were the modes of communication. Even in 1958, a migrant from Britain to Australia faced a voyage of more than a month, the cost of which was enormous relative to average income (which is why fares were subsidized) and during which several stops would punctuate the passage. These would, by their exoticism, remind the traveller of the distance and variety of cultures separating the old and new countries. The host nation made the immigrant's transition formally easy because of the need for labour power.

In contrast, if someone left a backward or poorer area for a more affluent area in their own country (as was the case as late as the massive post-1945 migration from the South to the industrial triangle of Italy), the emphasis on settlement was not crucial, as it was always possible to return home. The same applied to intra-European migrations such as those from Poland to Germany in the late nineteenth century, or from Southern Europe to the core industrial areas of Europe after 1945. The 'guestworkers' were expected to return home, and citizenship rules within the nation-state were not affected. Exceptions were made in special circumstances: French industrialists and politicians supported the 1889 revision to French nationality codes because the low domestic birth rate made it imperative to secure immigrants both as workers and as soldiers.

But those who made the long voyage from Europe to the Americas, Australia or New Zealand were often (although not always) leaving their birthplaces for ever. ('Farewell to old England for ever' runs the refrain of a song that was sung long after its first meaning no longer had any basis.) Migration was usually from a limited number of source countries similar in culture to the dominant group in the receiving country, which tried to attract people as much like themselves as possible – those who belonged to the same 'family'. The only country for which this was not true in the nineteenth century was the USA, which drew in immigrants from all over Europe. However, even there the difficulty of travel meant that a long period of assimilation was possible and a 'melting pot' principle was conceivable. The approach of other white-settler colonies to granting nationality was close to countries of the *ius sanguinis*. The only way in which someone of differing origins could obtain nationality, and therefore citizen rights, was to show that he or she had joined the Anglo-Celtic value systems of the British national family or the Hispanic culture of Latin America. In Canada, this demand was less forceful because of the French Canadian minority.

Nevertheless, the need for labour in industrializing countries forced a continuing redefinition and enlargement of those 'aliens' who were acceptable as immigrants. From the mid-twentieth century onwards, more and more people of different ethnic origin started to be admitted to such settler worlds. At the same time, the older nation-states of Europe also became immigration countries, with large inflows from increasingly distant countries. From the receiving countries' point of view, this added up to waves of ethnically different and diverse newcomers, who did not intend to transfer their allegiance exclusively to their new homeland by giving up their old cultural identity. The newcomers, given their different origins, needed varying practices of insertion. In the process of immigration, countries turned themselves into multiethnic societies. Their populations came from everywhere and were polyglot. As they intermarried, the very notion of the original national 'family' disappeared.

Thus, the motives for migration may still be understood as economic and social, but no longer is it implied that migration means forgetting where one belonged before joining the host culture. This is so from both the emigration and immigration societies' points of view.

Multiculturalism

With a considerable time-lag and resistance, receiving states began from the 1970s to adapt their policies and state structures to such realities. Some countries started to promote multiculturalism in place of the notion that all newcomers should join the majority national culture. Australia and Canada have gone furthest in developing multicultural institutions and policies, but debates on multiculturalism are taking place in many immigration countries. Some European states – notably Scandinavia, the Netherlands and Britain – have introduced fairly general multicultural policies (although not necessarily under this label), while even countries that vehemently reject the concept in principle – such as Germany and France – have some multicultural elements in their social and educational policies.

The emergence of multiculturalism is linked to crisis management strategies of welfare states, which seek to secure integration and cohesion of the whole population (including minorities) through social policy measures. In contrast, countries with weak welfare states (for example, Switzerland) reject multicultural policies. The USA is a special case in that it combines a pluralist understanding of national belonging with a minimalist welfare state model. Our discussion of multiculturalism will focus on the USA and on Australia, a country with the largest immigrant share in population of any developed country,[1] and with a remarkable degree of ethno-cultural diversity.

Immigration, race and citizenship in the USA

The USA is widely seen as the world's most successful model for integrating a large number of immigrants as citizens in a democratic nation-state. The prevailing ideology of the USA for most of the twentieth century has been that of a 'nation of immigrants', in which people of diverse origins could be assimilated and 'Americanized'. That meant being re-formed in a great 'melting pot' to become a new people united not by a common ancestry (as in 'old' Europe) but by a common destiny to build a new nation based on freedom, equality and opportunity (Gitlin, 1995, pp. 39–59). Thus, people of any background could share the 'American dream' of 'a land in which life should be better and richer and fuller for every man, with opportunity for each according to his ability or achievement' (Adams, 1931, quoted here from Gitlin, 1995, p. 56). Since the 1960s, the nation of immigrants has been reconceptualized as a multicultural society, to which people of differing backgrounds can belong as citizens without abandoning their cultural distinctiveness.

Today, however, multiculturalism is being questioned by best-selling books with provocative titles such as *Alien Nation: Common Sense about America's Immigration Disaster* (Brimelow, 1995) or *The Disuniting of America: Reflections on a Multicultural Society* (Schlesinger, 1992). Conflicts about multiculturalism have given rise to 'campus wars' (Arthur and Shapiro, 1995) and 'culture wars' (Gitlin, 1995), and to polemics about 'political correctness'. Americans are becoming increasingly dubious about their capacity to absorb the new waves of global migrants in the same way as the massive pre-1920 European inflows. Immigration and ethnic diversity are increasingly seen as forms of fragmentation that threaten the nation.

To understand these developments, it is necessary to look at some of the contradictions underlying the ideal of nation-building through immigration, and to see how new types of immigration have brought these contradictions to a head. As Steinberg points out, the most fundamental of these contradictions goes back to the establishment of the USA as a democratic republic:

> When the nation's founding fathers betrayed the noble principles enshrined in the Declaration of Independence and the Constitution, and surrendered to temptation and greed by sanctioning the slave trade, they placed the nation on a calamitous path of racial division and conflict that continues down to the present. (Steinberg, 1995, p. 205)

Throughout the history of the USA, the question of race has been 'the wound in all American dreams' (Gitlin, 1995, p. 27). Since colonial times, America has been dominated by a white majority of mainly British heritage – the so-called WASPS (white Anglo-Saxon Protestants). This dominance was historically consolidated through the violent dispossession of the Native Americans (or American Indians) and the import and exploitation of slaves from Africa. As the USA expanded westwards in the nineteenth century, Mexican Americans were forcibly incorporated and subordinated. In the late nineteenth century, laws to exclude Chinese and other Asian immigrants were enacted. Thus, racist practices and ideologies were crucial to the formation of the nation; the 'American dream' of freedom, equality and prosperity was for white people only.

The great American success story of turning a vast number of immigrants (24 million between 1880 and 1920) into Americans was therefore based on the continued exclusion and racialization of millions of non-Europeans. Even after the abolition of slavery in 1865, the African-Americans in the South remained impoverished, segregated and oppressed. They were non-citizens, denied both civil and political rights. Although many migrated to the North (especially after the First World War) they found that the colour-line prevailed here too, albeit in a more covert form, keeping them out of all but the most menial jobs and forcing them into segregated neighbourhoods.

The 'huddled masses' of Europe – from Ireland, Italy, Germany, Poland, Russia and so on – experienced discrimination, exploitation and violence too, as they built the factories, railways and roads that were to make the USA the world's greatest power. They were, however, encouraged to become citizens and send their children to public school. Then the First World War triggered a wave of suspicion of anything foreign. An anti-immigration 'Nativist' movement developed, based on a mixture of anti-Catholicism and anti-radicalism. Foreigners were seen as dangerous anarchists or communists and ideas of Anglo-Saxon superiority were rife (Higham, 1974). In the 1920s, national origin quotas were introduced to keep out undesirable aliens (especially Southern and Eastern Europeans). Now, the willingness to assimilate and to speak English became the test of loyalty. It was assumed that second- and third-generation immigrants would become true Americans, and achieve the dream of upward mobility and prosperity in a rapidly expanding economy.

Assimilationist beliefs were strengthened by the participation of young Americans of differing national origin in the armed forces – even if this meant fighting against their parents' former homeland. In addition, African-Americans played a major role in the armed forces, although they fought in segregated units under white officers. The war also opened up Northern labour markets for blacks. It was widely believed that this experience of common struggle would lead to an end to segregation and discrimination when peace returned, but this was not the case (Steinberg, 1995, p. 210). It was not until the Civil Rights Movement of the 1960s that legal discrimination against African-Americans was ended and they became full citizens – at least in formal terms.

The mid-1960s were, in more ways than one, decisive years for US approaches to dealing with difference. The 1965 amendments to the Immigration and Nationality Act were a part of the civil rights legislation, which removed the discriminatory national origin quotas. These amendments unexpectedly led to an upsurge in Hispanic and Asian immigration, which was to bring about dramatic changes in the ethnic composition of the population. The 1960s were also the era of the 'ethnic revival', in which third- and fourth-generation descendants of pre-1920 immigrants rediscovered their cultural roots and began to make claims for equality and special treatment based on the notion of being ethnic communities (Glazer and Moynihan, 1975). Ethnic movements were following the lead of other minority movements of the time, especially the Black Power and Native American movements. Suddenly, the previously hegemonic principle of assimilation was being questioned. All this was happening in the context of growing disaffection of white youth caused mainly by the Vietnam War. Protest movements and counter-cultures burgeoned.

The initial reaction of the US political system was to try to use legal instruments and welfare to control and coopt protest. President

Johnson's 'Great Society' programme, with its compensatory educational and social assistance measures, put many black and ethnic leaders on government payrolls from the mid-1960s. Violent repression was still an option for those, like the Black Panthers, who refused to cooperate. Desegregation was enforced in the South, and a range of anti-discrimination laws were enacted, while affirmative action programmes were introduced in government departments, universities and private corporations to provide economic opportunities to minority members. African-Americans began to gain some local political power through joining the mainstream parties and winning election as mayors and Congress members. Discourses of assimilation for immigrants were replaced by the idea of ethnic pluralism: the maintenance of homeland cultures and languages by ethnic communities was no longer seen as being un-American.

In retrospect, it is clear that the measures of the 1960s and 70s failed in the most important area: despite the emergence of a small black middle class, the overwhelming majority of African-Americans remained poor and residentially segregated. The gap between white and black incomes actually grew. By 1990, blacks made up 12 per cent of the population, but 29 per cent of the poor. Nearly half of all black children were being raised in families below the poverty line (Steinberg, 1995, p. 213). It became obvious that the civil rights laws had not succeeded in combating the deep-seated structural racism of American society. The task had been made more difficult by the major changes brought about by globalization and economic restructuring since the 1970s. The employment opportunities for low-skilled workers – especially of minority background – shrank dramatically.

Moreover, the Reagan and Bush administrations of the 1980s implemented the neo-classical economic doctrine of small government by slashing welfare expenditure and rolling back affirmative action programmes. The new right approach was to stigmatize the poor and control them through the criminal justice system. By the 1990s, one out of every two young black males had a criminal record, and half of the US prison population was black. Virtually all black children grew up in segregated neighbourhoods, with inferior schools, poor services and high rates of crime and drug addiction (Carnoy, 1994, p. 5). America's inability to bring about racial equality and to deal with gross inequality could not be attributed to an economic or technological incapacity to do so. Instead, it arose from a failure of political will: politicians found it convenient to attribute economic and social problems to race, and to allow racial polarization to increase (Carnoy, 1994, pp. 9–11).

These major economic and political shifts coincided with dramatic changes in US population composition as a result of post-1965 immigration. By 1990, non-Hispanic whites made up only 75 per cent of the population, while the black, Hispanic and Asian populations were all growing. In Los Angeles, New York and other cities, ethnic minorities came close to overtaking the white population, and indeed made up the majority in many municipalities. Such trends – often exaggerated into mistaken predictions that non-whites would be the majority population of the USA by the middle of twenty-first century – gave rise to widespread panic about the 'colouring of America' (Gitlin, 1995, Chapter 4). The result was a backlash against immigration and multiculturalism. This took two main forms.

The first was what Sánchez (1997) has called 'a new racial nativism'. This has three main elements:

● an extreme antipathy towards non-English languages and a fear that linguistic difference will undermine the American nation;
● a belief that misguided and sometimes secretive government policies favour people of colour over whites through multiculturalism and affirmative action;
● the notion that immigrants are non-working loafers who drain public resources through the utilization of welfare, education and health-care services. (Sánchez, 1997, p. 1020)

Such attitudes have given rise to increasingly restrictive border control measures (see Chapter 3) and severe cuts to the welfare entitlements of resident non-citizens (see Chapter 5).

The second form of the white backlash has been a movement against multiculturalism, affirmative action and so-called 'political correctness', especially within the education system. Unlike Canada, Australia and Europe, where multiculturalism has been conceptualized mainly as a public policy model for dealing with immigration and ethnic difference, multiculturalism in the USA has referred mainly to attempts to question previously dominant understandings of American history and culture. Multiculturalism was an intellectual trend that emerged from the civil rights and counter-cultural movements of the 1960s and 70s. It questioned the 'deeply ethnoracialized Eurovision centred at the heart of monoculturalism [which] continued to dominate the "high culture" by which the US academy... took itself to be defined' (Goldberg, 1994, p. 4). Multiculturalists attacked the claim to universalism in American learning, claiming that it was based on a white Eurocentric perspective, which ignored the role of African-Americans, Native Americans, other ethnic minorities and women in history and culture.

Multiculturalism had brought about a considerable change in US universities, including the appointment of more women and minority professors, the establishment of ethnic and gender studies departments, and changes in the curriculum to include minority voices. Further changes included affirmative action policies, and codes of conduct to prevent sexual harassment as well as racist and sexist speech (Arthur and Shapiro, 1995, p. 1). An influential book by Allan Bloom (1987) has attacked such trends as being deeply threatening to traditional notions of scientific objectivity and excellence. Multiculturalism questions the idea of a common set of American values and a single way of life, and is therefore perceived by its opponents as a profound threat to national unity (Schlesinger, 1992). The struggle over multiculturalism has been a major issue throughout the 1990s. One of its main forms has been the lampooning of alleged excesses of 'political correctness' in the curriculum and in use of language (see Gitlin, 1995, Chapter 1).

Overall, the US model for managing difference has been profoundly destabilized. The old model of the nation of immigrants that assimilated newcomers and in return gave them the chance of freedom, equality and prosperity was undermined by the protest movements of the 1960s. The attempt to build a multicultural model recognizing the value of distinct cultures while offering social equality through welfare and affirmative action has also foundered through the economic changes of the 1970s and 80s, and the conservative backlash of the 1980s and 90s. The USA remains the most desired destination for millions of potential immigrants, but it is unclear what principles will in future be used to make them into citizens.

Multicultural citizenship in Australia

Multiculturalism in Australia is very different in character: it is a government policy for managing difference, which continues a tradition of government intervention in immigration and settlement that goes back to colonial times. It has evolved through a number of stages since it was first introduced in 1973. The most recent official definition was provided by the *National Agenda for a Multicultural Australia* in 1989 (OMA, 1989); this remains still valid, although there has been a shift away from multicultural policies in the past few years.

The *National Agenda* in effect provides a new notion of belonging for a multiethnic society:

> [Multiculturalism] is a policy for managing the consequences of cultural diversity in the interests of the individual and society as a whole. The Commonwealth Government has identified three dimensions of multicultural policy:
>
> • cultural identity: the right of all Australians, within carefully defined limits, to express and share their individual cultural heritage, including their language and religion;
> • social justice: the right of all Australians to equality of treatment and opportunity, the removal of barriers of race, ethnicity, culture, religion, language, gender or place of birth; and
> • economic efficiency: the need to maintain, develop and utilize effectively the skills and talents of all Australians regardless of background. (OMA, 1989, p. viii)

However, the *National Agenda* makes it clear that these three dimensions are to be realized within the context of the nation-state:

> There are also limits to Australian multiculturalism. These may be summarized as follows:
>
> • multicultural policies are based on the premise that all Australians should have an overriding and unifying commitment to Australia, to its interests and future first and foremost;
> • multicultural policies require all Australians to accept the basic structures and principles of Australian society – the Constitution and the rule of law, tolerance and equality, Parliamentary democracy, freedom of speech and religion, English as a national language and equality of the sexes; and
> • multicultural policies impose obligations as well as conferring rights: the right to express one's own culture and beliefs involves a reciprocal responsibility to accept the right of others to express their views and values. (OMA, 1989, p. viii)

The main point is that, with the arrival of multiethnic workforces, the requirement that someone belong nationally before obtaining citizen rights has been gradually given up. This trend away from the citizen who belongs as a national has in turn spelt the emergence of new civil, political and economic rights and practices, which have had to be introduced by the state to cope with a new reality in which its inhabitants do not share common cultural values.

In 1901, when the Commonwealth of Australia was created as a federation of six pre-existing colonies, 98 per cent of its population was Anglo-Celtic.[2] The population shared a strongly hegemonic British culture. The Celts had become Anglicized in that they shared the economic and social lifestyle and by 1901 spoke only English. As an isolated continent at the end of the Empire, very few people knew anything but Australia and New Zealand. They built their new nation on a firmly racist basis, adopting as one of its pillars the infamous 'white Australia' policy. Within Australia, the active genocide of the indigenous peoples, which went back to first settlement, continued as the more arid and distant parts of the continent were opened up from 1901 to 1939. In fact, Australia became more homogeneous culturally by 1945 than it had been up to 1901 when it was easy for non-Britons of European origin to obtain naturalization (Davidson, 1997).

It was this solidly Anglo-Celtic population who faced the massive influx of non-British migrants for the first time after 1945. Because Australia needed labour to develop, it gradually relaxed its rigidly exclusive plan to admit only one foreigner for every 10 British immigrants. First Northern and Eastern Europeans, then Southern Europeans, then Middle Easterners and finally Asians were encouraged to come to Australia. By 1996, 23 per cent of the population had been born overseas; there were over 100 ethnic groups, and 15 per cent spoke a language other than English at home. Moreover, Asian and Middle Eastern (Arabic) languages were those growing most quickly. The number of adherents to non-Christian religions also increased rapidly.

The position of the Anglo-Celtic majority at the beginning of the process was that it was doing these 'New Australians' a favour. In return, they were expected to turn their backs on the past and assimilate to what was seen as the higher British civilization. The Nationality and Citizenship Act 1948 defined an 'alien' as 'a person who is not a British subject, an Australian citizen, or a protected person'. Before becoming a British subject or an Australian citizen, 'aliens' had to show, by long residence, service to the Australian state and the acquisition of competence in English, that they had transferred their cultural ties from their community of origin to the Australian community. Any hint of divided loyalties, such as belonging to the Communist Party, proved un-Australian qualities. The oaths sworn at the naturalization ceremonies emphasized loyalty to the British monarch and a readiness to fight for Australia in any war.

It took a battle lasting 25 years to change the Act and the attitudes underlying it. The move to greater openness in citizenship rules was bitterly opposed by conservative forces, who often included members of the working class. The reform was basically forced by the change in the ethnic composition of the population itself and by ethnic minorities' resistance – particularly through voting power once citizens – to the notion that the institutional arrangements in Australia brooked no criticism. This had an enormous impact on the Australian Labor Party (ALP), which came to power in 1972. Gough Whitlam, the Labor Prime Minister, wrote that his electorate of Werriwa contained too many 'ethnics' to be ignored (Whitlam, 1994, p. 496). At the same time, 40 per cent of new migrants refused to naturalize and gradually, in the 1960s in a timorous sort of way – through the regular Citizenship Conventions – started to suggest that it was impossible to demand that they give up their past. Some sort of compromise and therefore dialogue was necessary. In particular, the oath to the Queen of England – that symbol of Britishness – was strongly challenged.

The evacuation of the nationality requirement to become a citizen was symbolized when the Nationality and Citizenship Act was renamed the Australian Citizenship Act in 1973. Further changes were gradually introduced. Today, only two years' residence is required for naturalization, and only one half of a couple has to have a basic knowledge of English. The oath to the Queen has disappeared. The oath now runs: 'From this time forward (under God [optional]), I pledge my loyalty to Australia and its people, whose democratic beliefs I share, whose rights and liberties I respect, and whose laws I will uphold and obey.' Vestiges of the requirement to belong to the nation – such as the requirement to serve in case of war – still exist, but the bulk of the communitarian content has been evacuated. A newcomer need only participate in the civil and political life of the state, and thus forge a unity – a political community – this is the extent of the belonging required. A transfer of cultural attachments is no longer required.

By 1978, it had become bi-partisan policy to promote multiculturalism and foster the different ethnic voices in the social debate, although vestiges of attachment to the old Britishness remained. Even in the 1980s, when ethnic press, state-financed radio and television, and multilingual facilities at all levels of the state machinery and legal system were established, the insistence on a knowledge of English by citizens was still voiced in parliament (Davidson, 1997, pp. 118–21). By that time, however, it was highly contested. This gradual elimination of the nationality or belonging prerequisite for citizen rights since 1945 – which corresponded to an estimated 3 million dual nationals in Australia by the 1990s – led to a fundamental reconsideration of the civil, political, social and economic arrangements in Australia and the creation of new citizen rights.

The limits of multicultural citizenship

Insofar as Australia's citizenship rules are now multicultural rather than national, and are therefore open to new voices on how to control risks at local, national and international levels, it should be an open republic, where everyone who subscribes to democratic rules can be a citizen. But it is not yet so. What the Australian experience makes clear is that the institutions of even a country that emerged from the *ius soli* to adopt a multicultural understanding of its society are inadequate to empower citizens in a global world.

It is true that, in the 1980s, a large number of institutional innovations were made, together with the setting up of a host of para-governmental organizations, to give the ethnic minorities a voice. In turn, pressure from minorities in a climate of general openness led to further innovations in administrative law, which were non-Anglo-Celtic: an Ombudsman; freedom of information acts; appeal tribunals for migrants; the use of languages other than English. Some ethnic spokespeople made it into decision-making élites. Perhaps the most significant of the innovations was the establishment of the Human Rights and Equal Opportunity Commission in 1986, which allowed minorities to demand their rights as established by the United Nations (UN; Gaze and Jones, 1990, p. 55) Unfortunately, in a constitutional system that allowed only the courts to make and enforce legal decisions, its findings are unenforceable.

It must be remembered that, for a minority, the problem in a multicultural society is that the old community will always be the majority, so the democratic privilege to make the laws, which lies at the basis of citizenship, will usually result in the minority point of view being rejected democratically or, at least, by a majority. The defence of the multicultural citizen thus shifts decisively to an assertion of rights. This privileges the legal system. Thus, in Australia, when a migrant or an indigenous person wants to assert rights, that person has to go to the courts. Their discourse is crucial to the outcome.

Legal tradition insists that the basis for decision be past decisions, or history, and that community standards be taken into consideration in innovation. While – in the last instance – the protection of migrant rights lies in the hands of the courts, these remain overwhelmingly Anglo-Saxon in composition and discourse. They are therefore unlikely to open up further by inserting new communal standards, those, for example, of the Vietnamese. The meaning of the international instruments, which state that no one may consult only national traditions in deciding what is right, are sieved through an exclusively Anglo-Celtic mind set and training. Inevitably, judges who know nothing of other worlds and are taught to care even less, however good-hearted and progressive they may be, cannot defend migrants. They themselves know this, and many have pleaded in the 1980s and 90s for the politicians to introduce a bill of rights so that they do not have to find more and more fantastic 'implied rights' in a constitution that was set up by an Anglo-Celtic élite to maintain itself forever in power.

Australia illustrates how a purely open republic based on the nation-state will not be sufficient to master the new risks posed by globalization. Even if we were to take France or the USA – the most successful examples of nation-state citizenship of the nineteenth century – the argument for multicultural citizenship in an 'open republic' within the nation-state as a sufficient solution to global pressure would not improve. Both demanded little more than adherence to democracy and human rights from those who wished to become citizens. However, precisely because they were so successful, both became increasingly less ready to subject their established nationality and citizenship practices to external criticism. The USA and France are at the same time the success stories of nation-state citizenship and the staunchest defenders of national sovereignty. The former is notorious for its refusal to subscribe to international – even UN – standards of human rights.

What happened in France and the USA was that their very democratic and human rights successes meant that they brooked no criticism of their norms in those areas. Over the two centuries when they were the light on the hill for all others, their very democratic and legal procedures became culturally specific through their closure to outside standards. Democracy and human rights became the 'American way of life' and '*la civilisation française*' (Delbruck, 1994; Karst, 1994). To ask newcomers to subscribe to them was like asking them to change their religion, to become affectively democrats along the ancient Greek rather than the modern procedural model. In other words, the open republic was itself a cultural artefact, a non-negotiable product of a history that was not that of the newcomer. This is the 'open republic' understood as the product of an 'original intent' of the constitution makers that operates to constrain the democratic revision of the document by new majorities – in our case, ethnically diverse combinations. Karst points out that any transition to a really open republic that continually modifies itself by reference to internal and external standards 'is certain to be painful, for – like the end of Jim Crow – it will threaten the psychological underpinnings of millions of individual identities' (Karst, 1994).

We note that, in the case of France and the USA, the defence of what are arguably the most advanced nation-state citizenship norms (and their promotion in massive civics programmes) rapidly slides into a defence of what is ours as specific difference and thence to extreme nationalism and racism of the sort advanced by Jean-Marie Le Pen. What is important to note is that no matter how advanced rights (even multicultural rights) are, once defined in national terms they become inadequate to cope with the development of globalization, unless something further is added. Fortunately, there are trends that tend to lead out of the stalemate in which the most advanced liberal democracies are most hostile to challenges to the practices of citizenship that they have elaborated.

Regional economies

Even the most developed countries have been compelled by the pressures of globalization to enter regional economic blocs. Thus, France belongs to the European Union (EU), the USA to the North American Free Trade Area (NAFTA), and Australia to the Asia Pacific Economic Cooperation (APEC) Forum. These are all free trade zones where increased trade and better utilization of capital and labour have brought about greater growth and overall more wellbeing than did the system of competing protected national economies. Their common characteristic is the ending of tariff barriers and therefore of national sovereignty in economic matters.

This is affecting citizenship. The new supra-national markets require new rules of law to regulate them. That is inevitable for economic and commercial transactions. Yet, they impinge directly on the workers who produce in those markets, either because there is a completely free movement of labour within the region irrespective of nation-state barriers – something that is completely new – or because even where that is still only a possibility, the cost of labour becomes all important to competitivity, and wage rates cannot be purely nationally referential.

The new rule of law that emerges is more than the traditional international law based on bilateral or multilateral trading. This is particularly so for nation-states that are already committed to democracy and human rights, and whose polities are not viable unless the rules there are observed. Most of the world's states formally accept democracy and human rights, but still rule coercively, against popular will. Only democratic states are obliged constantly to expand the list of rights to face up to new problems. Thus, when they set up a regional economic organization, they are obliged to move from passive rights to the granting of active rights to their inhabitants, from being given rights by law to making those rights. The EU is the clearest example of this progression. The experience there is not necessarily what it will be everywhere else, since the EU is made up entirely of states that are democratic and based on human rights. This is not the case with NAFTA, APEC, MERCOSUR (the South American free trade zone) or any other putative regional economy. However, its experience is illuminating, given the common starting point in a consumer-citizen.

The European experience

The first point to be made is that the intentions and motives of those promoting the Union of what are now 15 European nation-states with 370 million people of hundreds of ethnicities are less important to our account than are the unintended logics. The EU has grown in global significance because of its success in promoting economic and social wellbeing for the peoples of the Union. Its very success shows why there are now competing models in other parts of the world.

Its first institutional form certainly set some intentional parameters. The Council of Europe (1949) was established to oppose the negative experience of Fascist nationalism for citizens. Thus, all its members had to subscribe to democratic principles and to human rights. These were initially based on those of the UN, but the European Convention of Human Rights, and the Commission and Court set up to implement that Convention (1959), rapidly outstripped the World Court in efficacity and areas covered. The Social Charter of 1961 was notably advanced in economic and social rights. Today, the Council of Europe numbers 34 countries, and membership is a prerequisite for entry to the EU. Aspirants want to get into the latter because of the standards of living it has attained. It is this which has beaten the pretensions of national economic and social sovereignty in all except a few bastions, such as Britain.

While composed of liberal democracies, and in the majority of liberal-socialist democracies (Fabricius, 1992), what has driven European unification from the Treaty of Rome (1957) onwards has been a move to a free market in capital, goods and labour. All of these, particularly the last, have impinged on citizenship as nationals used to democratic citizenship have flowed into other countries of the EU to find work. As shown in Chapter 3, European states became multiethnic in the 20 years after the Treaty of Rome, with average foreign presences between 5–10 per cent, and much larger concentrations in certain urban areas. Since 1980, there has been a massive increase in the number of migrants from outside the Union as well. Intra-European Economic Community (EEC) migrants were, of course, guaranteed passive citizenship rights by the Rome Treaty (Meehan, 1993b; Soysal, 1994; Davidson, 1996a), but nothing more at the beginning. Regulatory political, legal and administrative institutions were, however, set up to manage the effects of the treaty.

Two processes to manage the multiethnic common market emerged. First, there was the establishment of a rule of law for market exchanges, which, despite nation-state resistance, had become paramount by 1970. Second was the increasing acquisition by citizens used to national democratic norms of the right to live under laws that they themselves made. In this second process, there emerged a European citizen whose rights in various domains overrode those of the nation-state of which he or she was originally a citizen. The first process shows that, even where politicians insist that such an economic union is no more than bilateralism or multilateralism writ large and therefore has no implications for national sovereignty, they have not been able to stop the development of overriding norms. The import of cases before the European Court of Justice (ECJ) in the 1960s has been summed up by one commentator thus:

> By contrast with ordinary international treaties, the EEC has created its own legal system which on the entry into force of the treaty, became an integral part of the legal systems of Member States and which their courts are bound to apply. By creating a Community of unlimited duration, having its own institutions, its own personality, its own legal capacity and capacity of representation on an international plane and, more particularly, real powers stemming from a limitation of sovereignty or a transfer of powers from the States to the Community, the member states have [albeit with limited areas] limited their sovereign rights and have thus created a body of law which binds their nationals and themselves. (Fontaine, 1991, pp. 9–10)

Since states were obliged to live under that new legal regime and its rule of law, they increasingly demanded an active voice. In particular, they were interested in protecting their workers, but that soon extended to the families of these workers. Some of the issues of interest to these workers were covered by decisions of the ECJ. Most of those concerning them and non-workers, as well as extra-communitarians, were covered by the European Convention of Human Rights, which saw the volume of cases balloon in the late 1980s and early 90s. This was partly because, once the domestic avenues for defending human rights were exhausted, the highest court to which an individual could turn was the European Court of Human Rights (ECHR).

There were two novelties to this avenue of redress for individuals belonging to minorities. First, both courts were always made up of non-nationals. This meant that a person who went to the ECHR was never judged by the nationals whose values he or she might be questioning. Second, it was established after a series of struggles with nation-states that opposed the trends of decision in that court, that the latter would not follow national traditions of jurisprudence (especially that of the common law). Nor would national understandings of margins of appreciation be followed, which allowed nation-states to deviate from the Convention where that was considered necessary in a democratic society. The result was a double rupture with the nationality principle, since it meant that no nation could be a judge in its own cause where an individual of a minority sought to defend a citizen right. Conscious of how much more advanced the ECHR was in the defence of human rights that are at the basis of citizenship, ethnic minorities started to go past the national institutions directly to the Council of Europe and the European Parliament, as the *sans papiers* did in 1997 in France (Gomien, 1991; Davidson, 1996c; Steiner and Alston, 1996, p. 631ff). This indicates a transition from passive to active rights, without which citizenship is only half developed.

In the process of European integration, decision makers felt the need for a popular mandate in order to justify decisions in liberal-democratic terms, so they began to promote citizenship from above. The stages of this process were:

1. The Treaty of Rome in 1957, which referred to the 'peoples' of Europe (*Europe des hommes*). It was a heavily loaded reference for men and women brought up on the Rousseauian notion of the general will and the democratic tradition of the Resistance to the totalitarian nation-state.
2. The Paris Summit of 1974, which instructed a 'working party to study the conditions and time limits within which special rights could be granted to the citizens of the nine Member States of the Community'. Since such 'special rights' were the political rights to

vote and stand in elections, the proposal started the debate about a 'citizens' Europe'.

3. This led to the Tindemann report in 1975, which insisted that Europe could only be constructed if individual wills as well as state wills were involved. While the first step was the protection of worker and consumer rights, it pointed to a more active role for citizens of Member States.

4. In 1977, the European Parliament proposed that, after 10 years' residence, all 'foreigners' from Member States should be allowed to vote and stand in all administrative elections wherever they were in the EEC.

5. The European Parliament Florence Round Table in 1978 focused on the issue of 'special rights' and a European constitution with a bill of rights. The accession of the Community to the European Convention of Human Rights was mooted. This shows the convergence of the two structures. Understanding European citizenship as a bundle of rights implies considering both as being intertwined, given overlapping membership by nation-states.

6. The first direct elections to the European Parliament on the basis of universal suffrage were held in 1979 after 22 years of the selection of members by national parliaments. However, participation in elections fell at each election after that date.

7. The Fontainebleau meeting of the European Council (composed of heads of state plus the head of the European Commission) in 1984 decided that a committee should be set up 'to adopt measures intended to strengthen and promote the identity of the Community and its image in the minds of its citizens and the world as a whole'. This became known as the Addonino Committee after its first chairperson. Its two reports were made in 1985. The second concerned the 'rights of Community citizens'. Among them we note the right to vote and stand in municipal elections for Community citizens who have resided for a specified period in another Member State of the Community, and the adoption of symbols such as a flag and an anthem to strengthen the image of the Community in the minds of citizens.

8. The Single European Act, effective in 1987, guaranteed freedom of movement to nationals of Member States within the Community. It led to the introduction of the European flag and anthem (Beethoven's *Ode to Joy* without Schiller's words) and the burgundy-coloured European passport, which allowed freer movement in the European space.

9. The next landmark was the Maastricht Treaty of 1992. After lengthy debate on the democratic deficit, or dwindling participation in European elections, European citizenship was formally established in the following terms. Article 8a(i): 'Every citizen of the Union shall have the right to move and reside freely within the territory of the Member States, subject to the limitations and the conditions laid down by this treaty and by measures adopted to give it effect. Article 8b(i): Every citizen of the Union residing in a Member State of which he is not a national shall have the right to vote and stand as a candidate in municipal elections in the Member State in which he resides, under the same conditions as nationals of that State. Article 8b(ii): 'Every citizen of the Union residing in a Member State of which he is not a national shall have the right to vote and stand as a candidate in elections to the European Parliament in the Member State in which he resides, under the same conditions as nationals of that State.' It also created an Ombudsman and adhered to the ECHR. It created a Charter of Social Rights, which the ECHR did not cover.

The first striking characteristic of this new citizenship is how it severs citizenship rights from national belonging. Already, there is a push to extend the right to vote to national elections as well as local and European elections. It thus goes further than does the multicultural citizenship of nation-states, in which there is still a residue of the old demand for national belonging. Indeed, there is a regression to that demand in many countries faced by the economic and social crises provoked by the end of protectionism. The criteria for admission to citizenship were greatly tightened in the early 1990s. European nation-states have accepted the new rule reluctantly, except for European citizens in EU elections themselves. However, given the pre-eminence of Community law, the states will have to introduce this right for all EU citizens in national domestic legislation in the near future, even if they have not done so yet.

While Europe itself still has borders and therefore excludes outsiders, often in impermissible ways (see Davidson, 1996b), this radical severance with the nationality principle indicates the emergence of a new layer of citizenship. This was inevitable in a multiethnic world where the requirement that a person belong nationally was in contradiction to democracy, as it disenfranchised too many in the population of any state. Too much exclusion spelt too much social disharmony for states not to respond to it institutionally. What concerns us are the new practices and institutions for their expression that have been created to cope with a non-national notion of belonging and the corollary of empowerment of people within the political space.

New citizen practices

There are so many complex influences operating to decide what will be done in the EU that it is essential to recall that the major effect of regional economies is to create a space for political action that is geographically enormous, involves a vastly increased number of people of a vastly increased variety, and faces totally new problems. We can identify the way in which the EU is attempting to empower its citizens to cope with this under three headings:

- subsidiarity, that is, decentralization of decision making to the smallest unit consistent with the problem which is faced;
- segmentation of rights, that is, different regimes of rights for different areas and peoples and problems within its space;
- differentiated civic educations, to complement the outcome of people working together according to the two institutionalized practices above.

Once it is recognized that there must be citizen power in a population that does not share the same collective memories (and, indeed, if it does, sees other ethnicities as the traditional enemy and oppressor), that power has to express itself actively in novel ways.

The first level at which this could be attempted is that of representative democracy, something already tried in the large nation-state. However, this immediately encounters a problem even if we leave out nation-state reluctance to allow a really democratic European Parliament to emerge. Even were the European Parliament to end the outrageous malapportionment that results from completely discrepant national electorates, in which a Luxembourgeois has many times the voting power of a German, problems of scale would still remain. With the expansion of the Union – through which it is expected that the Parliament will have over 1000 members and myriad areas of complex jurisdiction – the legislative function would be too difficult to maintain even if relative majorities and a Council that became something like an upper house did emerge (Directorate General of Research/European Parliament, 1992, p. 10).

It is this reality which partly explains the devolution of power under the subsidiarity principle. Only matters with which the Member States cannot deal will fall within the competence of the European Parliament. Since most of those states have already devolved much decision-making power to their local regions and municipalities, this adds up to more democracy in more places. Decentralization of decision making is central to citizen procedures in any regional space.

This does not in itself add up to direct democracy, but what is significant is how much attention is now paid to the use of *electronic democracy*: the use of computer networks to increase citizen participation in decision making. This allows people in what is already an alienated space, even at the lowest level – for example, in a global city – to make decisions across time and space on the matters that interest them. This refers directly to the notion of segmented rights. Only certain issues at certain times will concern the citizens of, for example, Bologna, Kassell and Glasgow. They share a procedural world but not a unified cultural one. Computers will allow them to communicate with regard to the impact of the global market on them, and to make decisions and legislate on how to meet such challenges (Bonaga, 1995, pp. 2–3).

While mocked as little as 12 years ago as electronic fantasy by advocates of more democracy in more places (Bobbio, 1984, p. 43), these projects are now well advanced and endorsed as *the* complement to subsidiarity. Once this revived Greek direct democracy is implemented on a wider basis than at present, the traditional procedures of representative democracy will themselves change. This does not mean that they will disappear at any level from place of production to the European Parliament. Nor is this envisaged. Yet returning the right to legislate in a city to its citizens linked by computer as well as other media means 'Discussion groups in a network... without a hierarchy... to pinpoint and develop civic issues and invite views, make suggestions and forward proposals to the deaf and lifeless authorities'. This could fundamentally change legislative and administrative rules about what, when and where matters needed attention (Bonaga, 1995, pp. 2–3). It might help to end the domination of administrative expertise. The role of parties and the existing political hierarchies as politics, returned to the people, could become issue based (Rodota, 1993).

Overall, the principle of devolving democratic decision making to the base level was intended not only to allow decisions to be taken as close to the problem as possible, but also to return what immediately concerned them to minorities. In nearly all cases, the regional and communal areas of different European countries corresponded with ethnic, religious and other minorities. This would supposedly overcome the danger of majorities without an understanding of local culture or problems taking inappropriate decisions. Within the relative majority of a minority, an individual who felt discriminated against could use the Convention on Human Rights as protection, since this allowed him or her to appeal beyond the local majority, so to speak, outside its cultural community.

In sum, decentralization and local democracy were expected to protect group rights to some extent (see Delemotte *et al.*, 1996, for how this applies to extra-communitarians in France). However, the European experience also showed that the extension of civil and political rights to non-nationals at local or regional level could provoke nasty consequences if not accompanied by relative economic and social equality. This was made clear in particular by the *Lega Nord* of Italy, who, enjoying regional power to express themselves culturally as *Padania*, then excluded Southerners and adopted racist attitudes towards non-communitarians. Their progress towards such aggressive and socially dysfunctional views started out from the simple but deceptive fact that the North was richer than the South, coupled with the inference that this was explained by cultural characteristics specific to the North (Ruzza and Schmidtke, 1996).

Since there are enormous discrepancies in wealth per capita in different European regions, and even more so between the worst-off EU regions and all Eastern European countries aspiring to membership, a liberal-socialist policy of redistributing wealth to the more backward regions has been emphasized. The alternative is to shift old national racism to a new local level, as is clear in most European countries. The extreme has been reached in the policy of insisting that Eastern European countries reach a certain minimum economic viability before admission to the EU. In a regional economy, such differences will have to be minimized to avoid conflict – a social welfare approach is therefore imperative.

This brings us to the innovation of segmented or differential rights. Except for civil and political rights, which must always be equal to meet the requirement of democracy, segmented or differential rights have always been an essential feature of citizenship in a nation-state. This is because affirmative action in the economic, social, educational and health realms is required to create the neo-Kantian individual participant in the democratic process of the debate and vote on the collective good. The EU continues this. However, segmented civil and political rights are a novelty that it introduces by creating what in

French terms would be regarded as second-class citizens. Maastricht creates citizens who can only vote in local and European elections if they are residents but not nationals of the state in which they live. They thus have civil and political rights different from those of nationals. This has provoked moves to extend the rights of Section 8 of the Maastricht Treaty to cover national elections, which would end national sovereignty as it has been understood since the French Revolution.

One solution has been to define local government as something that is not part of national sovereignty, and therefore to accept the right to vote locally while maintaining that it does not affect the claim to national sovereignty. However, once that principle is accepted, it opens the gates to claims by non-EU residents to vote locally. As was pointed out in Chapter 5, this has been generally accepted in some European countries and applied locally in others (Delemotte *et al.*, 1996, pp. 45–52). Countries of the *ius sanguinis*, in judgments that highlight its reactionary quality in a globalizing world, refuse to consider this. The German Constitutional Court in 1990 refused to allow foreigners to vote in local elections, while recognizing that this was undemocratic. The French, after considering that it was allowed even for non-EU citizens in the Netherlands, and in Scandinavian countries that had not joined the EU, gave up the proposal to allow it. The best argument they could mount for disenfranchising significant parts of the population was that allowing the vote only at local level created second-class citizens (Bernard, 1993, p. 85).

But, even when the nationalist resistance is noted, segmented political rights cannot as a practice be avoided in the new multicultural society of the EU. To manage the complex, mainly urban, worlds of the multiethnic workforces, all states have had to admit non-nationals to administrative bodies dealing with rents, social security and so on. They have long sat on neighbourhood councils, even in Germany. What unites the members of such bodies – as is the case for municipal councils themselves – are issue-related matters rather than a basic commitment to the same set of cultural values or the nation. The motive in a nation-state is supposed to work in the other direction: from commitment to the nation back to common, day-to-day civic issues. So in yet another way, the rights of the citizen are becoming segmented. It is much easier to see how the proposed local and electronic democracies would work when they concern only local and extempore issues.

As this suggests, regional citizenship is very much interest based, eminently procedural and, for that reason, thin, where nation-state citizenship was thick in its expectation of commitment not to segmented, issue-based activity but to a unifying principle of common identity. In proposals to extend local government rights to foreigners from non-EU countries, the Council of Europe argued in such terms, and not primarily in those of belonging and civic commitment. Starting from the principle that multiethnicity was a fact, the Convention on the Participation of Foreigners in Public Life at Local Level (1992) advised all governments to set up bodies ensuring links between themselves and lawful foreign residents:

> to provide a forum for the discussion and formulation of the opinions, wishes and concerns of foreign residents on matters which particularly affect them in relation to local public life, including the activities and responsibilities of the local authority concerned, and... to foster their general integration into the community.

After five years of residence, they should be allowed to vote and stand in local elections.

It is clear from the extreme-right hostility to such proposals, and its readiness to challenge such moves even legally, that the fear of the old majority is that such newcomers – who could well control, for example, Kreuzberg in Berlin – are taking away the old national majority power. Yet since they could only do so as a coalition and as people with dual or multiple loyalties, it could not be for the benefit of another nationality. Rather, its real offence is that it cannot build civic commitment to the nation. It is required for management purposes whatever the position any state takes about nationality. Indeed, managing the public housing of Lille implies nothing about France, or Algeria, or Mali. In this sense, it heightens the need for civic commitments of a new sort. This is a third characteristic of regional economies: the development of civic educations, with the emphasis on the plural. We will discuss this in Chapter 9.

Conclusion

The European experience shows not only that rights grow in number in a regional economy, but also that the trickle-down logic of a purely economic approach such as that of Ohmae (see Chapter 1) and the cultural civilization patrimony theories we associate with Fukuyama and Huntington (Huntington, 1993; Fukuyama, 1995) are inadequate. Indeed, the notion of history as a patrimony to which the present is at least beholden is directly challenged. It is instead something that is made by social being, and all depends on how it is made.

That feeling of belonging that is at the source of civic virtue is understood as something consciously forged together rather than as an inheritance that is inescapable. This too is something that goes back to the French Revolution and the 'open republic', but it is understood as a never-closed entry of new voices into the debate speaking in their own idioms. It is implicitly in favour of porous frontiers between cultures or civilizations. A unity that is constructed in mutual respect and tolerance for difference is, of course, contractual, and the EU is the place for the new social contract, at multiple levels. It is also therefore a place of struggle and contestation, particularly against difference as past history. It is a refusal of determinism and in favour of agency, a place where unity is built on respect not for our dead but for the life of future generations.

Critics can still point to the limitations of the borders of Europe, and the increasing exclusion there of refugees produced precisely as a consequence of globalization's negative effects. Yet it is important to remember that even Europe is more porous than its caricature. Just as Germany retreats from welcoming all, the Italian Supreme Court allows outsiders who have entered to go free and then enter other European countries on the grounds that it is constitutionally wrong to deny them their liberty.

Moreover, the decline of national sovereignty is highlighted by this innovation. Each EU Member State depends on the next to secure its borders against the outside. A people no longer owns its territory according to the property criterion of the capacity to exclude. It cannot keep itself 'pure' even if it wishes to do so. No longer is it formally the final arbiter of its destinies or of those of others who enter. Their rights are governed by regional rules enforced by the ECJ, the ECHR and the vote.

Yet, if we can learn more from the practical achievements in Europe than from armchair post-modernists or prophets of doom who see an inevitable clash of civilizations preventing the attainment of democracy and human rights on a global scale, we must be cautious about assuming that European practices will emerge elsewhere. The logics should be the same for NAFTA, APEC and MERCOSUR. The regional consumer-citizen leads to regulation in his or her marketplace: a supranational rule of law. This in turn poses the issue of whose law it is to be. Must it be controlled from below by an active global citizen? European countries already committed to democracy and human rights logi-

cally faced that dilemma in a particular way. There had to be an active
European citizen, and this led to the innovations in citizen practices
described above.

In countries of Confucian and other Asian traditions, however, the
resistance to those logics will be stronger, as was evident even in the
refusal to accept the social clause in World Trade Organization meetings in Singapore in December 1996. There, as the writings of
Malaysian Prime Minister Mahathir make clear, a European solution is
itself seen as culturally specific and has been challenged widely in
Asia, where the bulk of the world's population lives. We discuss Asian
developments in the next chapter.

The struggle for even a regional citizen will thus be great. The EU
has only been a success because of its social welfare principles. If those
are not attainable elsewhere, misery will be the outcome of globalization for much of the world. If a Singapore solution is accepted on the
grounds that the new risk society cannot be controlled (that is, that all
the multiple new social contracts together will not add up to a new form
of order), chaos or a revolutionary situation could also be the outcome.

Notes

1. Except Israel, which is, however, a special case since admission is based
   on Jewish origins.
2. 'Anglo-Celtic' is a term used in Australia to denote the dominant group,
   with its mixture of English, Welsh, Scottish and Irish ethnic origins.
   However, within this hybrid group, identities often diverge. For example,
   conflicts between the English and Irish have been of great historical
   importance in Australia.

8

Globalization and Citizenship in the Asia-Pacific Region

It has been made dramatically clear in earlier chapters that citizenship, if it is equated with the development of democracy and human rights, is primarily a western notion. Globalization affects the whole world, albeit unevenly. This chapter attempts a preliminary discussion of the evolution of both globalization and citizenship in one part of the non-western world: the Asia-Pacific region. This region is chosen as an example because of its size and its significant role in current globalization processes. The discussion will, we hope, suggest how enormous and culturally specific the problems of various world regions are where citizenship is concerned. Any project that attempts to extend citizenship to the global realm to cope with the new global problems faces a mammoth task. Indeed, as the final chapter of this book will discuss, conditions in many areas are so chaotic that it is not even possible to think in terms of democratic citizenship, since functioning states and the rule of law are virtually absent.

Globalization and migration in the Asia-Pacific region

When we leave the minority of peoples of mainly European culture, who comprise only a dwindling 20 per cent of the global population, our account of becoming a citizen in a globalizing world changes radically. This is first of all because globalization takes on a quite different form among the 50 per cent of the world who live in the Asia-Pacific region. The Asian area had known extraordinary growth in per capita income in the 1980s, outstripping many Organization for Economic Co-operation and Development countries, while the rest of the world had fallen radically behind. One journalist's summation is that: 'Asia was once the center of the world, and now the center is again returning to Asia.... The modernization of Asia – economically, politically and culturally – is by far the most important event taking place in the world today' (Naisbitt, 1997, pp. 16–18).

Whatever reservations we might have about a renewed centre/periphery theory of this sort, we must nevertheless concede that it is in Asia that the biggest populations and markets exist, and where the greatest trade, investment and migrations of the next half century can be expected. Asia already outstrips most other regions in all those figures. Moreover, if we look at the power-houses driving the globalization processes, we see that they are not only found in the 'white' world, but are also heavily concentrated in Asia. Of the three 'global cities' where most of the important information and financial transactions take place, Tokyo is at least as important as New York and London (Sassen, 1991, 1994). The role of the four tiger economies – Hong Kong, Taiwan, Singapore and South Korea – is also extraordinary. Yet more significant is the emergence of China, where a quarter of the world's population lives, and whose markets are crucial to the growth of a global economy. In the 1980s and 90s, growth rates have been phenomenal, almost twice those in OECD countries.

Thus, Naisbitt is probably correct when he claims that the west needs Asia economically much more than the converse. Treated as part of the global economy, it is also correct to think of Asia as a whole, rather than of the separate countries that make up Asia, as there are some common patterns between the dynamos that are driving its development. Basic to these patterns is an awareness that, until the 1997–99 crisis, Asia was an economic success when Europe and the USA with their 'white' outposts were flagging economically. The other regions of the world are disaster zones. Asians are aware that the number of people living in poverty in the region was reduced from 400 to 180 million during the region's drive to prosperity, without either democracy or social welfare. Emblematic of such feelings are these lines from Singapore's Prime Minister, Goh Chok Tong:

> Singaporeans today enjoy full employment and high economic growth, and low divorce, illegitimacy and crime rates. You may think decline is unimaginable. But societies can go wrong quickly. US and British societies have changed profoundly in the last 30 years. Up to the early 60s they were disciplined, conservative, with the family very much the pillar of their societies. Since then both the

US and Britain have seen a sharp rise in broken families, teenage mothers, illegitimate children, juvenile delinquency, vandalism and violent crime. (cited in Sheridan, 1995, p. 138)

He went on to warn Asia against imitating the west – societies that – like the USSR – had 'imploded'. He insisted that if Singaporeans thought for themselves, they would stay away from policies that had brought a plague of social and economic problems to those countries (Sheridan, 1995, p. 138). What needs to be noted here is the belief that Asian economic success is owed to the different cultural characteristics of Asian societies, notably their rejection of western policies.

Goh Chok Tong would certainly admit that the rapid Asian development, particularly in China, which he extolled, was uneven. Even figures provided by the most sanguine prophets of the Asian miracle show that with an overall increased gross national product went enormous discrepancies in wealth, as between regions and between countries (Ohmae, 1995, p. 82). In Shenzen, the main Chinese global development area, per capita income reached US$5695 when the Chinese average was US$317. Moreover, the massive development was accompanied by huge unemployment: official unemployment figures for China reached 30 million, while unofficial figures suggested as many as 100 million.

The effect of such economic discrepancies has been massive legal and illegal migration from poorer to richer regions, above all to boom cities. In China, this has been mainly internal migration because of the size of the country. Similarly, the *transmigrasi* programme in Indonesia involved relocating 6.5 million Javanese to other islands, giving rise to ethnic tensions that were to break out violently in East Timor, Kalimantan and Irian Jaya during the Asian crisis.

Elsewhere migration has been international. As we discussed in Chapter 3, millions of labour migrants have left Asia since the 1970s in search of a livelihood, with destinations ranging from the USA to the Gulf oil states. Millions more have migrated as workers within Asia. They do the '3-D jobs' (dirty, difficult and dangerous) in Japan, the tiger economies, Malaysia and Thailand. Some areas, such as South Asia, the Philippines, Indonesia and China, are becoming labour reserves for the faster-growing economies. A large number of women have migrated as domestic workers, entertainers or sex workers. There are also flows of highly qualified workers in both directions between highly developed and less-developed economies.

Large-scale refugee movements have also taken place. The exoduses from war-torn Indochina and Afghanistan were among the largest forced migrations in history, and have had an enduring legacy of displacement and resettlement. There have been many smaller movements: for example, a large proportion of the majority Indian population of Fiji has been forced out since 1987, and many refugees from Burma are to be found in Thailand and Bangladesh. The potential for ethnic conflicts and political upheavals in Indonesia and other countries gives rise to fears of new exoduses in the region.

This movement of the poor in search of better conditions in the global society would be unremarkable were there not one peculiarity to the region: its long history of migration. The Chinese diaspora stretching down the Malay peninsula is the biggest and richest in history (Naisbitt, 1997, p. 19). Malays traded with Australian Aborigines before Europeans knew that Australia existed. For centuries, merchants, fishermen and other travellers circulated in the maritime world of what is today Indonesia, Malaysia and the Philippines. Languages stretch across oceans covered in mythical epic voyages. Today, indigenous people from Hawaii, the Cook Islands, the Marquesas and New Zealand share the Maori language, and if you know *Bahasa Indonesia* you are at home in many countries. This millennially old multiethnic context was further fostered by the imperial powers when they arrived, as they imported labour careless of traditional lines of division. The Indians in Fiji soon outnumbered the ethnic Fijians; Malaysia was soon full of Chinese and Indians; Indochinese and Japanese worked in French and American colonies throughout the Pacific.

While global migration can be linked to past patterns in South East Asia and the Pacific, it is, however, a completely new experience in North East Asia. The result for citizenship is extraordinarily important, and in fact shifts the debate about citizenship into the region as much as it shifts the focus in the global economy. North East Asia comprises states that are unusually ethnically homogeneous compared with practically any other country in the world: Japan: 99 per cent Japanese; Hong Kong: 98 per cent Han Chinese; South Korea: 99 per cent Korean; China: 93 per cent Han Chinese (Bradshaw and Wallace, 1996, p. 95). As these figures show, Asia's leading states in globalization are ethnically homogeneous to a high degree. They are facing the influx of foreign labour from different 'civilizations' or ethnic groups on a large scale, labour that they cannot do without. It is visible in the large numbers of Filipinas, Bangladeshis or Indonesians at any of their airports.

When the leaders and the people of such states feel, like Goh Chok Tong, that their wellbeing is a product of a particular Asian culture, they understand that assertion even more radically than he did.

Culture

Asian (and indeed Pacific) leaders' statements that the wellbeing of their populaces rests on the adoption of the 'Asian' model, and that a rejection of the policies of the West explains economic success, means a defence of certain claimed cultural characteristics. These are often labelled 'Confucian' but are also, apparently, 'Islamic' and sometimes even animist (Mahathir, 1993; Chan, 1996, p. 6). We will go into the implications of these different positions later. Here we wish only to focus on what seems essential for understanding citizenship in the Asia-Pacific region. Goh Chok Tong hinted at it this way:

> We intend to reinforce the strength of the family. The Government will channel rights and benefits and privileges through the head of the family so that he can enforce the obligations and responsibilities of family members. We will frame legislation and administrative rules towards this objective. (cited in Sheridan, 1995, p. 138)

As this suggests, the family is very important in the Asia-Pacific region. Through it, and not through a system of social welfare, the state informed by 'Confucian' values claimed that it would cope with the problem of those left out by the drive to prosperity. The debate over the applicability of western values to Asia apparently centres on whether a social safety net is required to protect those who do not share in the general prosperity. On a first inquiry, Asians are justified in querying whether more than a helpful family is needed as a protective shield. The figures show that the distribution of income in Asian countries is now just as good as in the USA. Indeed, Japan has long been better than any European country in that regard (Bradshaw and Wallace, 1996, pp. 101, 105). How far reliance on the family will continue depends on the continuation of the extended or clan family in the region, a social institution that is in many places collapsing under modernity. Indeed, one reaction to the mass unemployment and impoverishment of urban workers during the 1997–99 Asian crisis has been a call for the establishment of social safety nets by the states.

Reliance on the family may, however, be sustained by the very ethnic homogeneity of some states, which encourages a blood familial notion of the nation itself. In such places, there is a further effect for citizen-ship: a profound attachment to the land or territorial space itself, as if it were not separate from the families and clans who draw sustenance from it. This attachment can be most clearly seen in the Aboriginal rela-tion to the land in Australia, New Zealand, Fiji, Vanuatu and the Pacific generally (Saussol, 1979; Boengkih, 1997; Davidson, 1997, Chapter 6; Spoonley, 1997). However, it can also be seen in many Asian societies, particularly among their indigenous minorities. Thus, Suzuki and Oiwa (1996, pp. 71–91, 209) remind us that it is fundamental to Shintoism, albeit today mainly adhered to by people such as the Ainu and Okinawans faced by a determinedly modernizing and assimilationist Japanese state. Land or territory conceived in this fashion can never be alienated: the people and the land are understood as one.

This again has profound repercussions on how someone can become a national in such places. Obtaining nationality is a formal preliminary act to exercising most citizen rights today.

Becoming a national

We can divide the nation-states of the Asia-Pacific region into two groups when addressing ways of becoming a national. The first group of states are those which formerly belonged to one or other of the European empires. The second are those which remained formally autonomous. In the first group, we find Australia and New Zealand, South Asia, Indochina, all the states in the Malay peninsula, Indonesia and practically all Pacific islands. In the second, we find China, Japan, Korea, Taiwan and Thailand. In the first group, the state borders were defined by the imperial power, while in the second, those borders were established in the process of an internal historical evolution.

Colonized countries typically had weak borders that were highly porous, while the second group were hermetically closed to outsiders for the four centuries up to about 1850. The result was a high degree of multiethnicity and a strong outward-looking quality within former imperial possessions, compared with a remarkable ethnic homogeneity coupled with an inward-looking quality in the non-imperial states.

The readiness of the imperial powers to encourage the importation of foreign labour, usually to guarantee economic profitability, was often grafted onto a pre-existing openness. This was especially so in the Pacific islands, where there had been no state in the western sense (Brown and Shue, 1969, pp. 15–37; Sack and Minchin, 1985) and there had been a millennially old migration of other ethnicities seeking solutions to overpopulation. Thus, the Fiji Islands are basically Melanesian west of Lau and Polynesian in the east, and Tongans from the North provided a large proportion of the *matai* or skilled workers long before cession in 1874. Again, the epic voyage of the great canoes from Hawaii and the Cook Islands to New Zealand meant the spread of a Maori culture way beyond any embryonic Polynesian state.

Conversely, the closed nature of the second set of states was legendary. Highly centralized, and in the sixteenth century still recognized as being more powerful and advanced than European states by the Europeans themselves, they rejected or limited drastically any intrusion of Europeans (or indeed other Asians) into their societies (Morris-Suzuki, 1996).

Former imperial possessions

In their colonies, the imperial power usually introduced the nationality rules that existed for its own subjects. Thus, throughout the British and American empires, *ius soli* rule became law, while in French and Dutch possessions that cross between *ius soli* and a modified *ius sanguinis* typically expressed in the 1889 French law on nationalities was established. This remains the case in Hawaii and the French Overseas Departments and Territories (DOM-TOM), which in one of the bizarre twists of history have been deemed part of the USA or France. Today, their constitutions and citizenship laws are those of metropole (Pacific Constitutions, 1991, Chapter 4).

Basically, a foreigner can only become French (New Caledonian) after five years' residence, when he or she speaks French as proof of belonging (*insertion professionnelle et linguistique*), is of good character, and is up to date on payment of taxes. If a foreigner marries a French citizen, nationality can be obtained after two years. A French citizen of a DOM-TOM automatically has the rights of European citizenship under the Maastricht Treaty. Similarly, a person can become a US citizen in Hawaii and other US possessions if that person is born there or has resided there for five years, has passed a test on the US constitution and the history and government of the US, and has taken an oath of allegiance to the US (Civitas, 1994, p. 35).

Apart from such places, where what applies in the metropole applies in the Pacific, there are now independent nation-states where a *ius soli* applies and it is formally very easy for a foreigner to obtain nationality. All are multiethnic, with both indigenous minorities and a large population of foreign labour; these are Australia, New Zealand, India, Singapore and the Philippines (see Pacific Constitutions, 1991, Section I; Constitution of India, Section II; Constitution of Singapore; Hill and Fee, 1995, pp. 41, 55; Hassall, 1999). In Australia, there is only a 2-year wait for naturalization, whereas in Singapore, it is 10 years. On the other hand, the language requirements in both places are very easy to meet. In New Zealand, obtaining citizenship is automatic for Cook and Niue islanders, and Samoans are also privileged (Aikman, 1982, p. 87; Quentin-Baxter, 1982, p. 97).

Such states may be regarded as highly progressive in the porousness of their citizenship rules, and are clearly distinguishable from those former colonies which have reversed the European rules in the direction of a racist *ius sanguinis* approach. This usually masquerades under the slogan of the defence of a local culture. Since the latter are all multiethnic, this means a suppression of minorities in favour of a majority culture. Among them we can number Malaysia, Indonesia and the two biggest Pacific nations – Papua New Guinea and Fiji. In all cases, it is extremely difficult for foreigners to obtain nationality.

In the case of Malaysia, the rule is that only those whose fathers are citizens can automatically be Malaysian citizens. There is also an openly pro-ethnic Malay section of the constitution masquerading as 'affirmative action'. Given the openly racist policy of the state around a supposedly Islamic principle, it is very difficult to meet requirements for citizenship. The British determination to protect ethnic Malays from Chinese settler dominance had meant a strong exclusionary intent that went back to at least 1948 (Lau, 1992).

Similarly, in the formerly Dutch multiethnic state of Indonesia, the adoption of *ius sanguinis* meant that foreigners had, and still have, great difficulty in becoming Indonesians if they were not within, or descendants of those within, Indonesia at independence. Where Singapore was born from the Malay rejection/expulsion of a predominantly Chinese area from within a federation, so post-1966 Indonesia was built on the slaughter of the Chinese minority. Today, despite the legacy of Dutch law, it is practically incomprehensible to the Indonesian state that a foreigner could become an Indonesian national. Being an Indonesian is built around such a complex of loyalties with an ethno-religious base that it is impossible to become Indonesian, even with name and religious and cultural change, as the remaining ethnic Chinese know. Article 26 of the Indonesian constitution certainly allows 'persons of other nations' to become citizens, but the emphasis has always been on being a 'native Indonesian person'.

When we enter the Pacific, the same tensions are also clear. In the largest Pacific state, Papua New Guinea, the law makes only the children of citizens automatically citizens, and while naturalization is possible after eight years' residence (s67(1) of the constitution), there is an exclusionary quality to the requirement that the vernacular of the country be spoken and that they have a respect for the customs and cultures of the country (Hassall and Singin, 1999, p. 106). The evidence of the case-by-case admission by local Citizen Advisory Committee, which is really unaccountable, has been summed up as extremely exclusionary (Hassall, 1999). Indeed, the strong attachment to the land led to a nearly racist attitude towards immigrants seeking citizenship, summed up in parliament in these words of 1992: 'If the government is genuine, we should not allow foreigners to become citizens of our country. We must send them back to where they came from... God created this country for me and my grandchildren, not foreigners' (Hassall and Singin, 1999, p. 116). Only 2000 people had naturalized by 1988.

Similarly, the Fiji constitution appears to make naturalization even easier, although it too limits citizenship, by birth, to the children of citizens. It does not require a knowledge of Fijian, but it too offsets the easy five years' residency requirement with a demand that 'he has been assimilated into the way of the life of the people of Fiji' (Article 27(2)d). This Fijian way, while most probably an invention of élite groups (Lawson, 1993), and a hybrid product of the local and imperial experience, is clearly exclusionary and racist when it becomes political practice (Lal, 1992, p. 98 *et passim*). Again, the main problem for inclusionary politics is the relationship with the land, *vanua*, which has almost sacred status (Bole, 1992, p. 76). Yet this feeling again leads to a blood/kin notion of Fijian nationality. How strong this could become was clear when a chiefly woman, Adi Samanunu, was divested of her nationality because she also held a British passport of convenience (Rashid, 1995, pp. 12–13). It is notable that all the countries discussed here prohibit dual nationality, while it is increasingly accepted in Europe and North America.

Asian economic giants

Throughout the Asia-Pacific region, the tendency towards a modified *ius sanguinis* is clear, even if the starting point was a more open policy. The significance of the choice of that nationality rule becomes fully clear when we situate it in the context of the Asian economic giants. As many of these countries are to an astonishing degree ethnically homogeneous, and none derive their systems directly from a colonial past, they bring an entirely different meaning to our discussion. Japan, China, two of the tigers (South Korea and Taiwan), Vietnam, Burma and other major emerging economies all adopt what appears to be a *ius sanguinis* rule.

It is extremely rare for anyone who is not regarded as being blood kin ever to become a national in such countries. Indeed, while all include indigenous minorities, these are still forced to assimilate in as brutal a way as that of Europe 200 years ago. More shocking still is the fact that it is a widely held belief that foreigners can never assimilate properly. As Yoshino writes: 'The Japanese subconsciously perceive themselves as a distinct "racial" community... Belief in the "immutable" quality of Japanese people is just as important as belief in distinctive Japanese culture in Japanese perceptions of their national identity' (Yoshino, 1997, p. 3; see also Yoshino, 1992).

Where the nation is a family and the latter is a genetic notion, it is not surprising that no foreigners, no matter how long they reside in Japan, can become nationals. The first (1899) Japanese Citizenship Law was based on German law and still retains the governing 'blood' notion of the latter. Morris-Suzuki points out that this made it so difficult to become a Japanese national that in 1900–59 only 298 foreigners became Japanese nationals (Morris-Suzuki, 1996, p. 13). Extremely restrictive immigration laws also applied. Nevertheless, a substantial Korean-origin population was established in Japan. Their treatment is emblematic of future problems. They constituted nearly 50 per cent (676 793) of all registered foreigners in 1994, and are treated as aliens no matter how many previous generations have lived in Japan.

Similar constitutional rules apply in China, Korea and Vietnam. Indeed, in the latter, the word 'compatriot' means kinship (Tran Van Binh, 1997, p. 2) in a genetic sense. In China, naturalization is really limited by Article 7 of the Nationality Law (1980) to descendants of ethnic Chinese. Only 70–80 people who are not covered by the *ius sanguinis* obtain Chinese nationality every year (Li Buyun and Wu Yuzhang, 1999). Once again, there is a prohibition on dual nationality (Article 3), which means that ex-Hong Kong citizens' use of British or other passports is regarded as no more than a convenience for travelling on business. The relative ease with which ethnic Chinese can regain Chinese nationality makes its *ius sanguinis* rule appear very strong. Indeed, the huge Chinese diaspora in the region explains – as in the case of Singapore – why such states are insistently nationalist *vis-à-vis* China's claims to represent a 'mother-land'. The dangerous irredentist implications of such a rule of nationality are very clear to the Taiwanese.

In China, Korea and, in fact, Japan, this 'blood' is assumed to pass only through the father, so nationality by descent can only be obtained if one's father was a national. In Japan, foreign brides even have difficulty obtaining residency permits for long periods. The anomaly of a Japanese mother with a foreign child exists (Moriki, 1996). While this was also possible in France under the late Pasqua and Debre laws, it was considered outrageous there.

The choice of ethnic nationalism and the *ius sanguinis* by the major powers poses fundamental problems for a global future in which there will be a high proportion of denizens, especially in growth areas. Where in Europe, and increasingly in North America, this has meant a decline in national sovereignty and increasingly easy access to citizenship over the past 50 years, there is little sign of a corresponding trend in the Asia-Pacific region.

Being a citizen

We have made it clear that it is very difficult for aliens to obtain nationality in any East and South-Asian or Pacific country, and certainly in the power houses of globalization. This is because of the strongly ethnic basis of nationality laws in most countries. Even in Indonesia (Constitution, Art 26 (1)), which appears to allow fairly easy citizenship for some ethnic groups (Dutch, Chinese and Arabs, who had been residents for centuries), the reality is that it is better to change both name and religion if one wants acceptance. In many Asian countries, discrimination borders on racism, especially if we accept Memmi's famous minimalist definition: 'racism is the use of difference to make profit' (Memmi, 1994, p. 14).

Overall, such exclusive 'nationalism' would make effective citizenship in the world of global migration almost impossible to attain for millions of foreign workers and denizens in Asia. To date, foreign workforces, while growing rapidly, are still small compared with those in western countries. The main problem is not yet that of a blood notion of nationality – but it probably will be in the future. Attempts such as that of Japan to find new workers among Latin-Americans of Japanese origin (15 per cent of Latin-American Japanese have already returned to Japan) cannot square the circle of dangerously exclusive nationality laws (Goodman and Peng, 1996, pp. 214–15).

It is the combination of exclusionary rules with the absence of citizen rights in Asia and the Pacific that really renders the notion of the citizen problematic in the region that is expected to be dominant in the world in the twenty-first century (Naisbitt, 1997, p. 10). Except for Japan, the Philippines and arguably the Republic of Korea and Thailand, none of the countries of the region is a democracy, and the three last are recent additions to the list. Moreover, not only do some refuse the notion of human rights explicitly, but also the records in that area are often appalling. It is important, in the face of books allowing statistical and structural claims to democracy to be decisive on the ground that there is never a pure democracy, and that indicators of its development can be identified and measured, to insist, when discussing citizenship, on the formally non-democratic nature of all these polities.

Typical of such books is Vanhanen's *Prospects of Democracy: A Study of 172 Countries* (Vanhanen, 1997). While it allows space for a criticism of its statistical approach, it mostly ignores the sort of approach essential to substantial citizenship – an understanding of the cultures into which terms such as 'vote' and 'democracy' are inserted. For example, Samoan contains neither word. More significantly, the word *shimi,* used *mutatis mutandis* in many major Asian countries for 'citizen', really only means town-dweller (Morris-Suzuki, 1996; Henderson, 1997, pp. 334ff). If citizenship is not understood as a combination of democracy and human rights – as we have defined it – it is useless. To deny rights on the grounds of cultural difference, as is the official position in China and most of the Muslim world (Conac and Amor, 1994), can only render people unfree. The poor record of Asian and Pacific countries is revealed in the Human Freedom Index, an international comparative classification that uses 40 indicators to compare access to a range of basic rights and freedoms. It is worth noting that almost all Western European countries rate higher than Australia and New Zealand on the Index (de Jonge, 1994, p. 564):

New Zealand	36	Thailand	14
Australia	33	Singapore	11
Japan	32	Malaysia	9
Papua New Guinea	30	Indonesia	5
Hong Kong	26	Vietnam	5
Republic of Korea	14	China	2

Almost certainly, Hong Kong, Papua New Guinea and Australia's positions have deteriorated since the table was compiled in 1991.

North East Asia

Japan stands out as the only longstanding Asian democracy. It meets all the criteria for a minimalist procedural democracy (Bobbio, 1984). There is full adult suffrage, a real choice between parties, a responsible government system and a rule of law. Japan subscribes to all the major United Nations (UN) conventions on human rights except those on racial discrimination and torture, and the constitution guarantees all significant civil and political human rights (UNDP, 1996, p. 215). It has established one of the two most egalitarian capitalist societies, in which disparities between income are the least in the developed world, and employment is guaranteed for life for most people (Bradshaw and Wallace, 1996, pp. 101–2). This makes it atypical in Asia.

A whole string of cases establish the basic principle of 'one vote, one value' in Japan, while allowing reasonable practical departures from such equality (Beer and Itoh, 1995, Chapter 6). While the superior courts defer to legislative and popular sovereignty, and are sometimes accused of being too servile, overall they ensure a rule of law that makes Japan one of the least insecure societies in the world.

While Japan has been extraordinarily prosperous, and its familial and private system of social support has worked up to the 1990s, the absence of the welfare state has not prevented a lively civil and political life with freedom of debate and participation at many levels of society and politics. It is, however, a country run like a company and with millennial traditions of respect for authority and the male. The former means that state-funded social and economic rights have not existed in a significant sense. State social welfare was gradually introduced after 1973 (after a few innovations in the immediate postwar period). It was made up of piecemeal borrowings from the west, and designed to maintain national homogeneity. Indexed pensions and free medical care for the aged were the most important novelties. In the 1980s, there were cutbacks to such welfare, without much opposition. Goodman and Peng write:

> This may be partly because the government has been very effective in raising public awareness about the aging society and the potential costs this will entail. Also, the idea of developing a Western-style welfare state was actually around only a fairly short period of time and perhaps never took root... it is also due to the way in which the state has fostered the social stigma that many Japanese still attach to statutory social assistance. (Goodman and Peng, 1996, p. 204)

The main problem for democratic citizenship in Japan arises from the definition of people within the cultural norms of the *nihonjinron*. The near-racist ethnic definition of nationalism based on Confucian and Shinto traditions politicized by leading groups has affected both politics and the legal system itself. Apart from foreigners, women and *burakumin* (traditional outcast groups) face structural discrimination. There is practically no space for non-conformity *vis-à-vis* the state.

To illustrate the way in which such attitudes impact on the understanding of individual rights to equality in the law, we refer to the judgments in the Aizawa patricide case, in which a young woman was tried for the murder of her father who raped her over many years. At issue was the constitutionality of Art. 200 of the Criminal Code, which stated: 'A person who kills his or her own ascendant or his or her spouse's lineal ascendant shall be punished with death or imprisonment for life at forced labour.' Other killings attracted lesser penalties. Its constitutionality was upheld, but the punishment it imposed was seen as unreasonably severe, and the lightest sentence for other killings – three years and six months' hard labour – was all that was imposed. The majority decision was that 'there naturally exists a certain order' in a family based on age:

> It must be admitted that respect and gratitude towards ascendants are basic to the morality of social life, and that the maintenance of such spontaneous affection and universal ethics deserves protection in criminal law... the killing of an ascendant [is] generally deserving of more severe social and moral denunciation than an ordinary homicide...

While several judges disagreed with the majority acceptance that past familial standards should be maintained, one made clear the connections in these words:

> 'Filial piety' in Confucianism did not regard the child as an independent entity. There, the relationship between parents and children was governed by the rule of authority and subordination, in contrast to relationships between independent personalities. The difference between '*son* (respect)' and '*hi* (disrespect)'... existed eternally, and observance of the unbreakable status order was an absolute demand. In a word, filial piety is a morality calling for children to obey their parents like slaves. Confucianism teaches that the favour of parents is higher than a mountain and deeper than the sea. To devote oneself with the fidelity of infinite and boundless service, to adore and obey them, and to serve them by denying oneself are the substance of Confucian filial piety. In its pure form, it requires that children should keep the attitude of children even when parents do not maintain the attitude of parents... Few words are needed to note that a filial piety which demands such a blind and absolute obedience is repug-

nant to contemporary common sense and is not compatible with democratic ethics based on individual dignity and equality. (cited in Beer and Itoh, 1995, pp. 160–3)

We would like to highlight that the state application of Confucianism did not mean the shutting down of a vigorous dissent in the courts. Nevertheless, the rigid patriarchal system means a systematic denial of women's rights. While Japan is listed as having the third highest average per capita income in the world, and the equality of distribution is matched only by Sweden, women fare badly on both measures of gender equality used by the UNDP. Japan is located 37th where gender empowerment criteria are concerned. China is conversely 29th, being 66th on the human development index (HDI) scale, on which Japan is in third place (UNDP, 1996, pp. 33–5). Women are thus significantly inferior where the economic and social requirements for citizenship are required, and are in fact excluded from office to an excessive extent.

In Japan, as in other Asian and Pacific societies, it is often indigenous minorities who suffer most from ethno-nationalist ideas on belonging. The long-established Korean minority, and the Ainu and Okinawans, have been either forced to give up their ethnic traditions or excluded totally from citizenship rights. Morris-Suzuki writes:

> the confiscation of traditional Ainu hunting and fishing grounds and the prohibition of traditional customs culminated, in 1899, in the passing of an act entitled (with eloquent ambivalence) the 'Former Natives Protection Law'... This sought to turn the Ainu into peasant farmers by settling them on small plots of infertile land, while at the same time giving the Japanese state immense power over their education, welfare and even use of financial assets. (Morris-Suzuki, 1996, p. 10)

This is strikingly similar to descriptions of what was done with Aboriginal people in Australia. It also reminds us of this sort of human tragedy once assimilation had been completed:

> a pretty teenage girl begged her mother to kill her. She resisted, but her daughter's frantic pleas finally overcame her maternal instincts and she complied by slitting her daughter's throat... Parents killed their children, then themselves... As they lit the flame, the Okinawans screamed 'Long Live the Emperor'. (cited in Suzuki and Oiwa, 1996, pp. 26–7)

Japanization has been refused to Koreans, who are to this day excluded from active citizenship in Japan because of *ius sanguinis* nationality rules. This exclusion has cultural bases. Nevertheless, were the *ius sanguinis* rules relaxed – as is being debated at present – Japan would provide all that is required for adequate democratic citizenship participation and avenues for the minority voice to be heard in the new century.

Japan is the only nation-state in the region to do this. The other major power, possibly the most important in the world together with the USA, is the People's Republic of China (PRC). Here what a citizen does and gets is insufficient. As a one-party Communist state dedicated to stifling all debate and opposition, China is one of the worst offenders in the world against human rights standards. Indeed, its insertion into the global capitalist market in its free trade zones, and more generally the absence of any adequate social welfare, means that even were civil and political rights recognized, the basis for popular participation in social welfare would not be present for decades. The PRC is explicitly committed to opposition to universal norms for human rights (Steiner and Alston, 1996, pp. 233–4).

China does not rest its rejection of democracy and human rights on cultural norms such as Confucianism, but such values are not inconsistent with its express positions. These usually rest on the inderogable right of national sovereignty, self-determination and non-interference. The 1954 constitution made clear, under the heading of the rights and duties of citizens, that all landlords, rich peasants, counter-revolutionaries, rightwingers and evildoers were not citizens. Since an independent judiciary and rule of law as understood in the west still did not exist, this added up to tyranny. In the 1982 amendments, all nationals were made citizens with equal constitutional and legal rights. When Hong Kong became part of the PRC, some of its residents continued legally to hold British-issued passports, which they use overseas. It appears that they do not have any additional privileges in China as a result (Li Buyun and Wu Yuzhang, 1999). China still fails to adhere to or implement the UN covenants on civil and political and economic, social and cultural rights.

These are the two super-powers of the region, and even the four tigers are minuscule in comparison. However, unlike Japan, the latter provide little more hope for global citizenship or even adequate citizenship norms in the future. None is really a democracy, despite some moves in that direction in South Korea. All are fiercely nationalistic and Confucian in inspiration. They reserve practically all offices for male nationals and only recognize the male line when out-marriage takes place. This is also the case in Japan (Hassall, 1999). Dissent in thought, word and deed is crushed as mercilessly in South Korea,

Taiwan and Singapore as it was at Tiananmen Square. The Human Rights ratings show systematic political imprisonment and torture (Humana, 1992). In South Korea, there is a readiness to endorse universal human rights and to write grandiose texts on world citizenship, which hides a practical reality that dissent is branded as pro-Communist (see, for example, Choue, 1986). Singapore has still to ratify many UN instruments; Taiwan is not even recognized by the UN.

The express commitment to the Confucian family model in all the tiger economies has meant a reduplication of the paternal system and a systematic exclusion of non-conformists. Indicative of the extremes to which this is taken is the Singapore leadership's policy of eugenic marriages and Draconian codes against breaches of state mores, such as sporting long hair. Where in Japan the vigorous and open debate and the democratic participation work to mitigate the state use of Confucianism, nothing can really oppose it in the tiger economies. The family model is expressly seen in many places as the opposite of individualism, and the stress is not on rights but on duties (Sheridan, 1995, p. 138; Kausikan, 1996; Milner and Quilty, 1997, pp. 233–5; Davidson, 1999).

In societies where all opposition to paternal authority is decried – so that there are only state unions, and strikes are banned – the idea of an antagonistic citizenry against the state is almost unknown. Since unofficial unions and strikes were banned until recently in the four tiger nations, opposition has to find other avenues. In the absence of a truly free press, unions and choice between political parties that have a real chance of winning – the civil institutions necessary for citizenship – the gap has been filled throughout Asia by an alternative. This is organized crime, which is closely linked with both capital and politicians at a very high level. Both the Chinese triads and the Japanese yakuza have spread and established themselves in the Asia-Pacific region and into America and Europe. It is to their local groups that individuals are often obliged to turn for help and protection (Posner, 1988; Kleinknecht, 1996). Such institutionalized corruption is also present as an alternative government in the European Mafia, but not to the same degree or significance for the global economy. While it exists as a major social and political force – whose leaders are able to have face-to-face meetings with US presidents when they visit – it remains an unsurmountable barrier to citizenship on two levels. First, it ends the single rule of law that is equal for all. Second, it creates a secret and occult governmental power that conflicts with the democratic requirement for open government.

Organized crime is unlikely to be challenged adequately while the present ethno-nationalism is dominant in Asia. Both the triads and the yakuza grow out of national resistance movements to foreign oppressors either in fact or in myth. It is a mark of commitment to the nation to join and support such patriotic organizations. This explains how ambivalent politicians are towards organized crime even in Japan. Again, the PRC was determinedly against such counter-governments and attempted to extirpate the triads in China, particularly because Chiang Kai Shek was a leader of one of them. However, the entire Taiwan government had been built on the triads for a generation, and once China opened its doors to global capitalism and reincorporated Hong Kong – the triad headquarters – into the PRC, the triads reestablished themselves as major powers in the free trade zones. As symbols of Chinese resistance to oppression, they also emerged in the Malay peninsula, gradually becoming acculturated. Most recently, they have moved into Australia and the Pacific to become the major organized crime networks operating in the region (Kaplan and Dubro, 1986; Posner, 1988; Booth, 1990; Kleinknecht, 1996).

South East Asia and the Pacific

The overall situation is similar in the states with large Muslim majorities – Indonesia and Malaysia – which still have one-party regimes, despite cosmetic changes. (At the time of writing, the outcome of current changes in Indonesia is unclear.) These are guaranteed by antidemocratic electoral systems in the constitution. Indeed, in Malaysia, ethnic Malays are favoured in practically all socio-political realms. It is in countries like these that the full degree of discrimination, masquerading as the right to maintain cultural difference and traditions, can be seen. It is particularly striking where women are concerned, despite a relatively good performance on social indicators and adherence to the UN conventions to protect women and children. Islamic law is used to justify the subordination of women to men, a characteristic of most Islamic societies.

Since it would be seen as treachery to attack Islam in favour of western human rights, women in opposition resort to a re-reading of Islam, without the institutional power to convert that into political effects. As Othman writes from a Malaysian perspective, after acknowledging the failure to actualize Islam in its liberating and democratic spirit: 'The challenge... is to begin a reformation of the methodology of interpreting the *shari'a* so that it may become applicable within contemporary nation-states' (Othman, 1994, p. 82). In this, the experience parallels that of Middle Eastern countries (Afshar, 1994; Helie-Lucas, 1994). One approach has been that of An Na-im, who argues that a pluralist Islam has to have various approaches to the relation of the *shari'a* (law) and the *umma* (faithful). As both Muslims and non-Muslims were citizens from independence onwards, citizenship and the *umma* cannot coincide. Since the first traditionally allows only passive citizenship to non-Muslims, the only way in which they can be protected is to give them minority rights. Again, since apostasy must be punished by death, a denial of freedom of conscience and its expression, the *shari'a* will have to be drastically revised to end its discriminatory hierarchies.

This lack of liberty is particularly marked for women. In Muslim countries and communities, the *shari'a* deprives women of the right to marry freely, submitting them to the authority of a marriage guardian. Islamic law deprives women of free access to divorce, allows the repudiation of wives by their husbands, permits polygamy and lays down inequality in inheritance rights. Women are deprived of the right to guardianship and custody of children in the event of divorce, although precise rules vary from country to country. Their mobility and access to paid employment is dependent on their father's or husband's permission. In some places, women are not even permitted to drive a car. Sex outside marriage is punishable – even by death in certain Arab emirates and Pakistan (Helie-Lucas, 1994, p. 263).

The reality is thus that nearly 10 per cent of the world's population have the status that they had when Montesquieu wrote *The Spirit of the Laws* (see Chapter 2). Indeed, overall, their condition has gone backwards from relatively emancipatory colonial legislation, and even when compared with Communist regimes such as that of Afghanistan (Montesquieu, 1964, pp. 567–8; Helie-Lucas, 1994, p. 264; Wahdud-Muhsin, 1994, p. 78). The failure to establish themselves as equals, or even to have minimal human rights in many Islamic countries, can be compared with the triumph of fundamentalist views of Muslim men seeking security in face of the changes imposed by globalization.

While the horrors of this trend in Africa, the Middle East and South Asia have not yet been characteristic of South East Asia, the feminization of migration is posing massive problems for retrograde Islamic systems. When thousands of Catholic and emancipated Filipinas arrive in the Arab emirates, the acceptance that there is little recourse against rapists has and will be increasingly challenged. This will bring Islamic and international standards into increasing conflict, as in some recent rape/murder cases in the Middle East. However, tyrannical nationalism, hiding behind Islamic slogans, has so far held back change, making the issue of citizenship for women one of the major issues of the 'Asian century'.

In many South East Asian and Pacific countries, considerable discrimination is experienced by the descendants of immigrants, indigenous peoples and those who are not of the 'national' religion. The most widespread minority is the Chinese diaspora, which extends throughout the region and, when combined, constitutes the fifth richest community in the world. It is tightly linked by kinship ties to many states in the region. There is formal and informal discrimination against Chinese throughout the Malay peninsula and Indonesia (Johnson, 1995, pp. 19–20). This came to a head with the slaughter of Chinese in Indonesia in 1965, and again with widespread violence at the time of the fall of the Soeharto regime in 1998. Since both areas refuse universal human rights norms in favour of a bogus national variety, the victims are practically defenceless if they do not resort to private force. Again, where Catholic minorities such as the Timorese, or Melanesians in Irian Jaya, refuse Indonesianization, they have no real alternative but armed resistance to martial law, state-approved oppression and the use of torture.

The anti-Chinese racism is paralleled by attitudes to the other major population of immigrant descent in the region, that from South Asia. The most striking example of the effects of insistence on national ethnic communitarian standards (the right to the land) on these people in recent years has been in Fiji. After the Rabuka coups (1987), ethnic cleansing resulted in the Indian population being reduced from more than half of the total population to a third by forced migration (Crocombe *et al.*, 1992; Lawson, 1993). While Fiji has recently adopted a more acceptable constitution and a rule of law to ensure readmission to the Commonwealth of Nations, it should be remembered that such norms do not add up to an adequate democracy for a world of global migration. Ethnic cleansing to ensure ethnic homogeneity and therefore a democracy without criticism is a negation of democratic citizenship. Conditions for South Asians are improving in Singapore and Malaysia, especially for Muslims, but even in Malaysia they are second-class citizens because of the constitutional privilege accorded the ethnic majority.

Faced with the widespread discrimination against minorities and the practical impossibility of securing outcomes that respect human rights or even justice from national instances, ethnic minorities from the Aborigines of Australia to the East Timorese and the Okinawans have tended in the 1990s to appeal directly to international bodies for redress, and favour the maintenance and establishment of institutions that allow them to go beyond national jurisdictions to obtain justice. This move parallels that of Muslims in Europe seeking to defend themselves as a minority (Bouamama *et al.*, 1992; Bouamama, 1994; Soysal, 1997). The allies of the UN turn out in Asia to be the oppressed groups, while the national state is supported by the oppressors.

It is regrettable that it is in Australia and French Polynesia, where standards on human rights scales are highest, that some of the worst discrimination against indigenous populations has taken place. Dishonouring decisions on land ownership and other matters was a feature of the Australian state in the 1990s, compelling approaches by the Aborigines to the UN and the ECHR, and other instances for redress. UN calls for a better observance of human rights have been rejected outright, and the government has dubbed such acts treason or disloyalty (Dodson, 1999). In the DOM-TOM, the demands for independence have led to massive rioting and a by-passing of the metropole to the EU and the Council of Europe, as it became clear that promises of independence referenda in 1998 were not likely to be kept or successful for Kanaks (Aldrich and Connell, 1992, pp. 220–32; Boengkih, 1997). As in Fiji, the problem that immigration has made the first peoples no longer unified majorities threatens an exclusionary racist response by the former.

In summary, at the beginning of the new century, the Asia-Pacific region shows little sign of adapting its citizenship models to respond adequately to globalization. Indeed, ethno-nationalism based on identifying people with land, and excluding all those of other ethnicities, leads to ridiculous racist explanations for financial and other problems. Unfortunately, the major regional powers are likely to dominate Asia in the next century, and their positions on both nationality rights and citizenship bode ill for the millions of foreign denizens who will provide labour in the region. For example, with the decline of Malaysian industry in 1998, even fellow Muslims from Indonesia and Bangladesh were sent home to add a million unemployed to the estimated 6 million who had become unemployed internally in Indonesia. Some Asian commentators recognize that the rights of migrants are menaced by an adherence to ethno-nationalism:

> In political terms, the intensification of intra – as well as extra – ASEAN migration flows has led to a heightened sensitivity and response to the prospect and

situation of migrants in these countries. On the one hand sending countries have now become more aware of the situations of their compatriots abroad and have taken steps within the bounds provided by international practice (and sometimes beyond) to remedy their current plight. The governments of such countries now insist that migrants become entitled as well to the dignity recognized by international statutes. On the other hand, receiving countries in the region tend to hesitate extending such rights to expatriates especially of the kind that performs menial and labour-intensive jobs. The worst responses are in the form of xenophobia and the outright injury and violence inflicted on foreigners. The milder and more common (and institutionalized) form of response for these countries is to impose stricter gatekeeping measures... The reality of the situation is that states merely attempt to insist on a sense of nationhood based on an ethnocentric context. (Tigno, 1995, p. 60)

What is interesting is that, faced with such nationalism, the myriad minorities are not asserting separate minority status, but instead going directly to the UN and elsewhere to obtain universal rights accorded to individuals and others as a sort of minimal threshold. Some leading Asian commentators have made it clear that insisting on cultural difference to exclude democracy and human rights hides the worst offences to human dignity. Minorities are realizing that too. There is thus an incipient alliance of the supra-national or global bodies and the subnational grouping even in Asia. This has long been the case in Europe.

Conclusion

Once developments in the non-western world have been examined, radical implications for citizenship in a global world follow. We have made it clear that citizenship, as discussed in this book, is a European notion that was carried to other parts of the world as whites occupied those new spaces. It was a theory and a practice that evolved and changed in response to altered contexts. As it is lived today, it is primarily the citizenship of nation-states that emerged in the eighteenth century. This bundle of human rights and a democracy that ensures the security of each individual and gives him and her power 'from below' has had a very brief history against all other forms of governance. As the product of a relatively homogenous culture, often described as Hellenic or Judaeo-Christian and of industrial capitalism that transcended national boundaries, citizenship was changed throughout that world without much dissension of a cultural sort between the different partners. This does not deny wars within states within that culture, or that national unity was built through enforced amnesia over several hundred years. When globalization posed a new challenge, new supra-national citizenship norms were evolved to cope with the novelty. We discussed this in all the previous chapters.

However, the economic, social and cultural transformations associated with globalization now affect the whole world. Far from seeing the solution to the new problems in a renewed or extended citizenship, non-western states have largely rejected this approach in favour of their own cultural values. Alternatively, where they have accepted, they have accepted half-heartedly, or not gone beyond the nation-state citizen found inadequate to cope with globalization by Europeans. Most Asia-Pacific nations have become firmly nationalistic in their immigration and nationality policies. When this is coupled with a *de facto* or *de jure* refusal to observe human rights or democracy within the polities, the newcomer is totally disempowered and at the mercy of the controlling national (usually ethnically based) majority.

Western scenarios for citizenship in a global world – which are also those of international agencies like the UN – must thus come to terms with the fact that even states benefitting from globalization, such as the fast-growing Asian countries, reject any valid model of democratic citizenship, or alternatively fail to implement it in prac-tice. One problem in trying to develop notions of democratic citizen-ship is that many Asian countries experienced the hypocrisy of western ideals during the colonial period and indeed since, when the 'civilizing mission' was a cloak for domination and exploitation. Nonetheless, it is essential to insist that individuals cannot be empow-ered as political subjects without democracy, human rights and the rule of law.

It is sometimes argued that a realm of civil society is opening up in such polities and that citizenship has its supporters. This is undeniable. However, it is significant that, in the Asia-Pacific, such opposition is either crushed by tanks as in China, or under house arrest or illegal as in Burma, Thailand and Indonesia – and even Singapore and Fiji when the state feels threatened. Those carrying the banner for citizenship are often forced into national liberation struggles, as in East Timor or Bougainville. They therefore parallel earlier national liberation move-ments. The literature shows that the national communitarian quality of such movements once in power was totally inimical to even the liberal-socialist tradition of citizenship. National fervour was always very strong, and nationality rules were such that foreigners were excluded from citizen participation.

So, when the elaborate, institutionalized citizenships of the west come up against the realities of non-western countries, it becomes necessary to reconsider the obviousness of the underlying notions and to elaborate new practices for conviviality between civilizations who meet in a global space. This leads us to our consideration of projects for a new global civic virtue.

9

Social Capital and the New Civics

It has been made abundantly clear that, in an age of globalization, citizenship has to deal with continuing difference of an economic, social, political and legal sort. This is due to the 'displacement' of populations that migrate to and fro in search of work and wellbeing in burgeoning but changing global markets. When these go into recession – as in the Asian financial crisis of 1997–99 – millions are obliged to return 'home' as employment collapses:

> We have entered a period of huge *displacement* of population. I use the word *displacement* deliberately, for when the populations of entire regions leave, this is not because they want to leave but because they are obliged to by the situation. In fact, what is called globalization, the extending of the economy to the globe, goes together with the uprooting of entire peoples, abandoned by the flight of productive structures, left to the blind forces of the world market. Even the rich countries undergo these changes fully... (Nair, 1997, p. 73)

In earlier chapters, we showed how these new challenges have been met in several ways. Since reforms to citizenship will, for the foreseeable future, be made primarily on the basis of an existing national citizenship, there have been attempts to bring it up to date by replacing the old ethnically based monist and exclusive understanding of the nation by multicultural versions. The latter do not require the assimilation or integration of immigrants into a national stereotype before empowering those individuals and groups as citizens. There is a novel multicultural citizenship emerging within former nation-states.

However, the nation-state's pre-eminence is in decline together with its effective sovereignty because of the globalization of spaces where power is exercised. At best, multicultural citizenship is a stop-gap or is insufficient by itself. More significant for the future, if not yet dominant at present, is the development of the supra-national regional citizenship, which is itself necessarily multicultural and severed from notions of national 'belonging'. It exists in its most developed form in the European Union and the Council of Europe, but it is nevertheless also emerging in the North American Free Trade Area, the Asia-Pacific Economic Cooperation, MERCOSUR (in Latin America) and other regional economic free trade areas.

As we showed in earlier chapters, the policy in such regional polities has been to have more democracy in more places by (a) devolving decision making to communes and local regions, and (b) establishing parliamentary and other authorities at the level of the supra-national entity. These are usually popularly elected even though malapportionment as a reault of national interest sometimes makes their representativity less than democratic.

This solution to the management of difference functions according to the subsidiarity principle. Decisions are made as close to the problem as possible, and only a very few universal or general issues are tackled at the summit of what resembles a federal system. While the effect is clearly to undermine national sovereign power by redistributing it to local regions as well as supra-national authorities (see, for example, Labasse, 1994, pp. 7–8), and this provokes central state resistance, it reinforces stability because ethnic and other local difference is allowed to manage itself according to its own cultural norms. Yet there is clearly also a danger with returning management to national minorities and ethnicities. By making policy corporate in interest, this power 'from below' can rapidly turn into a new and more narrow exclusivism. When the *Lega Nord* took control of the rich Italian regions, it adopted exclusionary and then racist policies, first against Southern Italians and then against foreign labour. The latter were deemed to be not sufficiently industrious. Thus, the community that produced and that made the wealth was entitled to exclude the newcomers from that wellbeing (Ruzza and Schmidtke, 1996). It became essential to protect the new minorities from the assertions of those who had won regional power on the basis of their difference. Wherever these experiments of devolving power to the local level have been tried, it has become obvious that racism is not just a phenomenon of nation-states, and more is needed than more democracy in more places to manage the problem of difference.

The further problem of difference within difference – for example, a member of an ethno-national majority who now finds him- or herself

living in an area where a former minority has majority power politically – is addressed by extensive and ever stronger human rights
regimes that protect both individuals and collectivities against state or
majority power. This again means by-passing national instances for
redress or giving the last instance to the supra-national level. Typical is
the European Convention of Human Rights and its institutions. A
member of a minority within a majority (for example, a Corsican in
France), after going through the court system of the majority, can
appeal to a supra-national body beyond the nation for protection. It is
important to note that it is the supra-national body that decides. Where
nation-states are forced to introduce such systems domestically, they
can legislate them away when they want. This is what has happened to
the Human Rights and Equal Opportunity Commission of Australia.

Minorities within majorities are increasingly using such avenues to
defend their difference against majority norms. Soysal (1997) has
identified the widespread use of such techniques by Muslims living in
Europe, and it is also the preferred avenue of the indigenous peoples
of the Asia-Pacific region where they have access to such authorities.
It has greater than legal effect. The moral force of the recent European
Union (EU) condemnation of the conservative Australian government's attempt to overturn the Wik decision establishing native title
over leasehold land is great. National calls for such people to keep
their noses out of Australian business are backward looking in a world
where, as with Europeans, it is accepted that the principle of non-
interference in domestic affairs has had its day (Council of Europe,
1993). As Catherine Lalumiere, Secretary General of the Council of
Europe, stated in 1993:

> The state should be the principal custodian of human rights; its role is to respect
> and enforce those rights. But experience teaches us that it can be not only the
> protector but the gravedigger of human rights. It was because the state has often
> failed in its role as custodian of human rights and been transformed into an
> instrument of oppression that the international community was given a watching
> brief over the behaviour of states. These can no longer shelter behind the cosy
> screen of non-interference. Human rights have ceased to belong to the domain of
> 'domestic affairs'. Respect for human rights is a duty of every state, not only
> towards its people but also towards the international community. (Council of
> Europe, 1993, p. 11)

Such principles are applied unevenly, and backward states resist
them fiercely, claiming to defend national sovereignty. These norms of
international law overriding nation-state sovereignty to protect difference look lopsided when the Israeli regime is equally in breach with its

Arab neighbours and seldom sanctioned. It is also true that the USA, probably now the most hypocritical in its rejection of international human rights at home while insisting on them abroad (typical being the widespread and increasing use of the death penalty), is most responsible for such double standards. Nevertheless, they exist as a basis for direct interference in even USA affairs.

In calculating which trend will predominate – the new internationalism or the new nationalism – it is important to realize that the regional polities already use interference as their principle, as their law overrides that of the nation-states where public matters of human rights are concerned. Minorities consistently appeal to them to override national legal norms and practices. In France, the *sans papiers* are an example. The Debre-Pasqua laws' systematic use of police to expel foreigners who did not meet national requirements was clearly against international human rights standards and even against the constitutional and other rules of the French state itself (*Hommes et Migrations*, 1996; Davidson, 1997; Nair, 1997). Despairing of a hearing by the government, the *sans papiers* turned to human rights activists and finally to the European Parliament for redress, making their treatment internationally notorious. Their predicament made clear the impossibility of thinking these issues to be national any longer. In great majority Muslim or black, their forced repatriation meant in most cases unemployment, in many starvation and in some death – as in Algeria (Bouamama, 1997a). The French problem was that of the source countries of its migrants as well. Moreover, their protagonist in the European Parliament, Dany Cohn-Bendit, also became the most forceful, later insisting that the Algerian government be subject to international scrutiny over the massacres allegedly by Muslim fundamentalists.

These practical techniques of managing difference – more democracy in more places and universally applied human rights regimes – are already established. We can anticipate that they will prevail in more and more places despite the new nationalist resistance as international migration increases. That trend is countervailed by the tendency towards chaos. They are all measures that leave a need to establish conviviality across difference. What such practical measures do at best is to allow redress for solving wrongs in the last instance by the imposition of law. This always provokes resistance and is therefore dangerous. What is needed is an everyday capacity to live and work with difference in a world where all hope of cultural homogenization of peoples who live and work cheek to cheek has gone for ever. This will possibly be no more than the principle of the cold porcupines who discover in trial and error that when it is freezing they must huddle together and give each other warmth, but if they come too close, they pierce each other with their cultural spines. Gradually, case by case, depending on the ambience, they figure out the correct relationship. This working out of ways of living with others who will remain different at more than an international level is the main focus of this chapter.

Ethnoscapes

The new global world is aptly described by Appadurai's notion of 'scapes':

> By ethnoscape, I mean the landscape of persons who constitute the shifting world in which we live: tourists, immigrants, refugees, exiles, guestworkers and other moving groups and persons constitute the essential feature of the world, and appear to affect the politics of and between nations to a hitherto unprecedented degree. This is not to say that there are not anywhere relatively stable communities and networks, of kinship, friendship, of work and of leisure, as well as of birth, residence and other filiative forms. But this is to say that the warp of these stabilities is everywhere shot through with the woof of human motion, as more persons and groups deal with the realities of having to move, or the fantasies of wanting to move. What is more, both these realities as well as these fantasies now function on larger scales, as men and women from villages in India think not just of moving to Poona or Madras, but of moving to Dubai and Houston, and refugees from Sri Lanka find themselves in South India as well as Canada, just as the Hmong are driven to London as well as Philadelphia. And as international capital shifts its needs, as production and technology generate different needs, as nation-states shift their policies on refugee population, these moving groups can never afford to let their imagination rest too long, even if they wished to. (Appadurai, 1990, p. 297)

For such people – even if they constitute only a minority of a global population – a new civic ethic is required that is quite different from the jealous warrior-citizen personality fierce in the defence of his or her and their rights. States and regional polities have become aware of this in the past two decades and developed many strategies on how to attain it. Apart from the obvious argument that it is acquired in living and working together in a strong democracy, which we have discussed earlier, the centrality of a need for a new sort of civic education can be found in many places.

What was regarded as essential for civic virtue among the old nation-state citizens was a sense of shared identity. States who claimed to be the cradles of democracy and human rights, such as France, the USA and Britain, made it policy to inculcate that sense through the project of creating a new nation out of the different disparate parts (see Chapter 2). It usually took the form of the development of a single language, even when that language had to be invented, as it was in Israel. Then it took the form of a national schooling system in which a single partial history or collective memory of the past was drilled into all children. It also took the form of symbols such as flags, hymns and other shared icons. Over more than a century, a single nation community was created in which the particular differences of the past were eliminated. As Schnapper put it, the project was 'to transcend by citizenship particular biological... historical, economic, social, religious or cultural belonging; to define the citizen as an abstract individual without particular identifying qualities, as beyond all his/her cultural determinants' (Schnapper, 1994, p. 49).

Thus, a single national definition of self was added, in an ongoing project of education, to the particular differences that were protected behind the notion of individual rights. As Art. 1 of the Declaration of the Rights of Man and the Citizen proclaimed, no social distinction that was not useful was permitted in establishing and enjoying rights. While there was no incessant flux of migration and arrival of newcomers, the project was mainly successful despite real exclusions – in 1789, other races, women and the mentally deficient were not included as possible citizens. It was eventually possible to say to nearly any newcomer that all he or she had to do to join the community was to be a democrat and believe in the rights of all to human dignity. This is totally unexceptionable as a principle. Nor can we see it wrong to educate children to express their views while respecting the dignity of others, which is what the immense civic programmes in France and the USA have done throughout the century.

However, the reality was rather different, especially for the imperial possessions that experienced the European warrior-citizen as someone who was a genocidal destroyer of culture and tradition. Indeed, as such colonial peoples revolted to defend their community against imperial oppression and then won, an insoluble problem arose for the notion of nation-state civic education and citizenship. It only became clear when the newly liberated migrated in huge numbers as labour to the former metropoles.

For example, what happened was the arrival of 3 million Muslims, many of them Algerians, in France. To ask those people to turn their backs on their cultural traditions in becoming French citizens was to ask the impossible. In effect, former enemies were asking a minority to accept the obliteration of their community identity, which had been forged in a struggle against them. Citizenship as an abstraction from all difference could not easily be accepted. Even the carrot of approval for those who denied their origins ('the good Beur') did not work (Bouamama *et al.*, 1992; Bouamama, 1994). Where the internal minorities had centuries to forget the obliteration of their own distinct cultures, these newcomers had actually fought against the French. Moreover, their global migration continues and will continue in waves into the foreseeable future.

Practically, the notion of a nation as the creating of a new community by turning one's back on the specific collective was too difficult. An endless literature from Memmi through to Fanon makes clear the psychological impossibility of this in a short period of time, even given goodwill. It is an experience that extends into the second generation *after a national civic education*, as these words of a Bangladeshi from London show: 'I know they say "Your home is where your heart is" but I don't know where my heart is so that makes it difficult' (Eade, 1997, p. 159). It is in recognition of such split realities or multiple belongings that the system of dual nationality has been recognized formally, even by those countries who regarded having only one nationality as a basic right only 30 years ago. Among them can be numbered Britain, Canada, New Zealand, Italy, Ireland, Greece, Turkey and France. The notion of a single nationality makes no sense in the EU; many other countries accept the reality in practice.

What these lived realities add up to is the impossibility of equating civics education exclusively with teaching people to love their country, as the community of its citizens. As we have pointed out, such education comes primarily through participation in politics and then through formal education in schools, where the 'nation' is instituted. Giving up the notion of civics as an education in loving one's country thus has implications for the nature of political participation. This can no longer be designed to simply attach discrete individuals to the state.

When defenders of the 'open republic' – the most advanced form of national citizenship – argue that all people can only be included if all particular differences are ignored, their goal of inclusiveness is as strong as that of the multiculturalists. What they do not take into account – or regard as a harsh necessity – is how difficult this is, for example, for a traditional patriarch from another culture. It appears to be their judgment that the transit has to be abrupt so that the individual and the state are brought face to face and the nation thus formed (see, for example, Schnapper, 1994). This is why they stress participation as participation in a democratic selection of national representatives in national parliaments. They are hostile both to supra-national projects, as being too large to sustain civic commitment, and to intermediate associations between the individual and the state, as this undermines the strength of national unity.

Their multicultural critics share their desire for inclusiveness but regard the nation as traditionally conceived (for example, France as one and indivisible), as passed up by globalization. Thus, they argue that to include newcomers, intermediate associations or more democracy in more places is essential. Here the minority voice will be heard in its economic, social and political accents. The central state is certainly undermined, together with national representative democracy and the vote as the first right and duty of a citizen. However, the public space is much more livable if concentrated minorities can manage their affairs in their own way rather than be subject to abstract rules that the majority has already evolved over centuries.

On the other hand, the spokespeople for such migrant minorities realize the danger of too much unilateral insistence on such devolved democracy to advance community cultural rights. It can lead – as French authors point out – to a reassertion of the right of the national majority community to its traditions. Le Pen's neo-Fascist movement builds on such a policy of France for the French understood as values, such as Christianity, that few newcomers hold. He merely reverses the communitarian argument, just as the *Lega Nord* does in Italy. Thus, in their plea for a new multicultural citizenship for France, leading ethnic minority specialists on citizenship link the denial of a need to belong to the cultural nation before enjoying citizen rights to a claim that the best way to protect minorities is not through affirmative action but through totally equal treatment with all other residents. The juxtaposition of the multicultural and universal citizen only appears strange when the logic of its argument is not followed (Bouamama, 1997b).

So the equation of reasonableness, and therefore, formal civics education, with the acceptance of democracy and human rights within the community of the nation-state is rejected practically by the new minorities. For them, the acceptance of even such public norms can only work by 'inclusion through exclusion' if the context remains that of national belonging (Bouamama *et al.*, 1992, p. 188). As they point out, in the civics of a nation-state even *reason* is a national patrimony, and only the host society is believed to have its key. Any attempt to debate it shows a quality that requires re-education (Bouamama, 1991). This can only be lived as majority oppression and provoke resistance.

There is nothing open about a situation in which all may participate in the democratic game, but only one party is allowed to decide what that game is. In fact, what an alien who wants French citizenship is asked is not whether he or she believes in democracy and human rights, but to abide by existing French laws produced in such a regime from the moment of application for nationality. Yet these very laws, the result or expression of democracy and human rights, may well be the continuing source of his or her oppression as a human being (Davidson, 1997). It is a request that ignores what is essential to a just rule of law: equality not merely *before* the law but *in* law.

While such minority speakers are multiculturalists in the way described in earlier chapters, they are, however, also universalists:

> The interdependence of the contemporary world, its complexity, the increasing mobility of humans with their cultural baggage and not only as labour power, makes unifying the complex totality without denying its constituent parts inevitable. Universality is a necessity in a contemporary world. It is both something 'already there' and a project. An 'already there' because the different cultures have already progressively been brought, consciously or not, voluntarily or not, to open up to the other, to make cultural borrowings, to recognize the plural and to agree on a certain number of values. (Bouamama, 1991, p. 66)

Not only is 'the right to difference without social, economic and political equality... only a project designed to maintain injustice' where there are majorities and minorities (Bouamama, 1994, pp. 19, 102–3), but also the universal cannot be coterminous with the nation-state. A new citizenship requires that 'the present link between nationality and access to rights be broken' (Bouamama, 1994, p. 10).

In other words, the new civics to complement existing practice must be sought beyond the system of nation-states. It must be more than loving your fellows and a single country, even if they claim democracy and human rights to be the basis of their community. As this implies, the way forward to a new civics lies in the global space and its overriding relation *vis-à-vis* the reason, norms and wisdom evolved with the nation-state.

The authors of the new civics identify virtue, not in the readiness to fight and die for a principle, which we may find praiseworthy when it is democracy but not when it is a Jihad, but in qualities such as tolerance, trust, mildness and love. We might sum this up as the way of coping with difference when it is met at a cultural or community frontier. In a realm of nation-states, it was assumed that difference was outside. Today and henceforth, it is assumed to be inside. Quite different mechanisms are needed to cope with it.

Social capital

The research group led by Robert Putnam has been most important in showing that there can be no simple institutional solution to the problem of ensuring conviviality. More democracy in more places does not guarantee civic virtue. They have also identified what must underlie those institutions, which are certainly a condition for civic virtue and underpin expanded democracy. This they call social capital, which is created by history and social context over a long period. Since it lies in the realm of altruistic values, it can only be attained against self-interest and hence advanced by civic education. Thus, the central problem of living with the difference of a global society has become, in the past decade, what sort of education or ethics should be taught. Moreover, while it thus becomes a project, since it is against self-interest or 'bad' history, it has to be seen as being contested in a struggle with opponents who wish to continue the traditional citizen ethics that go back to Pericles.

The new virtues, when combined, are the social capital that makes it possible to resolve differences by seeing what is common to all neighbours. That notion is as old as citizenship itself, but the work of Putnam and his followers – who studied the Italian history of more democracy in more places over 30 years – completely changes what people should be taught to value as the universal that even advanced multiculturalists agree is essential to any shared community. Social capital is what must be created: 'Social capital... refers to features of social organization, such as trust, norms and networks, that can improve the efficiency of society by facilitating coordinated actions' (Putnam, 1993, p. 167). He points out that it develops through networks of interaction such as sporting clubs, rotating credit associations and above all a reciprocity in care of the commons that does not expect an immediate or corollary, but a long-term, recompense when others behave in the same way. Civic virtue requires altruism or a cost in the short term to oneself and any particular interest.

Putnam and his research team make clear that it is such attitudes and values that make local democracy work, rather than vice versa. The value of his work is that it is a rare example of longitudinal research. It was made by research over 30 years into Italian experiments in devolved democracy, which worked in some places but not elsewhere in stimulating civic virtue of the sort needed to live with others. This research showed that where there was not a millennial history of social capital, democratic procedures did not change civic interaction. It was, of course, almost impossible where there was no democracy or horizontal attachments. Thus, in the traditionally clientelistic south of Italy, left-wing democratic local government had not ended the lack of trust and conviviality. Past history is crucial where such matters are concerned. Putnam writes:

> Where norms and networks of civic engagement are lacking, the outlook for collective action appears bleak. The fate of the Mezzogiorno is an object lesson for the Third World today and the former Communist lands of Eurasia tomorrow, moving uncertainly towards self-government... Without norms of reciprocity and networks of civic engagement, the Hobbesian outcome of the Mezzogiorno – amoral familism, clientelism, lawlessness, ineffective government, and economic stagnation – seems likelier than successful democratisation and economic development. Palermo may represent the future of Moscow. (Putnam, 1993, p. 183)

In the absence of a history of virtues such as trust rather than war, where can such virtues come from? Certainly, learning by doing in participatory democracy will bring slow changes, and they can only come from inside or below. Other than that, a civic education focusing on the sort of marketplace virtues first extolled by Kant, but used as models by Putnam, seems the most promising in its low-level, weak systems of tolerance, trust, mildness and love.

The reversal of values that should be taught as civics from those extolled by leading theorists of the communitarian nation-state built on the exclusion of difference is striking. Renan wrote critically in 1882 that 'the Turkish policy of separating nationalities according to religion... caused the ruin of the Orient' because it created communities 'with almost nothing in common between them'. The new civics, however, requires an understanding of what made such multiethnic communities work together. This requires in turn giving up the search for a common memory or history. It means the end of an education towards the Periclean warrior defence of the cultural patrimony, whether it is a defence of democracy or of Islam. In its place, there must be an educational project of working with all others as if there were no prehistory of cultural predeterminations.

Practically no attention has ever been paid to promoting such values of tolerance and trust in all the history of civics education in modern nation-states. Indeed, since the modern citizen was created against the status-based society backed by the Church, such values were regarded as religious and to be abhorred in favour of enlightened reason. Only today, when minorities note that that reason itself is in practice exclusionary (Bouamama *et al.*, 1992), do its claims to be an exclusive guide to life become suspect.

The absence of such teaching in existing school civics programmes could be the result of the dead hand of the past, what Putnam calls 'path dependence', which clearly conditions us all as we are caught in our cultures and their demands. Within a rationalist west, to be told that we should bid farewell to Aristotle and return to the Gospels (as the originators of the new civics suggest) (Las Casas, 1992; Davidson, 1996c) is doubly difficult, particularly when we are told that it is more reasonable.

It is important to identify briefly what these new civic virtues are before turning to how they are being considered and implemented. First, there is the new notion of *tolerance*. This is much more than the old notion of the toleration of two vying religious faiths on pragmatic grounds or grounds that seek to reconcile two verities. It is instead showing where an inacceptance of the Other rests on inveterate, emotional, irrational prejudices (Bobbio, 1990b, p. 236). Yet this does not mean that all has to be accepted as equally of value, even if, in the first instance, even the intolerant or those who refuse to abide by democratic rules of debate have themselves to be tolerated. No shutting down of debate or use of repression is possible. It is, of course, open to someone to refuse to speak with such people (Eco, 1994). As this suggests, it requires a refusal to subscribe to a strong Cartesian reason and a weak thinking approach coupled with a readiness to revise one's own opinions. Virtue is no longer backward looking in the sense of loyalty to past opinions. This has implications for trust, which we discuss below.

The second notion is that of *mildness* in exchanges with others. The quality of mildness is less difficult to grasp than is what it leads a person to do. It is that attitude which we will hypothesize in the following preliminary way: it is holding to our belief about the Good in the face of rival and disputing views, and yet not *imposing* our own view even when we have the desire, the anger or the power to do so. It is thus an ethical attitude rather than a legal duty with a corollary right. Yet without it, it is difficult to see how a rule of law rather than of men, and therefore tyranny, could exist as a practice. It can usefully be compared with the canon that if you know what is right, you should act upon it against those who disagree, who must be opponents of the Good (Bobbio, 1995; Davidson, 1996c).

The third proposed notion is that of *trust*, but not in the contractual sense traditional to the social contract. In that use it assumed a compact with consideration all round that could be exacted. This was the foundation of the notion of rights and duties, and thus of the rule of law. Trust as demanded in the new civics is altruistic and therefore mutually traded and traded as mutual, against what at best is a non-immediate recompense and perhaps an incommensurate value. As this indicates, the prudential quality of Aristotelianism that Las Casas rejected in his dealings with the Indians of Latin America in favour of the Gospel, did not totally preclude the sort of trust found in a family – which has little to do with calculus and is also in Aristotle. Indeed, the new social contract with the irreducible Other may have to be rethought away from its denial of the familial model that was at the source of citizen theory (Bobbio, 1989, p. 4).

The shift in focus from a hard bargain to mutual trust of the sort whose quality is more Biblical than Enlightenment, brings us to the fourth notion, which is that of *love* in the sense of *caritas*. It flows from and completes the other three. The main characteristic of this value is a refusal to reduce anyone to their cultural characteristics – to take them simply at 'face value'. As Levinas wrote in a chapter headed 'The Citizen of the Modern State', in a passage that is of great importance in a book whose key lies in global migration:

> The first relation between man and being passes through his relation with man... The Jewish man discovers man before he discovers countrysides and towns. He is at home in a society, before he is so in a house. He understands the world starting from other people rather than the ensemble of being as a function of the land. In a sense he is exiled on this globe, as the psalmist says, and he finds a meaning for it starting from human society. This is not an analysis of the contemporary Jewish soul, it is the literal teaching of the Bible where the world is not individually owned, but is God's. Man starts in the desert where he inhabits tents, where he worships God in a temple he carries about with him... From this existence, which is freed with regard to countrysides and architecture, from all those heavy sedentary things which one is tempted to prefer to man, Judaism recalls, throughout its history, that that existence becomes rooted in countrysides and towns... Freedom from sedentary forms of existence is, perhaps, the human way of being in the world. For Judaism, the world becomes intelligible in a human face and not, as in a great philosopher who sums up one aspect of the West, in houses, temples and bridges... There is nothing sickly about this freedom, nothing tense and nothing upsetting. *It places the values of rootedness on a secondary level and institutes other forms of faithfulness and responsibility.* Man is after all not a tree and humanity is not a forest. (Levinas, 1976, p. 41, emphasis added)

The insistence that common humanity consists in refusing to reduce individuals to the general characteristics of their 'culture' by looking at them in the face and taking them at 'face value' (compare Finkielkraut, 1984) is, once again, not a denial of the Enlightenment. Striking indeed, is the similarity with Voltaire's famous words in his essay on tolerance: 'I possess a rank and power created by ignorance and credulity. I step on the heads of the men who are prostrate at my feet; if they get up and look me in the face, I am lost; I must therefore keep them fastened to the ground with chains of iron' (Voltaire, 1971, p. 392).

While the promoters of such views recognize that they are contested by the new nationalist and racist communitarians, and that a battle will be required for them to become the norm in civics training so much are they redolent of 'old values', they are slowly passing into civics literature (Global Commission, 1995; Autrement, 1997). A particularly notable discussion was that held in 1993 on the proposed Bill of Obligations of the Council of Europe. Since this document was not open to the public, only its broad lines can be traced here. The discussion document made clear that 'duties', understood as obligations to distinguish them from the corollaries of rights, were moral and ethical rather than legal; that they were required in the face of the Other; and that they were barely discussed in the great Bills and Conventions of Rights that had founded the rights of man and the citizen. Their origins lay in Judaeo-Christan teachings. They were matters that required an extensive civic education as they could not be legislated. The discussion document therefore proposed that a formal bill not be introduced. The obligations suggested went much beyond the respect for others that human rights required. What was needed was acceptance of the Other as a human being rather than a cultural artefact. This meant solidarity and sharing, and the qualities we have called mildness and tolerance.

Again, we see further evidence of their translation into policy in the rediscovery of the UNESCO project of Jeanne Hersch, which the Secretary General of the Council of Europe cited in the preparations for the 1993 Vienna Human Rights Conference in this context:

> The fundamental principle of the universality of human rights is not only inadequately practised and applied; it is openly disputed, even rejected, by certain movements advocating cultural relativism in the human rights field. According to them, the cultural, social or religious context gives rise to different and yet equally valid conceptions of human rights. In 1981 the Swiss philosopher Jeanne Hersch wrote in an article entitled 'Is the concept of human rights a universal concept?': '...in a vivid, diffuse and deeply felt form, there is in all individuals and all cultures a need, an expectation and a sense of these rights... The main point is that this fundamental requirement is perceptible everywhere: something is due to the human being simply because he is a human being... to advance the diversity of cultures as a reason for refusing to recognize the universality of human rights can only be a very poor pretext'. (Council of Europe, 1993, p. 8)

Hersch's strong assertion rested on a vast comparative survey of attitudes towards the Other drawn from most cultures (notably with the omission of South East Asia and the Pacific) over our recorded history. Grouped in categories that overlap our four key values, the replies showed the basis for conviviality if such norms were inculcated and followed. Indeed, among the people, they always had existed in folk and other 'low' traditions (Hersch, 1968).

In summary, the new civics required for living with difference is not only advanced by most significant and influential thinkers, and has roots back into history, but is also gradually being taken up by civics promoters. The focus on tolerance, trust and other virtues in the videos for schools now provided by European authorities is quite different from the continued stress on the militant citizen who insists on his or her rights to be found in national civics literature.

It is difficult to rethink categories and to return to such old apparently religious notions, especially when they can appear to subordinate the citizen to his duties to the state rather than make the latter his servant. Yet, despite even left-wing resistance, in regimes of difference, which wish to be moral, there can be no reduction of individuals to their social environment. Since Levi-Strauss pronounced his famous report to UNESCO on racism in 1951, Enlightenment historical developmentalism had been in the dock precisely because of its cultural relativism. Culture exists in the head and is the source of exclusions. The remarkable shift from the time when progressives supported cultural difference against universals, to the present use of cultural difference by ultra-conservatives to attack claims to the possibility of world peace through democracy and human rights, is evidenced by Samuel Huntington.

His pessimistic forecast about the relations between cultures is, regrettably, shared by many major Asian economic powers, as we have seen. Basing their positions on the existence of distinct Asian cultural values, leaders such as Mahathir Mohamed of Malaysia simply regard as western notions like human rights and democracy, and reject them as being inappropriate to their cultural traditions. Since they can only do so by caricaturing what citizenship means today in the West, projects like those of Hersch, which show massive overlaps in civic virtues, have an invaluable bridging function when global citizenship norms are proposed.

Global virtues

The notion that conviviality in an age of difference can come from education to a global citizenship is now also well-advanced both in regional polities and in the United Nations (UN) projects. For example, one document argues:

> Perhaps the time has come... to focus attention explicitly on *global citizenship*. This does not mean striking out in a new direction, but rather pursuing more deliberately a process that is already under way. The starting point was '...recognising that all human beings have certain fundamental rights'... codified in the Universal Declaration which had been made concrete by ignoring national borders as '...demands for human rights have been taking precedence over claims to national sovereignty'. (UNRISD, 1995, pp. 168–70)

This meant making further moves towards global governance to control unaccountable global decision making affecting all levels of life. The germs existed in the UN and other transnational organizations. The representativity of all these bodies should be strengthened politically as a major task of the UN. Such exhortations are accompanied by schemes such as the Global Commission's recommendation that the UN create a representative Forum of Civil Society, end the Security Council veto, consider a system of civil petition, and ultimately establish a people's chamber that controls the globe democratically (Global Commission, 1995, pp. 255–6, Ch. 7).

The UN promotion of civic education in that direction is paralleled in the vastly extended schemes of the Europeans, whose emphasis on a civic education that preaches tolerance of the Other, the recognition of community rights, and a non-national perspective in the allocation of rights has become stronger in recent years. In earlier eras, the Rousseauian/Kantian understanding of a world of individuals and states, rather than a tripartite scheme of individuals, communities and state machinery, had been the exclusive focus. Again, we find the theme that the best defence of difference is universal rights and that the way to reconcile multiculturalism and universalism as everyday conviviality is through extensive education programmes, especially among the very young.

These projects for global citizenship build on the network of international agreements on democracy, human rights and other matters that pertain to empowering people against chaos. The UN instruments now comprise not only the Universal Declaration of Human Rights (1948) and the two Covenants on civil and political rights (1966) and

economic, social and cultural rights (1965), but also those against genocide (1948), for the protection of refugees (1956), anti-discrimination
against women (1979), against torture (1984), and for the rights of the
child (1989). While not universally subscribed to, much less observed,
as we have shown, they are nevertheless signed by between half and
two-thirds of the world's states (UNDP, 1996, pp. 214–16). Together,
they establish an international rule of law. It is not entirely without
sanctioning power, and this would grow greatly the more popular power
grows at the UN at the expense of state power.

These instruments have parallels in those of the European Community. Apart from the Convention on Human Rights (1950) and its
multiple protocols (No. 6 abolishing the death penalty), it too has
Social Charters (1961) and a Convention Against Torture (1987). It will
soon have ratified conventions to protect women and children as well.
These are all seen as applications of UN standards, but they carry sanc-
tions and have therefore radically altered national policy in the areas
covered (see, for example, Council of Europe, 1995, pp. 115ff).

In addition, while the UN has as yet no political representation for
the people, Europe does, and thus adds to the judicial bodies and
administrative bodies that exist for both political bodies. Together, all
are being used more and more.

Notable has been the UN readiness to intervene to force its rulings
in different parts of the world. The Gulf War was an episode that split
opinion. On the one hand, it was seen as no more than a cover for a
US-led punitive gunboat diplomacy or a fight for oil. On the other, it
was seen as official UN documents portrayed it – as an extension
of the rule of law to a global space (Global Commission, 1995,
pp. 236–7). The first position seems less tenable after the recent role
played by the UN in defusing a second intervention in Iraq. In the bitter
debate on the intervention in Italy, Norberto Bobbio, before this a paci-
fist, highlighted the importance of the emergence of a law-making
body at an international level. He insisted that it was a matter of efficacity rather than establishing a just war thesis (Bobbio, 1991). His
views were shored up by the neo-Kantian belief that once democracy
was extended to all people, war would become unlikely as it was tyrannical regimes that historically made war.

While undoubtedly worthy, the institutions and proposals for a new
level of global citizenship come up against the sort of criticism made
by Schnapper: that the size of the global or regional multiethnic
constituency is too great to imagine any real civic commitment and
civic virtue. People will at least feel that they belong to a nation-state,

although not to a globe of kaleidoscope difference. Richard Falk, whose views were not without influence on the UN positions at the beginning of the 1990s, has changed his position radically over a period of seven years. In the aftermath of the Gulf War, he argued for global citizenship on the grounds that 'the global citizen... adheres to a normative perspective' and that economic integration, awareness of the limits to global resources and transnational militancy were reinforcing that development; 'an African baby is a powerful symbol of the vulnerability and solidarity of the species as a whole' (Falk, 1994, pp. 131–3). In 1996, he argued contrarily that a global, and even a regional, space was too great for there to be anything but a civic commitment that was so thin as to be inefficacious unless people were attached economically and socially to it. This did not seem to be globalization's trend. Instead, there was a fragmentation of citizenship everywhere. No education would overcome that. The world of the Internet and global traveller was destroying even national sense of attachment (Falk, 1996).

Even if we assume only regional rather than global spaces, it is fatuous and difficult for an Australian child to relate to a child in a country never before heard of. It is also impossible to expect any satisfactory 'global' education even in the major cultures of the world, so vast is the volume of information. Quick and facile solutions such as the indication of the emergence of vehicles for the transmission of information such as English as a global language (Crystal, 1997), now a lingua franca of a fifth of the world's population and of the development of the Internet, currently available only to a small (albeit fast-growing) minority of the world's 6 billion people, should not mislead us. Both only function by the expulsion of affect – which is needed for civic commitment – and still reach only a small minority.

More importantly, for there to be democracy, a regular dialogue is required to reach the common consensual norms or rule of law across cultures. So far, even a putative electronic parliament that avoids the problems forecast by the Europeans (see Chapter 7) runs into the argument of Bruce Ackerman. He recognizes that each culture believes in the values of its community and cannot really divest itself of them. To live with the Other, it has to engage in political dialogue with it, as the only way to discover where the Other has gone wrong is to talk with it. This leads him to assert that 'Somehow or other, citizens of a liberal state must learn to talk to one another in a way that enables each of them to avoid condemning their own personal morality as evil or false' (Ackerman, 1989). The only way to do this is through conversational restraint, which removes from the agenda what divides them morally or obliges them to say that what they feel is affirmatively false. Thus, dialogue is used only to discover what all political participants find not unreasonable, so as to be pragmatically productive. While any issue can be raised, restraint must be exercised concerning answers, and procedures for conflict resolution must be agreed. Ackerman believes that his conversational restraint has at least the advantage that while every time the debate takes place people have to repress many things that they think are true, they are not obliged to accept and express what is false for them. They learn to play the role of citizen, which is a partial role, like that of a lawyer in court (Ackerman, 1989).

I suspect that most diplomats would say that this has been diplomatic practice since its origins. The problem is not only that with thousands of different players, the unmentionable areas will soon shrink the possible space of agreement, but also that to set up institutions for global governance, the debate must establish positive agreement in many areas. Do they correspond with the unmentionable? How is the necessary affect to be created in the absence of community as traditionally understood?

Yet, despite the thinness of global citizenship and the problems posed about a shared language that is sufficient even to arrive at some elementary common agreement, some set of values greater than those demanded of a nation-state citizen is clearly required. The major problems of the twenty-first century – migration, pollution, crime, global epidemics – will be uncontrollable within nation-states. These are issues that cannot be coped with by a Periclean citizen ready to defend his or her national patrimony, even if it is democracy and human rights. The warrior-citizen is not enough if it means no more than a defence of what is ours against the Other.

Fortunately, in developed countries, that position appears to be held more by the older generation than by those who will decide in the next century. The first believe in the notion of citizenship as a heritage. A recent survey in France showed that such people believed, for example, that:

> It [citizenship/nationality] is the totality of traditions, customs, in fact it is tied to the family in the wide sense. To received tradition, to our history, to the history of our country. To a certain ethic vis-à-vis one's country. A certain ethic vis-à-vis what the family, in earlier generations, has been able to do. (Duchesne, 1997, pp. 46, 55, 85)

This explained why they felt that its basis was a similarity of past lived experience, and why migrants could not integrate completely. The strong sense of debt to the past and to the shared history was accompanied by a recognition, even among such people, that the nation-state might have seen its heyday. The notion of obligation to one's forebears was not a view shared by younger people, for whom 'you are a human being, others are the same' and that being sure 'that what comes from outside puts our system in peril is the opposite of progress and nonsense in human terms' (Duchesne, 1997, pp. 105, 107, 112, 117, 132). However, both groups agree on what civics should be. It is about 'the feelings that make a good citizen' rather than 'the devotion of a citizen to his country' (Duchesne, 1997, p. 194). Thus, the changing context is the ultimate arbiter.

This necessitates new virtues beyond those of the warrior-citizen of the past. The context is no longer one of homogeneous peoples who have fought to establish their freedom(s), and whose virtue is measured by their readiness to fight to defend them against outside and menacing Others for whom they are 'unreason'. As we have seen, several authors and opinion leaders are today developing a new civics for a global world of difference. While increasingly influential, what is most important is the complementarity of their views. These recall the somewhat unheroic and peaceful conviviality of the marketplace where difference meets to trade values. This goes back to Kant's cosmopolitan citizen. Kant wrote that perpetual peace might be expected as 'a commercial spirit cannot coexist with war and sooner or later the first captures every people'. He argued that, when pushed to associate, humans are driven to establish law everywhere and to adopt the practice of 'universal hospitality' (Kant, 1985, pp. 26, 16). Of course, nineteenth- and twentieth-century history belied that hope as nation-states fought for economic dominance. As we showed earlier, however, the new globalism and most certainly regionalism of the European sort is designed precisely to avoid such conflict.

10

Postscript: Citizenship or Chaos?

We conclude this book at the beginning of the new millennium. All the major forecasts suggest that globalization will continue and grow in the next century. There will be a continued shake-up of old stabilities, and a reproduction of societies and states as difference rather than homogeneity. The battle for the empowerment of human beings in the political realm will continue. Indeed, the Asian financial crisis that started in 1997, with its consequent unemployment and misery for millions, suggests that the good period may be over. The belief that the new global reorganization of capital would end the contradictions that condemn the majority of the world's people to poverty can only be in doubt today.

The problems to be managed are increasing, as is the challenge for exponents of citizenship. Foremost among these problems is the growth of multiethnic states everywhere in the globe. This undermines any sense anywhere that an individual can always be expected to belong exclusively to one national family and thus to support its nation-state. Instead, multicultural policies to manage the new difference, owed to the migration of huge 'alien' workforces, have brought humanity face to face with the need for new policies to attach human beings to their patrimony, and to breed in them a new set of rights, duties and obligations to each other and to a rule of law.

We have shown throughout this book that there are two main positions in the debate on how to manage globalization through citizen power. These overlap and complement each other, so the debate ends as a matter of emphasis. One school really wants to revamp and amplify the existing nation-state citizenship as the nation-state changes and adapts to a new role in the global economy (Cerny, 1990; Palan,

1996). Then there is a second school that believes we must go beyond nation-state citizenship and supplement it with a new regional or global citizenship.

We find two groups of people within the global-citizenship camp, who reflect the opinions found at nation-state level. There are the free marketeers, who nevertheless want a rule of law within that market-place and are sometimes ready to consider a modified democracy (Reich, 1991; Ohmae, 1995). Then there are the global liberal social-ists, who can see no hope of a commitment even to regional parlia-ments without adequate economic, social and cultural investment in the global constituency (Falk, 1994). At the nation-state level, the economic rationalists seem to be ascendant, but in the much less-developed regional and global sphere, we find both more democracy and also a greater demand for third-generation (social) rights.

As we have shown, only a few countries among those benefitting from globalization seem to be in favour of promoting the democratic and human rights of citizens. Often, they too are half-hearted. Even among the group that believes in nation-state citizenship, a majority (especially among Asian countries) rejects proposals that globaliza-tion would best be challenged by extending democracy and human rights. Instead, they claim that their traditional cultural way of managing their societies is preferable. Typical is the Singapore solu-tion, in which an autocratic state, run by an administrative élite, imposes a high level of accumulation of wealth and provides good economic and social conditions for all inhabitants, who are not expected to do anything but obey.

In summary, the very notion of citizenship as traditionally under-stood is highly contested by the emerging centres of power, who favour management by a technological élite. They have an increasing number of allies within the former bastions of democratic citizenship among supporters of the post-modern position that no universal values can be found in a world whose sense as a totality escapes us. There is increasing post-modern insistence that we must learn to live with 'risk'.

Yet, it is the human misery that has accompanied globalization, and that has worsened in the past 20 years, which is the source of an even graver problem for the expansion of democratic citizenship. The fear of chaos, as we showed in Chapter 2, is why there is a drive for citizen-ship as humans seek security and a calculable world in which risks are minimized. Today, it has become starkly clear that the main problem is not the rival position of different states, or even peoples, on how to establish a better rule of law. At best, 40 per cent of the world's population lives in places where the rule of law is more or less established. It is the other 60 per cent who are caught in the downside of the global world.

What is happening to the majority of the global population is the threat of imminent social chaos of a type and a scale not seen since the Middle Ages. They face, and often already live in, situations that evoke the state of 'war of all against all' described by the political philosopher Thomas Hobbes (1968) in the seventeenth century. In many areas, there is certainly no rule of law, even under a total autocrat. The recognition of this condition is materially visible in the emergence of walled cities protected by private armies not only in Third World countries, but also in the developed centres of globalization (Davis, 1990; McKenzie, 1994; Kuntsler, 1996). Outside them are the threatening 'hordes' of the impoverished and dispossessed.

It cannot have escaped readers that Africa, Latin America, the Middle East and most of South and Central Asia have not figured in this book. We have attempted to cover the globe in a discussion that has ranged from Europe, North America, Oceania, Japan and the 'tiger economies', to mere dots in the Pacific Ocean, such as Fiji. We did this in an endeavour to show not merely the success of globalization, but also its failures, and to demonstrate how difficult and how varied are attempts to empower individuals to meet globalizations' challenges as citizens; but it was clearly beyond one book to deal adequately with the whole world.

Yet, this is not the main reason for the glaring absence of some of the largest and most populous regions on the globe. Instead, their absence can be explained by the fact that they are already in the throes of a return to barbarism. The Global Commission states:

A disturbing feature of the contemporary world is the spread of the culture of violence. Civil wars brutalize thousands of young people who are drawn into them. The systematic use of rape as a weapon of war has been an especially pernicious feature of some conflicts. Civil wars leave countless weapons and a legacy of continuing violence. Several political movements, ostensibly dedicated to the liberation of people, have taken to terrorism, showing scant regard for the lives of innocent civilians, including those in whose name they are fighting. Violence is sometimes perceived as an end in itself....

A hopeful scenario portrays the present level of violence as a transitional phenomenon. In this view, the world is likely to become much more peaceful and secure for most of its inhabitants once it recovers from the disruptions caused by the sudden end of the Cold War. Another scenario envisages a world divided into two: a prosperous and secure part that would include most of Western and

Central Europe, East Asia and North America, and a larger part of impoverished and violently conflicted territories without stable governments, which would include large areas of Africa, the Middle East, and South Asia and possibly bits of Central and South America. (Global Commission, 1995: pp. 16–17)

It is true that India is the world's largest democracy and still more or less successfully meets the requirements of a rule of law. However, both Africa and parts of South and Central Asia are already outside the scope of a book about the contest between globalization and citizenship. If they are certainly among the worst victims of globalization and illustrate how adverse globalization has been for the lives of the people who live in such areas, they do not have a place in a book that is about citizenship. In such areas, the state has practically collapsed; citizenship presumes a state and the rule of law.

Barbarism finds expression more and more each day in such places as Rwanda, Sierra Leone, the Congo, Sri Lanka, Afghanistan, Algeria and Iraq in a loss of all norms, of all security, in the emergence of societies where the war of all against all descends to the widespread and growing use of torture, where child armies are common. Menchu's description of the torture by burning alive and flaying of her brother only years ago is so typical of Central America and other chaotic regions that similar cases fill the dossiers of Amnesty International's reports (Menchu, 1984; Amnesty International, 1997).

The most excluded and weakest in this Hobbesian world are women and children, who are an absolute majority subject to horrendous abuse and exploitation. *States of Disarray* (UNRISD, 1995 pp. 145ff) notes the enormous growth in the number of female heads of families as men migrate for work. The gender-related development index of the United Nations Development Program shows that gender disparity in wellbeing is worst in Nigeria, Sierra Leone, Afghanistan, Burkina Faso and Mali. The figures for India are almost as bad (UNDP, 1996, pp. 32–5). The trafficking of women and children for prostitution is a fast-growing form of migration closely linked to organized crime. Moreover, a large number of children in poor regions are obliged to work. This struggle for existence ends all hope of public participation or even the literacy that underpins it.

Restructuring of the economy by global capital, together with large-scale migration, often spells the end of the traditional societies or civilizations that had already been undermined in the colonial period. The old order disappears, and the new order has been in crisis for many years. The post-colonial state finds itself confronted with ethnic separatisms and unable to implement the democratic and human rights norms proposed by the UN and many of their own leaders (Mamdani, 1996; Ashforth, 1997) What ensues is often general violence, displacement and death.

In places where traditional structures are breaking down and the new state has lost control – or never gained it – the chaos is sometimes masked as a search for ideological purity or a return to cultural origins. Fundamentalist Islam is typical of this trend, its outcomes in the slaughters of Algeria and Afghanistan being notorious (Kepel, 1994; Turner, 1994; Touati, 1996). Another development is the proliferation of criminal organizations. Typical are the Medellin and Cali cartels that have world-wide links in the drug trade. Building on the *violencia* that has been typical of the non-state of that region of Colombia where people are regularly murdered in the most brutal fashion, it has imported a culture of violence into its world. Again, we find that children and youths are among the main actors (Odquist, 1980; Salazar, 1990; Comment, 1993).

Both fundamentalists and criminal organizations become the groups to which the impoverished turn in the absence of the state and citizenship. They provide what social welfare and education, what order, is possible at the price of a denial of autonomy. Their militants share a cult of death. So uncontrollable does life seem to them that they believe that the impure or disloyal must be purged from the earth. We see this carelessness of death in the human bombs of Hamas and Sri Lanka, and in the enforcers of the drug cartels. It has spread to the killers of street children throughout the world (Salazar, 1990; Touati, 1996). Even Hobbes pointed out that it is from the refusal of death that rights start.

So desperate are conditions in such parts of the world that there has been a massive and unprecedented outflow from them. Nearly half of the world's refugees are in Africa, and many more are in South and Central Asia. Labour migration is also very high. Sooner or later, many of these people make it to the rich countries. Today, the highest inflow to Europe comes from Eastern Europe and the former Yugoslavia, with North African and Middle Eastern countries following. Latin Americans cross the 'tortilla curtain' to the USA and Canada.

Thus, while it is clear that the chaos is found above all in underdeveloped regions, it has spread to the metropoles through globalization. With the massive growth of the drug trade, the mores of Medellin have become those of parts of North America, and those of the Moscow mafia, those of parts of Western Europe, while those of fundamentalist Islam thrive in the former Yugoslavia and in Moscow (Klein, 1995; Kleinknecht, 1996). Drugs are second only to the arms trade as money earners, beating oil into third place. They create a subculture of their own: for children in the street gangs of Sao Paulo, Bangkok or New York, for example, drug consumption is a part of a ritual of belonging and obligation that further marginalizes them from mainstream society (UNRISD 1995, p. 87). With the spread of drugs comes the spread of disease, particularly HIV–AIDS, which takes on epidemic proportions both in the poorest countries (where there is practically no medicine) and in enclaves of global cities. An endless cycle of impoverishment and marginalization is set up, even in the rich part of the world.

Added together, such life experiences do not add up to the drive for citizenship as human rights and democracy. Instead, there is a yen for security, and for solutions that seek authoritarian regimes emphasizing law and order. As collective human bonds disintegrate in many places, the challenge that is faced is two-fold. On the one hand, there is the struggle to have stable but authoritarian regimes such as those of South East Asia turn in a democratic direction and show more respect for human rights. On the other, there is the much greater threat of anarchy or chaos. It is too pessimistic to argue, as Kaplan (1996a) has done, that democracy was merely a brief hiatus in human history. There is a common cause on a global level to be made against the threat of chaos by all those who think that a rule of law is preferable to the war of all against all. Finding the political will, the organizational capability and the new institutions to achieve this is the great human challenge of the new millennium.

Bibliography

Ackerman, B. 'Why dialogue?', *Journal of Philosophy* **86**, 1 (1989) pp. 5–23.

Adams, J. T. *The Epic of America* (Boston: Little, Brown, 1931).

Adelman, J. 'European migration to Argentina, 1880–1930', in R. Cohen (ed.) *Cambridge Survey of World Migration* (Cambridge: Cambridge University Press, 1995) pp. 215–19.

ADL. *Hate Groups in America* (New York: Anti-Defamation League of B'nai B'rith, annual).

Afshar, H. 'Fundamentalism and women in Iran', in O. Mendelsohn and U. Baxi (eds) *The Rights of Subordinated Peoples* (Delhi: Oxford University Press, 1994) pp. 276–95.

Aikman, C. 'Constitutional developments in the Cook Islands', in P. Sack (ed.) *Pacific Constitutions: Proceedings of the Canberra Law Workshop VI* (Canberra: Law Department, Research School of Social Sciences, Australian National University, 1982) pp. 87–97.

Alcorso, C. 'Economic stocktake: trends and issues for non-English speaking background women since 1982', *Australian Feminist Studies* **18** (1993) pp. 49–66.

Alcorso, C., Popoli, G. P. and Rando, G. 'Community networks and institutions', in S. Castles, C. Alcorso, G. Rando and E. Vasta (eds) *Australia's Italians: Culture and Community in a Changing Society* (Sydney: Allen & Unwin, 1992) pp. 106–24.

Aldrich, R. and Connell, J. *France's Overseas Frontier: Départements et Territoires d'Outre-mer* (Cambridge: Cambridge University Press, 1992).

Ålund, A. 'Wrestling with ghosts: transcultural bricolage and new communities', in A. Ålund and C.-U. Schierup, *Paradoxes of Multiculturalism* (Aldershot: Avebury, 1991) pp. 89–112.

Amnesty International. *Algérie: le livre noir* (Paris: La Découverte, 1997).

Anderson, B. *Imagined Communities* (London: Verso, 1983).

Andric, I. *The Bridge over the Drina* (London: Harvill, 1994) [first published in Serbo-Croatian, 1945].

Anthias, F. and Yuval-Davis, N. 'Introduction', in N. Yuval-Davis and F. Anthias (eds) *Woman–Nation–State* (London: Macmillan, 1989) pp. 1–15.

Appadurai, A. 'Disjuncture and difference in the global cultural economy', in M. Featherstone (ed.) *Global Culture: Nationalism, Globalization and Modernity* (London: Sage, 1990) pp. 195–311.

Appleyard, R. T. 'International migration and developing countries', in R. T. Appleyard (ed.) *The Impact of International Migration on Developing Countries* (Paris: OECD, 1989) pp. 19–45.

Aristotle. *The Politics* (Hardmondsworth: Penguin, 1986).

Arthur, J. and Shapiro, A. (eds.) *Campus Wars: Multiculturalism and the Politics of Difference* (Boulder: Westview Press, 1995).

Ashforth, A. 'Lineaments of the political geography of state formation in twentieth century South Africa', *Journal of Historical Sociology* **10**, 2 (1997) pp. 101–26.

Autrement. 'Le civisme: vertu privée d'utilité publique', *Autrement* **19** (1997).

Bade, K. J. 'Germany: migrations in Europe up to the end of the Weimar Republic', in R. Cohen (ed.) *Cambridge Survey of World Migration* (Cambridge: Cambridge University Press, 1995) pp. 131–5.

Baldwin-Edwards, M. and Schain, M. A. *The Politics of Immigration in Western Europe*. Special issue of *West European Politics* **7**, 2 (1994).

Balibar, E. 'L'Europe des citoyens', in O. le Cour Grandmaison and C. Wihtol de Wenden (eds) *Les étrangers dans la cité: expériences européennes* (Paris: La Découverte, 1993).

Balibar, E. and Wallerstein, I. *Race, Nation, Class: Ambiguous Identities* (London: Verso, 1991).

Ball, W. and Solomos, J. (eds) *Race and Local Politics* (London: Macmillan, 1990).

Barbelet, J. M. *Citizenship* (Milton Keynes: Open University Press, 1988).

Basch, L., Glick-Schiller, N. and Blanc, C. S. *Nations Unbound: Transnational Projects, Post-Colonial Predicaments and Deterritorialized Nation-States* (New York: Gordon & Breach, 1994).

Bauböck, R. 'Changing the boundaries of citizenship: the inclusion of immigrants in democratic polities', in R. Bauböck (ed.) *From Aliens to Citizens* (Aldershot: Avebury, 1994) pp. 199–232.

Bauböck, R. and Rundell, J. (eds) 'Globalization and the ambiguities of national citizenship', *Blurred Boundaries* (Aldershot: Ashgate, 1998).

Beer, L. and Itoh, H. *Japanese Constitutional Law* (Seattle: University of Washington Press, 1995).

Bernard, P. *L'immigration* (Paris: Le Monde, 1993).

Björgo, T. and Witte, R. 'Introduction', in T. Björgo and R. Witte (eds) *Racist Violence in Europe* (London: Macmillan, 1993a) pp. 1–16.

Björgo, T. and Witte, R. (eds) *Racist Violence in Europe* (London: Macmillan, 1993b).

Bloom, A. *The Closing of the American Mind* (New York: Simon & Schuster, 1987).

Bobbio, N. *Il futuro della democrazia* (Turin: Einaudi, 1984).

Bobbio, N. *Thomas Hobbes* (Turin: Einaudi, 1989).

Bobbio, N. *L'età dei diritti* (Turin: Einaudi, 1990a).

Bobbio, N. 'Le ragioni della tolleranza', in N. Bobbio (ed.) *L'età dei diritti* (Turin: Einaudi, 1990b) pp. 135–52.

Bobbio, N. *Una guerra giusta?: sul conflitto del Golfo* (Venice: Marsilio, 1991).

Bobbio, N. 'In praise of meekness', *Convivio* **1**, 1 (1995) pp. 21–38.

Body-Gendrot, S. 'Migration and the racialisation of the postmodern city in France', in M. Cross and M. Keith (eds) *Racism, the City and the State* (London: Routledge, 1993a) pp. 77–92.

Body-Gendrot, S. *Ville et violence* (Paris: Presses Universitaires de France, 1993b).

Boengkih, J. 'Citizenship in the French Pacific', paper presented to the Conference on Globalisation and Citizenship (UNRISD/Swinburne), Melbourne, 6–9 May (1997).

Bole, F. 'Fiji's chiefly system and its pattern of political self-reliance', in R. Crocombe, U. Neemia, A. Ravuvu and W. vom Busch (eds) *Culture and Democracy in the South Pacific* (Suva: University of the South Pacific, 1992) pp. 67–79.

Bommes, M. 'Migration und Ethnizität im nationalen Sozialstaat', *Zeitschrift für Soziologie* **5**, 23 (1994) pp. 364–77.

Bonaga, S. *Bologna 'CityCard' Project Seminar on Electronic Democracy* (Paris: Senate, République Française, 1995).

Booth, M. *The Triads: The Chinese Criminal Fraternity* (London: Grafton, 1990).

Bouamama, S. *Vers une nouvelle citoyenneté: crise de la pensée laïque* (Lille: Boîte de Pandore, 1991).

Bouamama, S. *Dix ans de marche des Beurs* (Paris: Desclée de Brouwer, 1994).

Bouamama, S. 'The view of the pariah (interview with Alastair Davidson)', *Eureka Street* **7**, 6 (1997a) pp. 14–15.

Bouamama, S. 'For a new multicultural and universal citizenship', paper presented to the Conference on Globalisation and Citizenship (UNRISD/Swinburne), Melbourne, 6–9 May (1997b).

Bouamama, S., Cordeiro, A. and Roux, M. *La citoyenneté dans tous ses états: de l'immigration à la nouvelle citoyenneté* (Paris: l'Harmattan, 1992).

Bovero, M. and Bobbio, N. *Società e stato nella filosofia politica moderna* (Milan: Il Saggiatore, 1979).

Bradshaw, Y. and Wallace, M. *Global Inequalities* (California: Pine Forge, 1996).

Breton, R., Isajiw, W. W., Kalbach, W. E. and Reitz, J. G. *Ethnic Identity and Equality* (Toronto: University of Toronto Press, 1990).

Brimelow, P. *Alien Nation: Common Sense about America's Immigration Disaster* (New York: Random House, 1995).

Brown, P. and Shue, H. *Boundaries: National Autonomy and its Limits* (Totowa, NJ: Rowan & Littlefield, 1969).

Bryce, J. *Promoting Good Citizenship* (Chicago: Houghton Mifflin, 1909).

Burnley, I. 'Immigration, ancestry and residence in Sydney', *Australian Geographical Studies* **32**, 1 (1994) pp. 68–89.

Carnoy, M. *Faded Dreams: The Politics and Economics of Race in America* (Cambridge: Cambridge University Press, 1994).

Castells, M. *The Rise of the Network Society* (Oxford: Blackwell, 1996).

Castles, S., with Booth, H. and Wallace, T. *Here for Good: Western Europe's New Ethnic Minorities* (London: Pluto Press, 1984).

Castles, S. 'The guest-worker in western Europe: an obituary', *International Migration Review* **20**, 4 (1986) pp. 761–78.

Castles, S. 'How nation-states respond to immigration and ethnic diversity', *New Community* **21**, 3 (1995a) pp. 293–308.

Castles, S. 'Contract labour migration', in R. Cohen (ed.) *Cambridge Survey of World Migration* (Cambridge: Cambridge University Press, 1995b) pp. 510–14.

Castles, S. 'The racisms of globalisation', in E. Vasta and S. Castles (eds) *The Teeth are Smiling: The Persistence of Racism in Multicultural Australia* (Sydney: Allen & Unwin, 1996) pp. 17–45.

Castles, S. 'Underclass or exclusion: social citizenship for minorities', in E. Vasta (ed.) *Citizenship, Community and Democracy* (London: Macmillan, 1999).

Castles, S. and Kosack, G. *Immigrant Workers and Class Structure in Western Europe* (Oxford: Oxford University Press, 1973, 1985).

Castles, S. and Miller, M. J. *The Age of Migration: International Population Movements in the Modern World* (London: Macmillan/New York: Guilford Books, 1998) (second edition).

Castles, S., Foster, W., Iredale, R. and Withers, G. *Immigration and Australia: Myths and Realities* (Sydney: Allen & Unwin, 1998).

Cerny, P. *The Architecture of Politics* (London: Sage, 1990).

Chan, J. 'The task for Asians: to discover their own political morality for human rights', *Human Rights Dialogue* **4**, March (1996) pp. 5–7.

Choue, Y. *Textbook on World Citizenship* (Seoul: Kyung Hee University Press, 1986).

Çinar, D. 'From aliens to citizens: a comparative analysis of rules of transition', in R. Bauböck (ed.) *From Aliens to Citizens* (Aldershot: Avebury, 1994) pp. 49–72.

Civitas. *National Standards for Civics and Government* (Calabasas: Centre for Civic Education, 1994).

Cohen, R. *The Cambridge Survey of World Migration* (Cambridge: Cambridge University Press, 1995)

Cohen, R. *Global Diasporas: An Introduction* (London: UCL Press, 1997).

Cohn-Bendit, D. and Schmid, T. *Heimat Babylon: Das Wagnis der multikulturellen Demokratie* (Hamburg: Hoffmann und Campe, 1992).

Collins, J. *Migrant Hands in a Distant Land: Australia's Post-War Immigration* (Sydney: Pluto Press, 1991) (second edition).

Collins, J., Gibson, K., Alcorso, C., Castles, S. and Tait, D. *A Shop Full of Dreams: Ethnic Small Business in Australia* (Sydney: Pluto Press, 1995).

Collins, P. H. *Black Feminist Thought: Knowledge, Consciousness and the Politics of Empowerment* (New York: Routledge, 1991).

Comment. *Coca, Cocaine and the War on Drugs* (London: Catholic Institute for International Relations, 1993).

Conac, G. and Amor, A. *Islam et les droits de l'homme* (Paris: Economica, 1994).

Condorcet, M. J. A. *Esquisse d'un tableau des progrès de l'esprit humain* (Paris: Flammarion, 1988).

Connor, W. 'From tribe to nation', *History of European Ideas* **13**, 1/2 (1991) pp. 5–18.

Constant, B. *Political Writings* (Cambridge: Cambridge University Press, 1990).

Council of Europe. *Human Rights at the Dawn of the 21st Century* (Strasbourg: Council of Europe, 1993).

Council of Europe. *Human Rights: A Continuing Challenge for the Council of Europe* (Strasbourg: Council of Europe, 1995).

Crocombe, R., Neemia, U., Ravuvu, A. and vom Busch, W. (eds) *Culture and Democracy in the South Pacific* (Suva: University of the South Pacific, 1992).

Cross, M. 'Race, class formation and political interests: a comparison of Amsterdam and London', in A. Hargreaves and J. Leaman (eds) *Racism, Ethnicity and Politics in Contemporary Europe* (Aldershot: Edward Elgar, 1995) pp. 47–78.

Cross, M. and Keith, M. (eds) *Racism, the City and the State* (London: Routledge, 1993).

Crystal, D. *English as a Global Language* (Cambridge: Cambridge University Press, 1997).

Dahrendorf, R. 'The changing quality of citizenship', in B. van Steenbergen (ed.) *The Condition of Citizenship* (London: Sage, 1994) pp. 10–19.

Dalton, R. *Citizen Politics in Western Democracies: Public Opinion and Political Parties in the United States, Great Britain, West Germany and France* (Chatham, NJ: Chatham House, 1988).

Davidson, A. 'Expansionary citizenship: the European experience', paper presented to the Conference on Globalisation and Citizenship (UNRISD/Swinburne), Geneva, 9–11 December (1996a).

Davidson, A. 'Paper cleansing', *Eureka Street* **6**, 9 (1996b) pp. 10–12.

Davidson, A. 'Mildness: a new civic virtue', *Humanist* May (1996c) pp. 2–10.

Davidson, A. *From Subject to Citizen: Australian Citizenship in the Twentieth Century* (Cambridge: Cambridge University Press, 1997).

Davidson, A. 'Never the twain shall meet?: Europe, Asia and the Citizen', in A. Davidson and K. Weekley (eds) *Globalization and Citizenship in the Asia-Pacific* (London: Macmillan, 1999).

Davidson, A. 'Fractured identities: citizenship in a global world', in E. Vasta (ed.) *Citizenship, Community and Democracy* (London: Macmillan, 1999).

Davis, M. *City of Quartz: Excavating the Future in Los Angeles* (London: Verso, 1990).

de Jonge, H. 'Democrazia e sviluppo economico nella regione Asia-Pacifico', *Rivista di studi politici internazionali* **61**, 244 (1994) pp. 547–65.

Delbruck, J. 'Global migration-immigration-multiethnicity: challenges to the concept of the nation-state', *Indiana Journal of Global Legal Studies* **2**, 1 (1994).

Delemotte, B., Chevallier, J. and Bayala, A. *Etranger et citoyen: Les immigrés et la démocratie locale* (Paris: l'Harmattan, 1996).

Demandt, A. 'Patria Gentium – das Imperium Romanum als Vielvölkerstaat', in K. J. Bade (ed.) *Menschen über Grenzen – Grenzen über Menschen: Die multikulturelle Herausforderung* (Herne: Heitkamp, 1995) pp. 22–37.

Directorate General of Research/European Parliament *Enlarged Community: Institutional Adaptations* (Luxembourg: European Parliament, 1992).

Dodson, M. 'Indigenous people and the globalization of rights', in A. Davidson and K. Weekley (eds) *Globalization and Citizenship in the Asia-Pacific* (London: Macmillan, 1999) pp. 203–18.

Dryzek, J. S. 'Political inclusion and the dynamics of democratization', *American Political Science Review* **1** (1996) pp. 475–87.

Dubet, F. and Lapeyronnie, D. *Les quartiers d'exil* (Paris: Seuil, 1992).

Duchesne, S. *Citoyenneté à la française* (Paris: Presses de Sciences Po, 1997).

Eade, J. (ed.) *Living the Global City: Globalization as a Local Process* (London: Routledge, 1997).

Eco, U. 'Tolerance and the intolerable', *Index on Censorship* **1**, 2 (1994) pp. 47–55.

Ehrenberg, V. 'The origins of democracy', *Historia* **1**, 4 (1950) pp. 515–48.

Esman, M. J. *Ethnic Politics* (Ithaca: Cornell University Press, 1994).

Esping-Andersen, G. *The Three Worlds of Welfare Capitalism* (Cambridge: Polity Press, 1990).

Essed, P. *Understanding Everyday Racism* (Newbury Park, CA: Sage, 1991).

European Parliament. *Committee of Inquiry into the Rise of Fascism and Racism in Europe: Report on the Findings of the Inquiry* (Strasbourg: European Parliament, 1985).

Fabricius, F. *Human Rights and European Politics: The Legal-political Status of Workers in the European Community* (Oxford: Berg, 1992).

Faist, T. 'From school to work: public policy and underclass formation among young Turks in Germany during the 1980s', *International Migration Review* **27**, 2 (1993) pp. 306–31.

Falk, R. 'The making of global citizenship', in B. van Steenbergen (ed.) *The Condition of Citizenship* (London: Sage, 1994) pp. 126–40.

Falk, R. 'The decline of citizenship in an era of globalisation', paper presented to the Conference on Globalisation and Citizenship (UNRISD/Swinburne), Geneva – December (1996).

Fehér, F. and Heller, A. 'Naturalisation or "culturalisation"?', in R. Bauböck (ed.) *From Aliens to Citizens* (Aldershot: Avebury, 1994) pp. 135–48.

Finkielkraut, A. *La sagesse de l'amour* (Paris: Gallimard, 1984).

Fontaine, P. *A Citizen's Europe* (Brussels/ECSC-EEC-EAEC, 1991).

Fukuyama, F. *The End of History and the Last Man* (London: Penguin, 1992).

Fukuyama, F. *Trust: The Social Virtues and the Creation of Prosperity* (London: Hamish Hamilton, 1995).

Gaze, B. and Jones, M. *Law, Liberty and Australian Democracy* (Sydney: Law Book Company, 1990).

Gilroy, P. *There Ain't no Black in the Union Jack* (London: Hutchinson, 1987).

Gitlin, T. *The Twilight of Common Dreams: Why America is Wracked by Culture Wars* (New York: Henry Holt, 1995).

Glazer, N. and Moynihan, D. P. 'Introduction', in N. Glazer and D. P. Moynihan (eds), *Ethnicity: Theory and Experience* (Cambridge, MA: Harvard University Press, 1975) pp. 1–26.

Global Commission. *Our Global Neighbourhood: Report of the Commission on Global Governance* (Oxford: Oxford University Press, 1995).

Goldberg, D. T. *Racist Culture: Philosophy and the Politics of Meaning* (Oxford: Blackwell, 1993).

Goldberg, D. T. 'Introduction: multicultural conditions', in D. T. Goldberg (ed.) *Multiculturalism: A Critical Reader* (Oxford: Blackwell, 1994) pp. 1–41.

Gomien, D. *Short Guide to the European Convention on Human Rights* (Strasbourg: Council of Europe, 1991).

Goodman, R. and Peng, I. 'The East Asian welfare states: peripatetic learning, adaptive change and nation building', in G. Esping-Andersen (ed.) *Welfare States in Transition: National Adaptations in Global Economies* (London: Sage, 1996) pp. 192–225.

Gregory, J. *Sex, Race and the Law* (London: Sage, 1987).

Grisel, E. 'The beginnings of international law and general public law doctrine: Francisco de Vitoria's *De Indiis prior* ', in F. Chiappelli (ed.) *First Images of America: The Impact of the New World on the Old* (Berkeley: University of California Press, 1976) pp. 305–25.

Guimezanes, N. 'Acquisition of nationality in OECD countries', in OECD (ed.) *Trends in International Migration: Annual Report* (Paris: OECD, 1995) pp. 157–72.

Habermas, J. 'Struggles for recognition in the democratic constitutional state', in A. Gutmann (ed.) *Multiculturalism: Examining the Politics of Recognition* (Princeton NJ: Princeton University Press, 1994a) pp. 107–48.

Habermas, J. 'Citizenship and national identity', in B. van Steenbergen (ed.) *The Condition of Citizenship* (London: Sage, 1994b) pp. 20–35.

Habermas, J. 'Der europäische Nationalstaat – zu Vergangenheit und Zukunft von Souveränität und Staatsbürgerschaft', in J. Habermas (ed.) *Die Einbeziehung des Anderen: Studien zur politischen Theorie* (Frankfurt/M: Suhrkamp, 1996) pp. 128–53.

Hage, G. 'At home in the entrails of the West', in H. Grace, G. Hage, L. Johnson, J. Langsworth and M. Symonds, *Home/World: Space, Community and Marginality in Sydney's West* (Sydney: Pluto, 1997) pp. 99–153.

Hammar, T. *Democracy and the Nation-state: Aliens, Denizens and Citizens in a World of International Migration* (Aldershot: Avebury, 1990).

Hargreaves, A. G. and Leaman, J. (eds) *Racism, Ethnicity and Politics in Contemporary Europe* (Aldershot: Edward Elgar, 1995).

Harris, N. *The New Untouchables: Immigration and the New World Worker* (London: Penguin, 1996).

Hartsock, N. 'Prologue to a feminist critique of war and politics', in J. Stiehm (ed.) *Women's Views of the Political World of Men* (New York: Transnational, 1984) pp. 123–50.

Hassall, G. 'Citizenship in the Asia-Pacific', in A. Davidson and K. Weekley (eds) *Globalization and Citizenship in the Asia-Pacific* (London: Macmillan, 1999) pp. 49–70.

Hassall, G. and Singin, S. 'Citizenship in Papua New Guinea', in A. Davidson and K. Weekley (eds) *Globalization and Citizenship in the Asia-Pacific* (London: Macmillan, 1999), pp. 104–18.

Häussermann, H. and Kazapov, Y. 'Urban poverty in Germany', in E. Mingione (ed.) *Urban Poverty and the Underclass* (Oxford: Blackwell, 1996) pp. 343–69.

Hegel, G. *The Philosophy of History* (Oxford: Oxford University Press, 1949).

Helie-Lucas, M.-E. 'Strategies of women and women's movements in the Muslim world vis-à-vis fundamentalisms: from entryism to internationalism', in O. Mendelsohn and U. Baxi (eds) *The Rights of Subordinated Peoples* (Delhi: Oxford University Press, 1994) pp. 251–76.

Henderson, J. 'Prospects of democracy in Oceania', in T. Vanhanen (ed.) *Prospects of Democracy: A Study of 172 Countries* (New York: Routledge, 1997), pp. 334–44.

Hersch, J. *Le droit d'être un homme: anthologie mondiale de la liberté* (Geneva: Lattes/UNESCO, 1968).

Higham J, *Strangers in the Land: Patterns of American Nativism, 1860–1925* (New York: Atheneum, 1974).

Hill, M. and Fee, L. K. *The Politics of Nation Building and Citizenship in Singapore* (London: Routledge, 1995).

Hobbes, T. *Leviathan* (ed. C. B. Macpherson) (Harmondsworth: Penguin, 1968).

Hobhouse, L. *Liberalism* (Oxford: Oxford University Press, 1964).

Hoffmann, L. *Das deutsche Volk und seine Feinde* (Cologne: Pappyrossa Verlag, 1994).

Hommes et Migrations. 'Réfugiés et demandeurs d'asile', *Hommes et Migrations* (1996) pp. 89–90.

HREOC (Human Rights and Equal Opportunity Commission) *Racist Violence: Report of the National Inquiry into Racist Violence in Australia* (Canberra: Australian Government Publishing Service, 1991).

Huguet, J. W. 'Data on international migration in Asia: 1990–94', *Asian and Pacific Migration Journal* **4**, 4 (1995) pp. 519–30.

Humana, C. *World Human Rights Guide* (Oxford: Oxford University Press, 1992).

Huntington, S. 'The clash of civilizations', *Foreign Affairs* **72**, 3 (1993) pp. 22–49.

Husbands, C. T. '"They must obey our laws and customs!": political debate about Muslim assimilability in Great Britain, France and the Netherlands', in A. G. Hargreaves and J. Leaman (eds) *Racism, Ethnicity and Politics in Contemporary Europe* (Aldershot: Edward Elgar, 1995) pp. 115–30.

Ibn Battuta. *Voyages* (Paris: Maspero, 1982).

IMR. 'Special issue: the new Europe and international migration', *International Migration Review* **26**, 2 (1992).

Irigaray, L. *Ethique de la différence sexuelle* (Paris: Minuit, 1984).

Johnson, C. 'The empowerment of Asia', *Australian Quarterly* **67**, 2 (1995) pp. 11–28.

Johnson, J. H. Jr, Farrell, W. C. Jr and Guinn, C. 'Immigration reform and the browning of America: tensions, conflicts and community instability in metropolitan Los Angeles', *IMR* **31**, 4 (1997) pp. 1055–95.

Jupp, J. and Kabala, M. (eds) *The Politics of Australian Immigration* (Canberra: Australian Government Publishing Service, 1993).

Kant, I. 'What is enlightenment?', in C. Friedrich (ed.) *Kant's Political Writings* (New York: Random House, 1784) pp. 132–40.

Kant, I. *Per la pace perpetua* (edited by N. Bobbio) (Rome: Riuniti, 1985).

Kaplan, D. and Dubro, A. *Yakuza* (New York: Addison-Wesley, 1986).

Kaplan, R. 'Was democracy just a moment?', *Atlantic Monthly*, December (1996a) pp. 55–80.

Kaplan, R. *The Ends of the Earth: A Journey at the Dawn of the 21st Century* (New York: Random House, 1996b).

Karst, K. 'Out of many, one?', *Indiana Journal of Global Legal Studies* **2**, 1 (1994).

Kastoryano, R. *La France, l'Allemagne et leurs immigrés: négocier l'identité* (Paris: Armand Colin, 1996).

Kausikan, B. 'Asia's different standard', in H. Steiner and P. Alston (eds) *International Human Rights in Context: Law, Politics, Morals* (Oxford: Oxford University Press, 1996) pp. 226–31.

Keith, M. and Pile, S. 'Introduction part 1: The politics of place', in M. Keith and S. Pile (eds) *Place and the Politics of Identity* (London: Routledge, 1993) pp. 1–21.

Kepel, G. *The Revenge of God: The Resurgence of Islam, Christianity and Judaism in the Modern World* (Cambridge: Polity Press, 1994).

Kepel, G. and Leveau, R. *Les banlieues de l'Islam* (Paris: Seuil, 1987).

Khor, M. 'Globalization: implications for development policy', *Third World Resurgence* **74**, 35 (1996) pp. 15–22.

Klein, M. *The American Street Gang: Its Nature, Prevalence and Control* (Oxford: Oxford University Press, 1995).

Kleinknecht, W. *The New Ethnic Mobs: The Changing Face of Organized Crime in America* (Glencoe: Free Press, 1996).

Klug, F. '"Oh to be in England": the British case study' in N. Yuval-Davis and F. Anthias (eds) *Woman–Nation–State* (London: Macmillan, 1989) pp. 16–35.

Kuntsler, J. 'Home from nowhere', *Atlantic Monthly* September (1996) pp. 43–65.

Kymlicka, W. *Multicultural Citizenship: A Liberal Theory of Minority Rights* (Oxford: Oxford University Press, 1995).

Kymlicka, W. and Norman, W. 'The return of the citizen', *Ethics* **104**, 2 (1993) pp. 352–81.

Labasse, J. *Quelles régions pour l'Europe?* (Paris: Flammarion, 1994).

Lal, B. B. 'The "Chicago School" of American sociology, symbolic interactionism and race relations theory', in J. Rex and D. Mason (eds) *Theories of Race and Ethnic Relations* (Cambridge: Cambridge University Press, 1986).

Lal, B. V. 'Rhetoric and reality: the dilemmas of contemporary Fijian politics', in R. Crocombe, U. Neemia, A. Ravuvu and W. vom Busch (eds) *Culture and Democracy in the South Pacific* (Suva: University of the South Pacific, 1992) pp. 97–116.

Lapeyronnie, D., Frybes, M., Couper, K. and Joly, D. *L'intégration des minorités immigrées: etude comparative: France – Grande Bretagne* (Paris: Agence pour le Développement des Relations Interculturelles, 1990).

Larsen, J. 'The judgement of antiquity on democracy', *Classical Philology* **49**, 1 (1954) pp. 1–14.

Las Casas, B. de *Brevisima relacion de la destruccion de las Indias* (Coyoacan: Fontamara, 1992).

Lau, A. 'The national past and the writing of history in Singapore', in K. Ban, A. Pakir Sim and C. Tong (eds), *Imagining Singapore* (Singapore: Academic Press, 1992).

Lawson, S. 'The politics of tradition: problems of political legitimacy and democracy in the South Pacific', *Pacific Studies* **16**, 2 (1993) pp. 1–29.

Layton-Henry, Z. *The Politics of Immigration: Immigration, 'Race' and 'Race' Relations in Post-war Britain* (Oxford: Blackwell, 1992).

Lever-Tracy, C. and Quinlan, M. *A Divided Working Class* (London: Routledge, 1988).

Levinas, E. *Difficile liberté* (Paris: Albin Michel, 1976).

Li Buyun and Wu Yuzhang 'The concept of citizenship in the People's Republic of China', in A. Davidson and K. Weekley (eds) *Globalization and Citizenship in the Asia-Pacific* (London: Macmillan, 1999) pp. 157–68.

Light, I. and Bonacich, E. *Immigrant Entrepreneurs* (Berkeley: University of California, 1988).

Lim, L. L. and Oishi, N. 'International labour migration of Asian women', *Asian and Pacific Migration Journal* **5**, 1 (1996).

Locke, J. *Essay Concerning Human Understanding* (New York: Dover, 1959).

Lutz, H., Phoenix, A. and Yuval-Davis, N. 'Introduction: nationalism, racism and gender' in H. Lutz, A. Phoenix and N. Yuval-Davis (eds) *Crossfires: Nationalism, Racism and Gender in Europe* (London: Pluto Press, 1995) pp. 1–25.

McAllister, I. 'Political attitudes and electoral behaviour', in J. Jupp (ed.) *The Australian People: an Encyclopedia of the Nation, its People and their Origins* (Sydney: Angus & Robertson, 1988) pp. 919–22.

McKenzie, E. *Privatopia: Homeowner Associations and the Rise of Residential Private Government* (New Haven: Yale University Press, 1994).

Mahathir, M. *Perspectives in Islam and the Future of Muslims* (Kuala Lumpur: Institute of Islamic Understanding, 1993).

Mamdani, M. *Citizen and Subject: Contemporary Africa and the Legacy of Late Colonialism* (Princeton: Princeton University Press, 1996).

Marcuse, H. *Negations* (Boston: Beacon, 1969).

Marcuse, P. *Is Australia Different? Globalization and the New Urban Poverty* (Australian Housing and Urban Research Institute: Melbourne, 1996).

Marshall, T. H. *Citizenship and Social Class* (Cambridge: Cambridge University Press, 1950).

Marshall, T. H. 'Citizenship and social class', in *Class, Citizenship and Social Development: Essays by T. H. Marshall* (New York: Anchor Books, 1964).

Martin, P. L. 'Labor migration in Asia: conference report', *International Migration Review* **25**, 1 (1991).

Martin, P., Mason, A. and Nagayama, T. 'Introduction to special issue on the dynamics of labor migration in Asia', *Asian and Pacific Migration Journal* **5**, 2–3 (1996).

Martiniello, M. 'Citizenship of the European Union: a critical view', in R. Bauböck (ed.) *From Aliens to Citizens* (Aldershot: Avebury, 1994) pp. 29–47.

Marx, K. *Collected Works* **3** (London: Lawrence & Wishart, 1975).

Massey, D. 'Politics and space/time', in M. Keith and S. Pile (eds) *Place and the Politics of Identity* (London: Routledge, 1993) pp. 141–61.

Mead, L. *Beyond Entitlement: the Social Obligations of Citizenship* (New York: Free Press, 1986).

Meehan, E. *Citizenship and the European Community* (London: Sage, 1993a).

Meehan, E. 'Citizenship and the European Community', *Political Quarterly* **64** (1993b) pp. 172–86.

Memmi, A. *Le racisme: descriptions, définitions, traitement* (Paris: Folio, 1994).

Menchu, R. *I, Rigoberto Menchu* (London: Verso, 1984).

Mill, J. *On Liberty and Other Writings* (Cambridge: Cambridge University Press, 1991).

Milner, A. and Quilty, M. *Comparing Cultures* (Oxford: Oxford University Press, 1997).

Mingione, E. 'Urban poverty in the advanced industrial world: concepts, analysis and debates', in E. Mingione (ed.) *Urban Poverty and the Underclass* (Oxford: Blackwell, 1996a) pp. 3–40.

Mingione, E. (ed.) *Urban Poverty and the Underclass* (Oxford: Blackwell, 1996b).

Mingione, E. 'Conclusion', in E. Mingione (ed.) *Urban Poverty and the Underclass* (Oxford: Blackwell, 1996c) pp. 370–83.

Moch, L. P. *Moving Europeans: Migrations in Western Europe since 1650* (Bloomington: Indian University Press, 1992).

Moch, L. P. 'Moving Europeans: historical migration practices in Western Europe', in R. Cohen (ed.) *Cambridge Survey of World Migration* (Cambridge: Cambridge University Press, 1995) pp. 126–30.

Montesquieu, C. de. *Oeuvres complètes* (Paris: Seuil, 1964).

Moriki, K. 'Citizenship and nationality of recent immigrants in Japan', paper presented to the Conference on Dealing with Diversity: Citizenship and Cultural Change in Australia and Japan, Australian National University, Canberra, 29–30 March (1996).

Morris, L. 'Dangerous classes: neglected aspects of the underclass debate', in E. Mingione (ed.) *Urban Poverty and the Underclass* (Oxford: Blackwell, 1996) pp. 160–75.

Morris-Suzuki, T. 'The origins of Japanese citizenship', paper presented to the Conference on Dealing with Diversity: Citizenship and Cultural Change in Australia and Japan, Australian National University, Canberra, 29–30 March (1996).

Moynihan, D. P. *Pandaemonium: Ethnicity in International Politics* (Oxford: Oxford University Press, 1993).

Münz, R. 'A continent of migration: European mass migration in the twentieth century', *New Community* **22**, 2 (1996) pp. 201–26.

Nair, S. *Contre les lois Pasqua* (Paris: Arlea, 1997).

Naisbitt, R. *Megatrends Asia: Eight Asian Megatrends that are Reshaping Our World* (New York: Touchstone, 1997).

New Community 'Special issue: New migration in Europe: dilemmas of mobility and control', *New Community* **22**, 2 (1996).

Nicolet, C. *Le métier de citoyen dans la Rome républicaine* (Paris: Gallimard, 1976) (second edition).

Noiriel, G. *Le creuset français: histoire de l'immigration XIXe–XXe siècles* (Paris: Seuil, 1988)

Odquist, P. *Violence, Conflict and Politics in Colombia* (London: Academic Press, 1980).

OECD *Trends in International Migration: Annual Report* (Paris: OECD, annual).

Ohmae, K. *The Borderless World* (New York: HarperCollins, 1991).

Ohmae, K. *The End of the Nation-State: The Rise of Regional Economies* (London: HarperCollins, 1995).

Okunishi, Y. 'Labor contracting in international migration: the Japanese case and implications for Asia', *Asian and Pacific Migration Journal* **5**, 2–3 (1996) pp. 387–409.

OMA (Office of Multicultural Affairs) *National Agenda for a Multicultural Australia: Sharing our Future* (Canberra: Australian Government Publishing Service, 1989).

Othman, N. 'Umma and citizenry: civil society in the new world order', in N. Othman (ed.) *Shari'a Law and the Modern Nation: A Malaysian Symposium* (Kuala Lumpur: Sisters in Islam, 1994), pp. 81–6.

Pacific Constitutions. *Pacific Constitutions* (Suva: University of the South Pacific, 1991).

Paine, T. *The Thomas Paine Reader* (Harmondsworth: Penguin, 1987).

Palan, R., with Abbott, J. and Deans, P. *Global Strategies in the Global Political Economy* (London: Pinter, 1996).

Park, R. E. *Race and Culture* (London: Collier Macmillan, 1950).

Parsons, T. 'Full citizenship for the negro American: a sociological problem', *Daedalus* 94 (1965) pp. 1009–54.

Pascoe, R. 'Place and community: the construction of an Italo-Australian space', in S. Castles, C. Alcorso, G. Rando and E. Vasta (eds) *Australia's Italians: Culture and Community in a Changing Society* (Sydney: Allen & Unwin, 1992) pp. 85–97.

Pateman, C. *The Sexual Contract* (Cambridge: Polity Press, 1988).

Phizacklea, A. *Unpacking the Fashion Industry: Gender, Racism and Class in Production* (London: Routledge, 1990).

Plato. *The Protagoras and the Meno* (Harmondsworth: Penguin, 1987).

Posner, G. *Warlords of Crime: Chinese Secret Societies – the New Mafia* (New York: McGraw-Hill, 1988).

Putnam, R. *Making Democracy Work: Civic Traditions in Modern Italy* (Princeton, NJ: Princeton University Press, 1993).

Quentin-Baxter, A. 'The constitutions of Niue and the Marshall Islands: common traits and points of difference', in P. Sack (ed.) *Pacific Constitutions: Proceedings of the Canberra Law Workshop VI* (Canberra: Law Department, Research School of Social Sciences, Australian National University, 1982) pp. 97–125.

Rashid, Y. 'The question of dual citizenship', *Pacific Islands Monthly* July (1995) p. 13.

Rawls, J. 'Justice as fairness: political not metaphysical', *Philosophy and Public Affairs* **14**, 3 (1985) pp. 223–51.

Raynal, G.-T. *Histoire des deux Indes* (Paris, 1794).

Reich, R. *The Work of Nations: Preparing Ourselves for 21st Century Capitalism* (London: Simon & Schuster, 1991).

Renan, E. *Qu'est-ce qu' une nation? et autres essais politiques* (introduced by J. Roman) (Paris: Presses Pocket, Agora, 1992).

Rex, J. *Race, Colonialism and the City* (Oxford: Oxford University Press, 1973).

Rex, J. and Drury, B. (eds) *Ethnic Mobilisation in a Multi-Cultural Europe* (Aldershot: Avebury, 1994).

Rex, J. and Tomlinson, S. *Colonial Immigrants in a British City: a Class Analysis* (London: Routledge & Kegan Paul, 1979).

Rials, S. *La déclaration des droits de l'homme et du citoyen* (Paris: Hachette, 1988).

Roche, M. *Rethinking Citizenship: Welfare, Ideology and Change in Modern Society* (Cambridge: Polity Press, 1992).

Rodota, S. *Sovereignty in the Age of Technopolitics: Interparliamentary Conference on 'Citizens, Representative Democracy and European Construction'* (Paris: Senate, République Française, 1993).

Rousseau, J.-J. *Oeuvres complètes,* vol. 2 (Paris: Seuil, 1971).

Rousseau, J.-J. *L'origine des langues* (Rome: Riuniti, 1989).

Rudolph, H. 'The new *gastarbeiter* system in Germany', *New Community* **22**, 2 (1996) pp. 287–300.

Rumbaut, R. 'The new Californians: assessing the education progress of children of immigrants', *CPS Brief* **8**, 3 (1996) pp. 1–12.

Ruzza, C. and Schmidtke, O. 'The Northern League: changing friends and foes and its political opportunity structure', in D. Ceserani and M. Fullbrook (eds) *Citizenship, Nationality and Migration in Europe* (London: Routledge, 1996) pp. 179–209.

Sachs, I. *The Discovery of the Third World* (Cambridge, MA: MIT Press, 1976).

Sack, P. and Minchin, E. (eds) *Legal Pluralism: Proceedings of the Canberra Law Workshop VII* (Canberra: Law Department, Research School of Social Sciences, Australian National University, 1985).

Salazar, A. *Born to Die in Medellin* (London: Latin American Bureau, 1990).

Sánchez, G. J. 'Face the nation: race, immigration and the rise of nativism in late twentieth century America' *International Migration Review* **31**, 4 (1997) pp. 1009–30.

Sassen, S. *The Mobility of Labor and Capital* (Cambridge: Cambridge University Press, 1988).

Sassen, S. *The Global City: New York, London, Tokyo* (Princeton: Princeton University Press, 1991).

Sassen, S. *Cities in a World Economy* (Thousand Oaks, CA: Pine Forge, 1994).

Saussol, A. *L'héritage: essai sur le problème foncier mélanésien en Nouvelle-Calédonie* (Paris: Société des Océanistes, 1979).

Schlesinger, A. M. Jr *The Disuniting of America: Reflections on a Multicultural Society* (New York: W. W. Norton, 1992).

Schnapper, D. *La communauté des citoyens: sur l'idée moderne de la nation* (Paris: Gallimard, 1994).

Seifert, W. 'Occupational and social integration of immigrant groups in Germany', *New Community* **22**, 3 (1996) pp. 417–36.

Seton-Watson, H. *Nations and States* (London: Methuen, 1977).

Shaw, J. W., Nordlie, P. G. and Shapiro, R. M. *Strategies for Improving Race Relations* (Manchester: Manchester University Press, 1987).

Sheridan, G. *Living with Dragons: Australia Confronts its Asian Destiny* (Sydney: Allen & Unwin, 1995).

Skeldon, R. 'International migration within and from the East and Southeast Asian region: a review essay', *Asian and Pacific Migration Journal* **1**, 1 (1992) pp. 19–63.

Smith, A. D. *National Identity* (London: Penguin, 1991).

Smith, S. 'Residential segregation and the politics of racialization', in M. Cross and M. Keith (eds) *Racism, the City and the State* (London: Routledge, 1993) pp. 128–43.

Solomos, J. and Back, L. *Race, Politics and Social Change* (London: Routledge, 1995).

Soysal, Y. N. *Limits of Citizenship: Migrants and Postnational Membership in Europe* (Chicago: University of Chicago Press, 1994).

Soysal, Y. 'Changing parameters and practices of citizenship in post-war Europe', paper presented to the Conference on Globalisation and Citizenship (UNRISD/Swinburne), Melbourne, 6–9 May (1997).

Spoonley, P. 'Migration and the reconstruction of citizenship in late twentieth century Aotearoa', in P. Spoonley and S. Castles, *Migration and Citizenship* (Auckland: Asia-Pacific Migration Research Network, 1997) pp. 21–40.

Stahl, C., Ball, R., Inglis, C. and Gutman, P. *Global Population Movements and their Implications for Australia* (Canberra: Australian Government Publishing Service, 1993).

Stalker, P. *The Work of Strangers* (Geneva: International Labour Office, 1994).

Stasiulis, D. and Jhappan, R. 'The fractious politics of a settler society: Canada', in D. Stasiulis and N. Yuval-Davis (eds) *Unsettling Settler Societies* (London: Sage, 1995) pp. 95–131.

Steinberg, S. *Turning Back: The Retreat from Racial Justice in American Thought and Policy* (Boston: Beacon Press, 1995).

Steiner, H. and Alston, P. (eds) *International Human Rights in Context: Law, Politics, Morals* (Oxford: Oxford University Press, 1996).

Stewart, J. *A Documentary Survey of the French Revolution* (New York: Macmillan, 1963).

Storey, H. 'International law and human rights obligations', in S. Spencer (ed.) *Strangers and Citizens: a Positive Approach to Migrants and Refugees* (London: Rivers Oram Press, 1994) pp. 111–36.

Streeten, P. 'Governance of the global economy', *Globalisation and Citizenship: an international conference,* 9–11 December (Geneva: United Nations Research Institute for Social Development, 1996).

Suarez, F. *Selections from Three Works, vol.* 2 (New York: Oceana, 1964).

Suzuki, D. and Oiwa, K. *The Japan We Never Knew: A Voyage of Discovery* (Toronto: Allen & Unwin, 1996).

Teitelbaum, M. S. and Weiner, M. (eds) *Threatened Peoples, Threatened Boundaries: World Migration and US Policy* (New York: Norton, 1995).

Thucydides. *The Peloponnesian War* (Harmondsworth: Penguin, 1964).

Tigno, J. 'Human rights and transnational migrants in South East Asia', paper presented to the Third Human Rights Colloquium on Human Rights, Labor and Refugees in ASEAN, Manila, February (1995).

Todorov, T. *The Conquest of America: The Question of the Other* (New York: Harper & Row, 1984).

Touati, A. *Démocratie ou barbarie* (Paris: Desclée de Brouwer, 1996).

Townsend, P. *Poverty in the United Kingdom* (London: Penguin, 1979).

Tran Van Binh. 'Citizenship in the process of renovation and development in Vietnam', paper presented to the Conference on Globalisation and Citizenship (UNRISD/Swinburne), Melbourne, 6–9 May (1997).

Tribalat, M. *Faire France: une enquête sur les immigrés et leurs enfants* (Paris: La Découverte, 1995).

Turk, D. 'How World Bank–IMF policies adversely affect human rights', *Third World Resurgence* **33**, 16 (1993).

Turner, B. 'Outline of a theory of citizenship', in C. Mouffe (ed.) *Dimensions of Radical Democracy: Pluralism, Citizenship, Community* (London: Verso, 1992) pp. 33–62.

Turner, B. *Orientalism, Postmodernism and Globalism* (London: Routledge, 1994).

UNDP. *Human Development Report* (Oxford: Oxford University Press, 1996).

UN ECE (United Nations Economic Commission for Europe) *International Migration Bulletin* 8 (Geneva: UN ECE 1996).

UNHCR (United Nations High Commissioner for Refugees) *The State of the World's Refugees 1995: In Search of Solutions* (Oxford: Oxford University Press, 1995).

UNRISD. *States of Disarray: The Social Effects of Globalization* (London: United Nations Research Institute for Social Development, 1995).

Vanhanen, T. (ed.) *Prospects of Democracy: A Study of 172 Countries* (New York: Routledge, 1997).

van Steenbergen, B. 'The condition of citizenship: an introduction', in B. van Steenbergen (ed.) *The Condition of Citizenship* (London: Sage, 1994) pp. 1–9.

Vasta, E. 'Immigrant women and the politics of resistance', *Australian Feminist Studies* **18** (1993) pp. 5–23.

Vasta, E. 'Community and the state', paper presented at the Australian Sociological Association (TASA) Conference, Wollongong, (1997).

Vogel, U. 'Marriage and the boundaries of citizenship', in B. van Steenbergen (ed.) *The Condition of Citizenship* (London: Sage, 1994) pp. 76–89.

Voltaire, J.- M. A. *Philosophical Dictionary* (Harmondsworth: Penguin, 1971).

Wacquant, L. J. D. 'Red belt, black belt: racial division, class inequality and the state in the French urban periphery and the American ghetto', in E. Mingione (ed.) *Urban Poverty and the Underclass* (Oxford: Blackwell, 1996) pp. 234–74.

Wahdud-Muhsin, A. 'The Qur'an, shari'a and the citizenship rights of Muslim women in the umma', in N. Othman (ed.) *Shari'a Law and the Modern Nation: A Malaysian Symposium* (Kuala Lumpur: Sisters in Islam, 1994) pp. 77–80.

Waldinger, R., Aldrich, H., Ward, R. *et al. Ethnic Entrepreneurs – Immigrant Business in Industrial Societies* (Newbury Park, CA: Sage, 1990).

Weber, E. *Peasants into Frenchmen: The Modernization of Rural France 1870–1914* (London: Chatto & Windus, 1979).

Weil, P. *La France et ses étrangers* (Paris: Calmann-Levy, 1991).

Whitlam, E. G. *The Whitlam Government 1972–1975* (Melbourne: Viking, 1994).

Wieviorka, M. 'Introduction', in M. Wieviorka, P. Bataille, K. Couper, D. Martuccelli and A. Peralva, *Racisme et xénophobie en Europe: une comparaison internationale* (Paris: La Découverte, 1994).

Wieviorka, M. *The Arena of Racism* (London: Sage, 1995).

Wihtol de Wenden, C. *Les immigrés et la politique* (Paris: Presses de la Fondation Nationale des Sciences Politiques, 1988).

Wihtol de Wenden, C. 'Generational change and political participation in French suburbs', *New Community* **21**, 1 (1995) pp. 69–78.

Wilson, W. J. *The Truly Disadvantaged: The Inner City, the Underclass and Public Policy* (Chicago: University of Chicago Press, 1987).

Wilson, W. J. 'Citizenship and the inner-city ghetto poor', in B. van Steenbergen (ed.) *The Condition of Citizenship* (London: Sage, 1994) pp. 49–65.

Wittfogel, K. *Oriental Despotism* (New Haven: Yale University Press, 1957).

Wobbe, T. 'The boundaries of community: gender relations and racial violence', in H. Lutz, A. Phoenix and N. Yuval-Davis (eds) *Crossfires: Nationalism, Racism and Gender in Europe* (London: Pluto Press, 1995) pp. 88–104.

Wrench, J. and Solomos, J. *Racism and Migration in Western Europe* (Oxford: Berg, 1993).

Yarwood, A. T. and Knowling, M. J. *Race Relations in Australia: A History* (Sydney: Methuen, 1982).

Yoshino, K. *Cultural Nationalism in Contemporary Japan: A Sociological Enquiry* (London: Routledge, 1992).

Yoshino, K. 'Nationalism, globalisation and issues of citizenship in Japan', paper presented to the Conference on Globalisation and Citizenship (UNRISD/Swinburne), Melbourne, 6–9 May (1997).

Young, I. M. 'Polity and group difference: a critique of the ideal of universal citizenship', *Ethics* **99** (1989) pp. 250–74.

Young, I. M. *Justice and the Politics of Difference* (Princeton NJ: Princeton University Press, 1990).

Zappalà, G. *The Parliamentary Responsiveness of Australian Federal MPs to their Ethnic Constituents*, research Paper No. 8 (Canberra: Department of the Parliamentary Library, 1997).

Zheng, Y. *Scarlet Memorial: Tales of Cannibalism in Modern China* (Boulder: Westview, 1996).

Zhou, M. 'Segmented assimilation: issues, controversies, and recent research on the new second generation', *International Migration Review* **31**, 4 (1997) pp. 975–1008.

Index